CONCEPTS IN
ARCHITECTURAL LIGHTING

CONCEPTS IN ARCHITECTURAL LIGHTING

M. David Egan

College of Architecture
Clemson University

McGraw-Hill Book Company

New York   St. Louis   San Francisco   Auckland   Bogotá   Hamburg
Johannesburg   London   Madrid   Mexico   Montreal   New Delhi   Panama
Paris   São Paulo   Singapore   Sydney   Tokyo   Toronto

CONCEPTS IN ARCHITECTURAL LIGHTING

234567890 HALHAL 89876543

ISBN 0-07-019054-2

This book was set in Univers by Intergraphic Technology, Inc.
The editors were Rodger H. Klas and David A. Damstra;
the designer was Merrill Haber;
the production supervisor was Diane Renda.
The cover photograph was taken by O. Baitz, Inc.
Halliday Lithograph Corporation was printer and binder.

Library of Congress Cataloging in Publication Data

Egan, M. David.
    Concepts in architectural lighting.

    Bibliography: p.
    Includes index.
    1. Lighting.   2. Lighting, Architectural and decorative.   I. Title.
TH7703.E33   1983   729'.28   82-20832
ISBN 0-07-019054-2

Martin James Egan
(1904—1981)

About the Author

M. David Egan, P.E., is associate professor at the College of Architecture, Clemson University. A graduate of Lafayette College (B.S.) and the Massachusetts Institute of Technology (M.S.), Professor Egan has also taught at Tulane University, Georgia Institute of Technology, University of North Carolina at Charlotte, and Washington University (St. Louis), and has lectured at numerous schools of design throughout the United States. He has worked as a consultant in architectural technologies for Bolt, Beranek and Newman in Cambridge, Massachusetts and for over ten years has been principal consultant of his own firm in Anderson, South Carolina. He is the author of several books in the area of architectural technologies, including *Concepts in Architectural Acoustics* (1972), *Concepts in Thermal Comfort* (1975), and *Concepts in Building Firesafety* (1978). In addition to teaching and consulting, Professor Egan is a fellow of the Acoustical Society of America (ASA), vice president of the National Council of Acoustical Consultants (NCAC), and a member of the lighting education committee of the Illuminating Engineering Society of North America (IES).

Contents

Foreword

Events of this decade have challenged many of the fundamentals of lighting design. The complexity of the art and science of architectural illumination demands that understanding the environmental consequences of lighting be a primary consideration in future energy-conscious design. As architects and designers we have the unique opportunity to create environments for people and by doing so to immeasurably enrich their lives. Both natural and electrical lighting are inseparably part of this responsibility, and it is the obligation of designers of buildings and places to realize and understand the significance of light in all their creative endeavors.

The late Richard Kelly, dean of American lighting designers, once said that every space should contain three qualities of illumination — "focal glow, ambient luminescence, and the play of brilliants." This poetic expression continues to challenge architects and designers throughout the world today and clearly describes the magic of light, which is so essential if we are to enjoy the places which surround us.

It is to this end that Professor M. David Egan's book on architectural lighting will be an invaluable source to students, teachers, and practitioners. The material presented herein is a comprehensive overview of daylighting and electrical lighting. The book is coherent and understandable, and utilizes a very clear graphic format to assist the reader with problem-solving techniques. Professor Egan has made a significant contribution to the growing awareness of the importance of lighting in the environment.

Richard C. Peters, AIA
Professor of Architecture
College of Environmental Design
University of California, Berkeley

Preface

The goal of this book is to present, in a graphical format, the principles of vision and of the behavior of light in the built environment. The illustrations are not supplements to the text, as is often the situation with traditional presentations; rather, they are the core of the book's coverage of vision and human perception, natural and electric light sources, lighting measurements and controls, lighting design and form, computations for quantity and quality of light, daylighting design techniques, and the use of illuminated models for daylighting and electrical lighting design.

It is hoped that the illustrations and example problems will lead students of architecture and interior design to an understanding of the conceptual background of light and vision, which is essential to achieve appropriate conditions for visual tasks and to produce illuminated spaces which satisfy human needs. In addition, the illustrations and practical checklists should aid architects, interior designers, and others with interest in lighting who have not had formal courses on illumination and do not have time to digest lengthy written descriptions.

The late John Flynn's book, *Architectural Lighting Graphics* (co-authored with Samuel Mills in 1962 and no longer in print), was an inspiration when used by the author nearly 15 years ago to teach lighting at Tulane University. Professor Flynn's later pioneering studies on the effects of brightness on the subjective impressions of space are presented in the chapter on lighting design and form. Bill Lam's writing and teaching efforts also have had considerable influence on the author. Lam's description of basic human biological needs for visual information, first published in his 1977 book, *Perception and Lighting as Formgivers for Architecture*, is presented in a checklist format and in example illustrations on light and form.

Several tables throughout the book have been reproduced or adapted from Illuminating Engineering Society of North America (IES) sources. The appendix contains several complete IES tables. For ease of communication, however, the reader is first introduced to computational concepts using shortened tables.

The book also contains an illustrated glossary of lighting terms and selected references organized into three important categories. The appendix includes an extensive metric-system conversion table for common lighting terms, electrical symbols for lighting layouts, and a listing of lighting organizations.

M. David Egan, P.E., FASA, MIES
Anderson, South Carolina

Acknowledgments

Thanks are due to many people who helped me during the preparation of this book.

Gratitude is extended to Professor Glen S. LeRoy, School of Architecture and Urban Design, University of Kansas, who prepared all the illustrations and margin art. Glen LeRoy's steadfast dedication to effective graphic-communication techniques is deeply appreciated. Glen also prepared the illustrations for the books *Concepts in Thermal Comfort* (1975) and *Concepts in Building Firesafety* (1978).

Dean Harlan E. McClure, FAIA supported the production of the Clemson University *Lighting Workbook* (1980), which was used to teach lighting design at the College of Architecture. John Dumas prepared the drawings for this publication.

Jeannie Egan edited the manuscript and illustrations and typed the manuscript.

Thanks to John Archea, Don Collins, Al Hart, Jim Jensen, Terry McGowan, Gordon Rowe, and Hank Williams for their reviews of various parts of the manuscript.

It is of course impossible to name all the people who influenced me in the field of lighting design, and thereby contributed to the preparation of this book, without inadvertently overlooking someone. Nevertheless, recognition should be given to the following people who kindly provided me with in-depth reviews of one or more chapters. Their invaluable comments, criticisms, and suggestions are appreciated.

Professor Charles C. Benton
College of Architecture
Georgia Institute of Technology

Professor Craig A. Bernecker, MIES
Department of Architectural
* Engineering*
Pennsylvania State University

Professor Donald J. Conway, AIA
Chairman, Interior Design
* Department*
Woodbury University

Mr. William M. Dombroski
University Facilities Planning Office
Ohio University

Professor Benjamin H. Evans, AIA
College of Architecture and
* Urban Studies*
Virginia Polytechnic Institute and
* State University*

Mr. W. S. Fisher, FIES
General Electric Lighting Institute
Nela Park, Ohio

Dr. Stephen Jaeger, P.E.
School of Architecture
University of Texas at Austin

Professor Henry Kowalewski, AIA
College of Architecture and
*   Urban Planning*
University of Michigan

Mr, Robert J. Lee, MIES
Lighting Systems Consultant
Atlanta, Georgia

Mr. Thomas M. Lemons, FIES
TLA-Lighting Consultants, Inc.
Salem, Massachusetts

Professor Marietta S. Millet
Department of Architecture
University of Oregon

Dr. Joseph B. Murdoch, FIES
Department of Electrical Engineering
University of New Hampshire

Professor Richard C. Peters, AIA
Department of Architecture
University of California at Berkeley

Mr. Gary R. Steffy, MIES, IALD
Gary Steffy Lighting Design
Ann Arbor, Michigan

Professor Samuel Wang
College of Architecture
Clemson University

Chapter 1
Vision and Perception

Primary Light Sources
(see Chapters 2 and 6)
- Daylight (clear, overcast, and partly-cloudy sky conditions)
- Incandescent lamps
- Fluorescent lamps
- High-intensity discharge lamps

Eyes (furnish color and brightness sensations to brain)
- Accommodation (ability to focus on near and distant objects)
- Dark adaptation (rods on retina increase in sensitivity)
- Bright adaptation (cones perceive color and detail)
- Presbyopia (loss of lens flexibility due to aging)

Seeing Light and Color

Secondary Light Sources
(all natural or manufactured objects which modify light waves)
- Atmosphere (water vapor, dust, and other impurities)
- Landscape elements (e.g., trees, ground cover, nearby structures)
- Baffles, louvers, and lenses of primary light sources
- Room surfaces and furnishings

Brain (combines, orders, and interprets sensations from eyes)
- Optic nerve (sends signals from retina to brain)
- Visual cortex (where visual sensations occur)
- Expectations, experience, and emotion of observer influence perception

SCHEMATIC OF HOW HUMAN EYE FUNCTIONS

The sketch below shows various parts of the human eye. The cornea and lens focus light on the multilayered retina which transmits impulses through the optic nerve to the brain. The size of the pupil is controlled by the iris — the larger the pupil, the greater the amount of light admitted into the eye. Under conditions of high brightness (e.g., bright skies outdoors) the reverse occurs — the iris reduces the size of the pupil so less light is admitted. The ability of the eye to control the amount of light it admits and to change the sensitivity of the retina is called *adaptation* (see page 16).

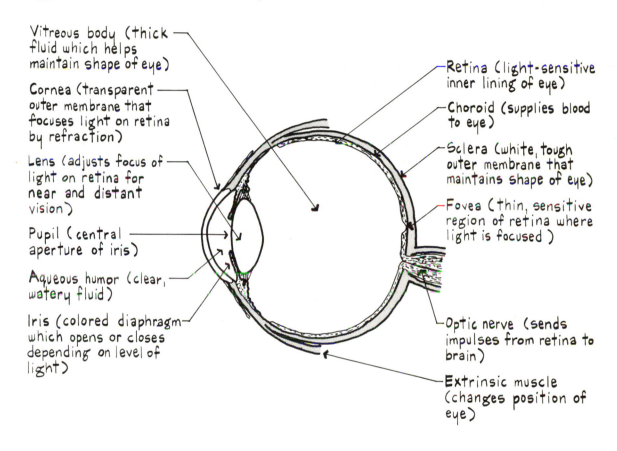

Vitreous body (thick fluid which helps maintain shape of eye)

Cornea (transparent outer membrane that focuses light on retina by refraction)

Lens (adjusts focus of light on retina for near and distant vision)

Pupil (central aperture of iris)

Aqueous humor (clear, watery fluid)

Iris (colored diaphragm which opens or closes depending on level of light)

Retina (light-sensitive inner lining of eye)

Choroid (supplies blood to eye)

Sclera (white, tough outer membrane that maintains shape of eye)

Fovea (thin, sensitive region of retina where light is focused)

Optic nerve (sends impulses from retina to brain)

Extrinsic muscle (changes position of eye)

Near and Distant Vision

The sketch below is a general description of how the human eye functions when viewing near and distant objects. The ability of the eye to focus light on the retina by changing the shape of the lens is called *accommodation*. For near vision (<20 ft), the curvature of the lens is increased, the pupil is constricted by the iris, and the lines of sight of both eyes converge on a common point.

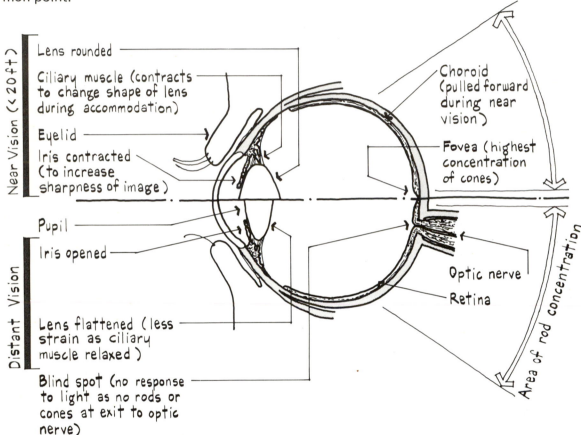

Blind Spot Test

Hold this page 8 to 12 in from your eyes. Cover your left eye and focus on the circle. Slowly move the page closer to your right eye. When the triangle disappears, it is focused on the blind spot of the right eye (i.e., point of exit of optic nerve where there are no rods or cones). The blind spot is not noticeable during normal vision because of the frequency of eye movements and because the view is seen by both eyes.

SCHEMATIC OF RETINA

There are several layers of retina between its inner surface, where light is focused (or scattered), and the light-sensitive rods and cones. *Cones* function in bright light, perceiving colors and detail. *Rods* function only in dim or low levels of light and are highly sensitive to motion (peripheral vision involves only rods) and to bright light, which bleaches their photosensitive pigments so that they become relatively inactive.

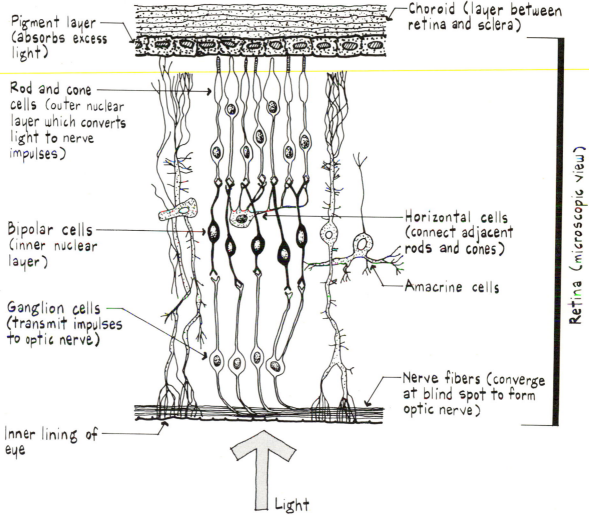

Pigment layer (absorbs excess light)

Choroid (layer between retina and sclera)

Rod and cone cells (outer nuclear layer which converts light to nerve impulses)

Bipolar cells (inner nuclear layer)

Horizontal cells (connect adjacent rods and cones)

Amacrine cells

Ganglion cells (transmit impulses to optic nerve)

Nerve fibers (converge at blind spot to form optic nerve)

Inner lining of eye

Retina (microscopic view)

Light

The brain's organization of sensations from the retina which enables recognition and understanding to occur, is called *visual perception*. Optic fibers from the two eyes follow the paths to the visual cortex as shown in the sketch below. At the optic chiasma, fibers from half of one retina cross to join fibers from the corresponding half of the other retina at the lateral geniculate body. The ability of the brain to perceive the images from both eyes as a single image is called *binocular vision.*

Experience, expectations, and emotion influence perception or evaluation of visual images. Because of expectations, a white object at low measured brightness, viewed indoors under electric light sources, will usually be perceived as being far brighter than a black object at considerably higher measured brightness, viewed outdoors under bright sky conditions.

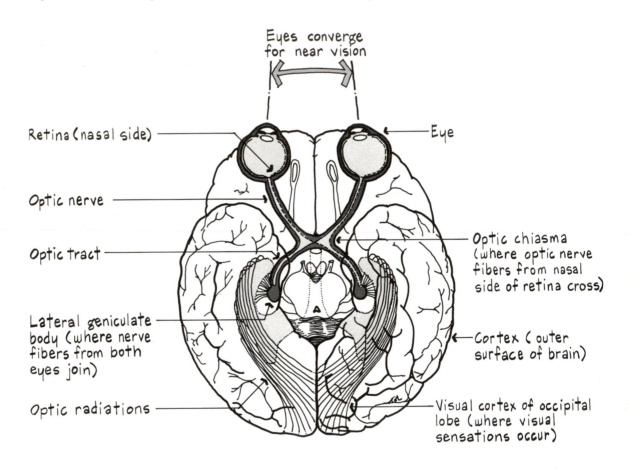

VISUAL FIELD

As shown below, <u>foveal vision is the detail acuity of the eyes. Foveal vision provides the best color response because of the concentration of cones in the fovea, the thinnest area of the retina.</u>

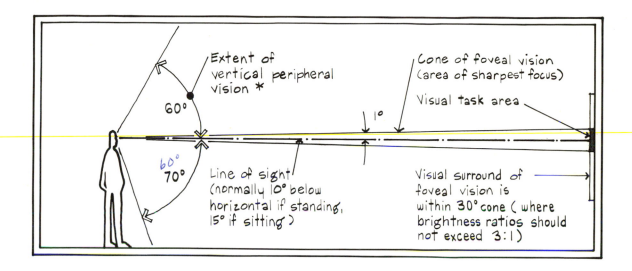

*Where eyes respond to changes in brightness and to motion. Central portion or near visual surround (i.e., about 30° above and below line of sight) provides relatively clear image perception.

BINOCULAR VISUAL FIELD PROFILE

The binocular visual field (i.e., vision by both eyes) extends vertically 130° and horizontally more than 120° when both eyes are focused on a fixed object. Vision by one eye alone is called *monocular vision.* The sketch below shows the extent of binocular and monocular visual fields.

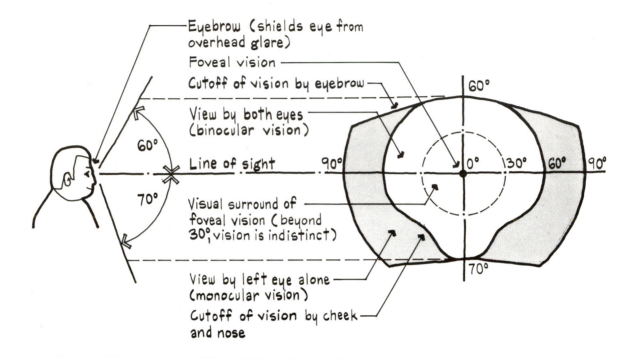

Eyebrow (shields eye from overhead glare)
Foveal vision
Cutoff of vision by eyebrow
View by both eyes (binocular vision)
Line of sight
Visual surround of foveal vision (beyond 30°, vision is indistinct)
View by left eye alone (monocular vision)
Cutoff of vision by cheek and nose

Visual performance decreases from the late twenties on. Old eyes have reduced visual acuity because of yellowing of the lens and other factors; require longer time for adaptation; and have increased sensitivity to glare. As age increases, normal-sighted persons need a higher illumination level and optimum contrast of visual tasks to achieve best visual performance (see graph on left). *Presbyopia* is the decrease in ability of accommodation due to loss of the ciliary muscle's effectiveness and the lens' flexibility, which normally occurs after age 40. The graph on the right shows this effect, as the near point distance (i.e., how close the task can be to the eyes and still be clearly focused) increases rapidly around age 40. This effect of aging can be corrected by prescription glasses.

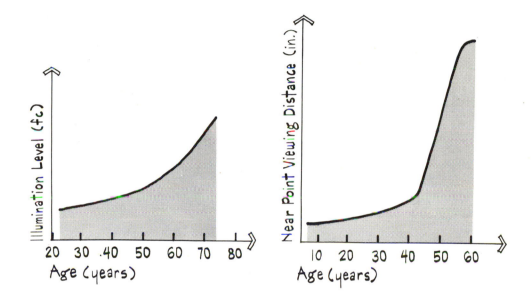

*Illumination level, measured in footcandles (fc), is the quantity of light reaching a surface.

Note: See page 37 for graph showing results of numerical recognition tests for 20-year-old and 50- to 60-year-old persons.

OBJECT SIZE AND VISIBILITY

The size of objects is usually estimated by comparing the unknown to the optical size of known objects in the visual field. The visual angle ($\angle\alpha$, in degrees) that an object subtends at a person's eye is more important than the physical size of the object. For example, visual angle can be increased by bringing the object closer to the eye. Visual angle is determined by

$$\alpha \simeq \frac{57h}{D}$$

where h = object height (ft)

D = distance from eye to object (ft)

Visual Lines of Sight

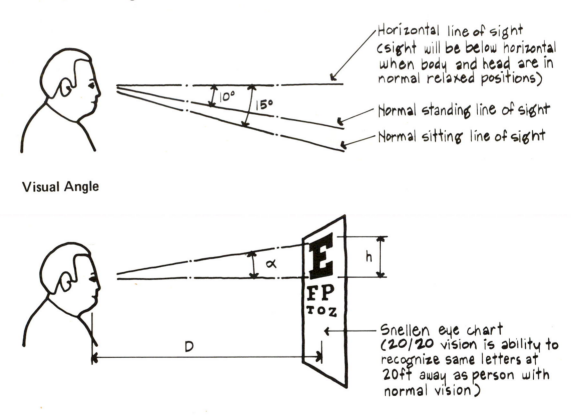

Horizontal line of sight (sight will be below horizontal when body and head are in normal relaxed positions)

Normal standing line of sight

Normal sitting line of sight

Visual Angle

Snellen eye chart (20/20 vision is ability to recognize same letters at 20ft away as person with normal vision)

The graph below shows that less illumination is needed when object size is increased (e.g., using large type, binocular loupes, magnifiers). In some classroom situations, moving 3 ft closer to the chalkboard can provide the same visual improvement as increasing the illumination level by 30 times. The required illumination level also decreases as the amount of time for viewing increases.

Illumination Level (fc)

Object Size (ft or in.)

COLOR SPECTRUM

The visible portion of the electromagnetic spectrum, which contains all visible colors, occurs at about 380 to 780 nm. The nanometer (nm), equal to 10^{-9} m, is used to express wavelength in the visible spectrum so that specific values will not have so many zeros. (The angstrom unit of wavelength is equal to 10^{-10} m.)

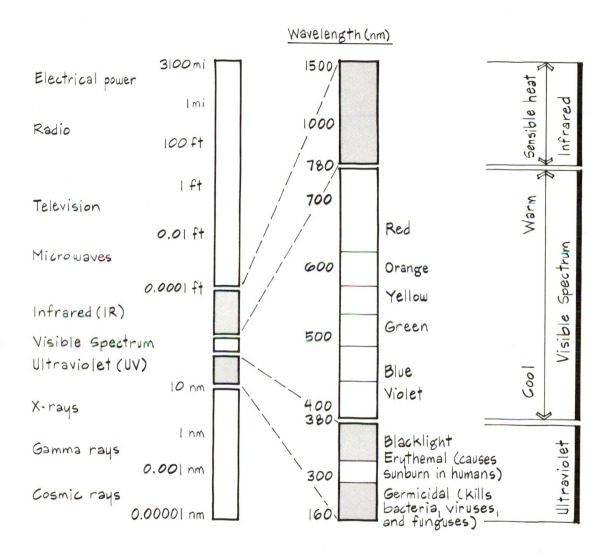

Note: Long exposure to ultraviolet (UV) wavelengths from 290 to 320 nm may cause skin cancer. Ordinary window glass normally filters out all UV wavelengths below 320 nm. However, special attention must be given to daylighted art galleries, as some wavelengths can damage paintings and prints. UV wavelengths cause fading of pigments and infrared (IR) cause deterioration of base material (e.g., canvas, paper, wood).

COLOR OF OBJECTS

Color perception by humans is personal. It depends on subjective factors such as expectations, experience, and the nature of the object being viewed. For example, a green carpet could be acceptable while green hamburger meat is not. Under conditions of normal adaptation, the color of an object is relatively independent of the spectrum (or color distribution) of its reflected light if the light source contains the entire spectrum. The color of objects can define form by contrasting with the surround. In addition, color can contribute a sense of weight, as dark-colored building elements appear heavy and light-colored elements appear lightweight.

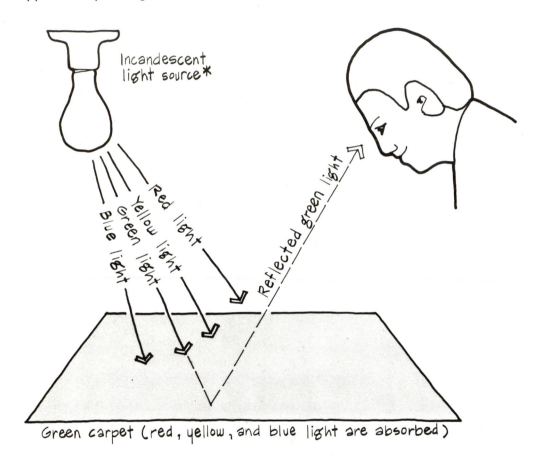

Green carpet (red, yellow, and blue light are absorbed)

*Light source emits wavelengths which surface (or object) reflects. Light which is relatively balanced among the visible wavelengths is called *white light.*

MUNSELL COLOR SYSTEM

The Munsell color system (Munsell Color Company, Inc., 2441 N. Calvert St., Baltimore, MD 21218) provides an accurate, universally understood vocabulary for object color. In the Munsell system of color classification, surface colors are ordered by specifying *hue* (basic family of colors), *value* (lightness or darkness), and *chroma* (saturation or vividness). As shown by the column axis below, value is the index of lightness or darkness; the higher the light reflectance, the higher the value of a color. Chroma, indicated along the spokes of the color wheels around the value axis, is the purity or richness of color (i.e., how much white or gray in the mixture). As chroma increases, the saturation or vividness of the hue increases. High chroma colors are used where light levels are high. The sketch below depicts a portion of the Munsell color solid, showing the variations in hue and chroma at a specific Munsell value. The complete color solid has the shape of an irregular globe.

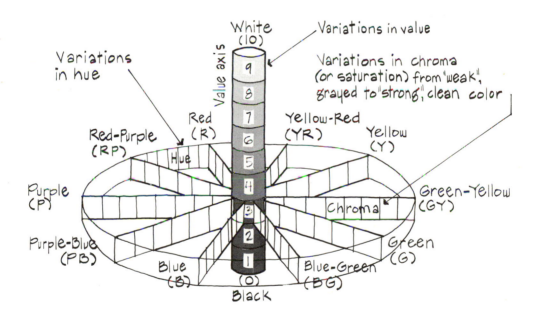

Note: When selecting color of paints and other finish materials, where accurate color judgments are required, be sure color evaluations are made under the lighting situation in which they are to be used.

COLOR CONTENT OF LIGHT SOURCES

The graph below shows the relative energy emitted at various wavelengths by three different sources of light. The curves are presented in terms of the relative energy of wavelengths for each light source on the graph and therefore cannot be directly compared to each other. For example, daylight can provide over 80 times the usual level of illumination of the other sources on the graph.

Observe the cover of this book under electric light sources and outside in daylight. Do the colors appear the same when illuminated by light sources of vastly different color content and light level? The following page presents the concept of color constancy, which allows color identity to be preserved under different illumination conditions if changes are not too fast or if light sources of different color content are not viewed simultaneously. For example, the blue of the sky will be distorted when viewed through clear glass and adjacent tinted glass, a combination which can also create artificial gloom.

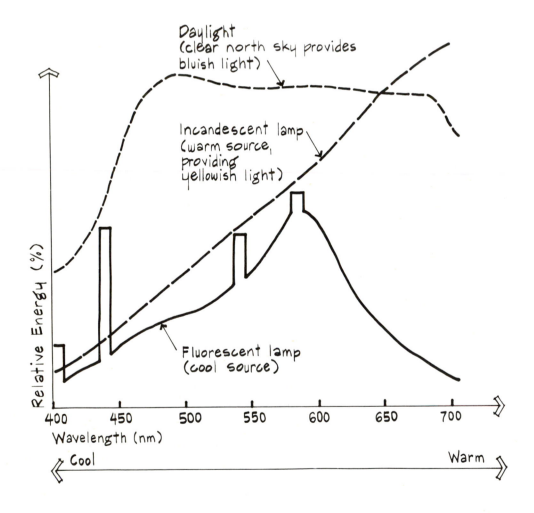

COLOR PERCEPTION

Color perception results from the complex interaction between a light source, an object, the eye, and the brain. The human eye detects a relationship among wavelengths rather than directly detecting a single wavelength. Therefore, the relationship between colors does not vary with changes of the color spectrum of light sources. When the color content of light changes, the color perception mechanisms of the eye adapt to a new neutral point so that the object color remains nearly the same. This phenomenon, called *color constancy,* is due to the ability of the brain to compensate for the color of light when judging color. Without this ability, visual chaos would be a routine occurrence.

In the example below, two adjacent rooms are illuminated by a blue light source (room 1) and a yellow light source (room 2). Two sheets of identical white paper are placed on the walls in each room. The sheets of paper will both be white when viewed for an extended period within the room containing them. However, when viewed through a small observation port between the rooms, the paper appears blue when viewed from room 1 and orange when viewed from room 2 because the color perception mechanism did not have time to adapt to the consequences of the different color spectra of the light sources.

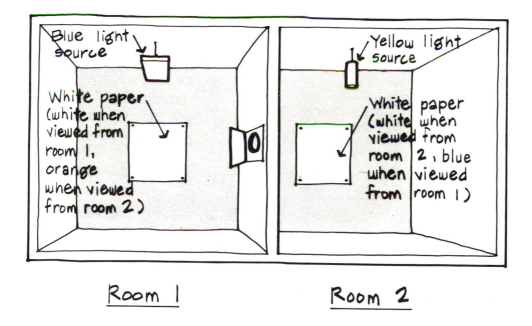

Room 1   Room 2

Reference

H. Yilmaz and L. C. Clapp, "Perception," *International Science and Technology,* November 1963, pp. 76-84.

Night vision conditions occur at low levels of brightness (less than about 0.01 fL). At low levels of light, rods in the retina increase in sensitivity — a process called *dark adaptation*. Adaptation to a dark theater on a bright, sunny day can take 2 min or more; complete dark adaptation can take up to 1 h. Light adaptation (e.g., walking onto a beach on a sunny day) is more rapid, but can be painful, causing eyes to squint and tear.

In the 1800s, Johannes Purkinje observed that on a sunny day red flowers normally seemed brighter than blue flowers. At dawn or dusk, however, the reverse occurred — blue flowers seemed brighter than red. This change in the color sensitivity of the eye, called the *Purkinje shift,* is due to the shift from perception by cones to perception by rods. Cones function in bright light and have greatest sensitivity to yellow-green wavelengths (red flowers). Rods function in low levels of light and have greatest sensitivity to blue-green wavelengths (blue flowers). The solid curves on the graph below show the Purkinje shift between day and night vision. The dashed day vision curve shows that rods, which are more sensitive to light than cones, require less energy for vision.

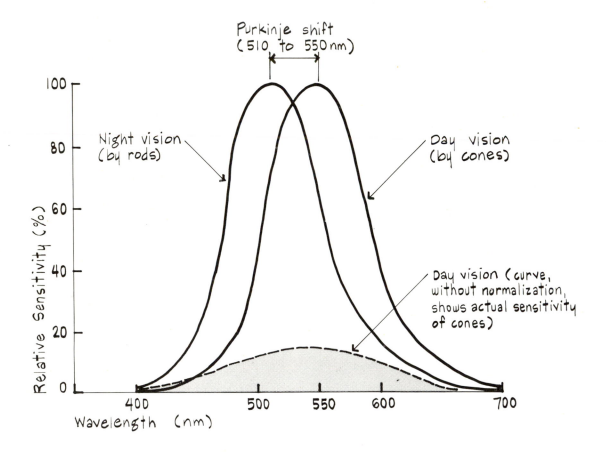

Note: The shape of the solid day vision sensitivity curve is similar to the relative energy distribution curve for sunlight reflected from green foliage (i.e., greenish-yellow light with peak energy at 550 nm).

WHITE-DOG EFFECT

The gray squares within the black and white stripes, called a *grating pattern,* have identical reflectance. In normal room light, the four squares in the white stripes appear darker than the corresponding squares in the black stripes, due to the phenomenon of simultaneous contrast (i.e., heightening of difference in brightness when objects are placed next to each other). In addition, small reductions in illumination do not appreciably affect contrast conditions. However, large reductions can cause a breakdown in *contrast constancy*. For example, at very low levels of illumination, the squares at the bottom of the grating pattern will appear lighter. This is an example of the white-dog effect, as white dogs are more conspicuous in the dark!

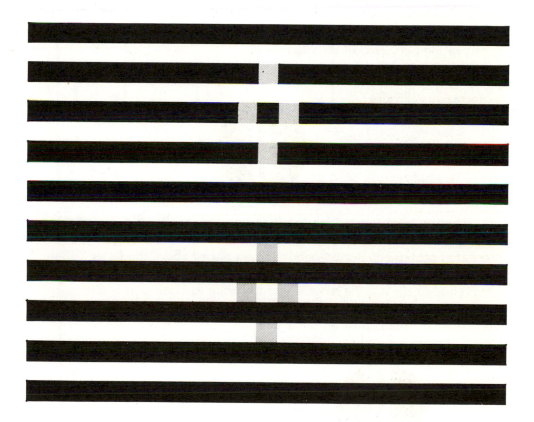

Note: Grating patterns can be used in visual performance studies as targets.

Reference

J. A. Lynes, *Principles of Natural Lighting,* Elsevier, Amsterdam, 1968, pp. 40-41.

According to Gestalt theory, the whole of a visual image is different from and greater than the sum of its parts. For example, the 12 dots shown above have been arranged to form a directional arrow and a circle. We perceive the arrow and the circle first, as whole forms are the highest level of organization perceived in the visual field.

Expectations/Closure

The acoustical consulting firm's corporate logo shown above, designed by graphic designer D. L. Collins, suggests an image of a tuning fork with elongated prongs and a short handle. When placed above the letter "u" in the word "architectural," the handle is lengthened by closure (see below). This is due to the natural tendency of the brain to close gaps and complete unfinished forms. We expect the handle to be complete, and so the unconscious mind completes the image.

ARCHITECTURAL ACOUSTICS & NOISE CONTROL

Brightness Contrast

Figure-background relationship of dark squares with white surround creates darkening or "spotting" at intersections of white stripes. Ceiling lighting fixtures can create similar spotting or "dazzle" effects when the lay-out consists of alternating dark and bright illuminated areas.

Figure-Background Ambiguity

Black and white stripes of identical width create figure-background ambiguity, as both contain equal information. Venetian blinds can create a similar pattern, but view stripes are more interesting than the uninforma-tive adjustable slat stripes.

Reversible Images

Observer will perceive either two faces silhouetted against white back-ground or a vase silhouetted against black background. How objects are per-ceived depends on context information such as expectations and nearby, familiar objects. When viewed for an extended time period, figure-background relationships can be reversed.

Bisection Illusion

Vertical and horizontal lines shown above are equal in length, but the vertical line appears longer. Window designs can create similar effects; however, wide windows are often preferred to tall windows because they provide a less restricted view of horizon.

Size Illusion

Open-ended line at top appears longer than closed line of identical length. Arrowheads at ends of lines distort perception of size. Sizes of objects in visual field are evaluated by comparison with perceived size of nearby, familiar objects. For example, the moon appears larger at the horizon because of the distance cues from buildings and trees, which are absent when the moon is viewed overhead.

Pattern and Expectations

Pattern established by rows of lines draws eyes to omitted line. Focus is due to expectation of completeness (or closure). Incomplete layout of lighting fixtures can be made more understandable by relating fixtures to structural elements, window openings, or furniture arrangement.

The level of sound in a room depends not only on the characteristics of the sound source but also on the sound-absorbing properties of the room surfaces, the size of the room, and the distance away the listener is from the sound source. The sound level is higher in a bare, hard-surfaced room than in the same room finished with soft, sound-absorbing materials. Sound levels indoors (near the source) decrease with distance according to the inverse-square law.

The same factors also apply to light in a room. Room illumination level is similar to sound level, light reflectance is similar to the sound absorption coefficient, and light, like point sources of sound, decreases with distance according to the inverse-square law.

For example, a small room with white-painted walls and ceiling is illuminated by a 50-W (800 lumens) incandescent lamp. Because of the high-reflectance room surfaces, this lamp could provide acceptable illumination levels. However, in a similar room with dark, low-reflectance surfaces, it would provide extremely low illumination. A 200-W (4000 lumens) lamp would be needed to provide acceptable illumination levels. Therefore, the level of ambient room illumination depends not only on the wattage (or lumen output) of the light source, but also on the light-reflectance properties of the room surfaces and the distance from the light source.

The eye can detect brightness over a range of greater than a trillion (10^{12}) to 1. At any one instant, however, brightness perception is normally within a range of only 1000 to 1. *Apparent brightness* is relative and subjective. For example, under identical illumination gray paper viewed on a black surface appears brighter than gray paper viewed on a white surface. (See example gray squares on page 17.) Nonetheless, its measured brightness (called *luminance*) in footlamberts would be the same. In the metric system, luminance is measured in nits or candela/square meter (cd/m^2); 1 nit equals 0.29 fL.

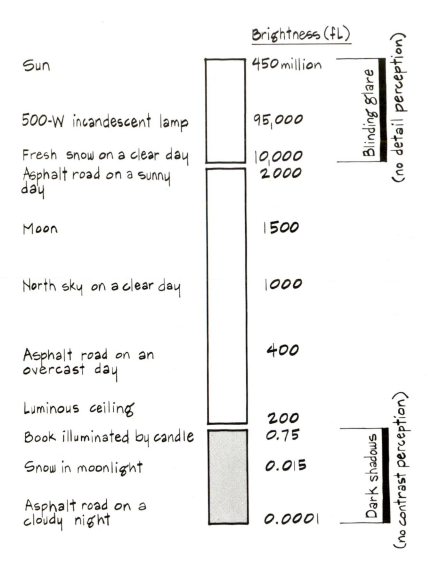

	Brightness (fL)	
Sun	450 million	Blinding glare (no detail perception)
500-W incandescent lamp	95,000	
Fresh snow on a clear day	10,000	
Asphalt road on a sunny day	2000	
Moon	1500	
North sky on a clear day	1000	
Asphalt road on an overcast day	400	
Luminous ceiling	200	
Book illuminated by candle	0.75	Dark shadows (no contrast perception)
Snow in moonlight	0.015	
Asphalt road on a cloudy night	0.0001	

Note: Above 2000 fL, objects listed on the scale above cause eyes to blink or squint. The upper limit of brightness tolerance for most persons is 10,000 fL (e.g., blinding glare from snow on a clear day).

BRIGHTNESS DIFFERENCES

Visual performance increases with contrast and other factors. Contrast is the brightness difference between the object being viewed and the immediate surroundings. Brightness perception, like color perception, depends on eye adaptation, expectations, experience, and so on. Nevertheless, for comfortable contrast in most situations, brightness difference (or *luminance ratio*) should be within the following limits. These limits on luminance, however, do not imply that uniform or unchanging lighting conditions are preferred or even desirable.

2:1   Perceptible brightness difference for focus

3:1   Between task and adjacent darker surroundings

10:1   Between task and remote darker surfaces; clearly noticeable brightness difference for focus and transition between adjoining spaces

20:1   Between lighting fixtures (or windows) and sizable adjacent surfaces

40:1   Should not be exceeded anywhere within normal field of view (exceptions would include crystal chandeliers)

50:1   Will highlight objects to exclusion of everything else in field of view

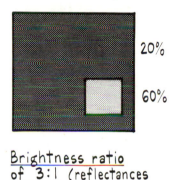

Brightness ratio of 3:1 (reflectances given in %)

To achieve desired brightness differences, light sources and reflectances of room surfaces must be carefully selected.

Brightness is a sensation which can be expressed as bright, brilliant, or light. The apparent or *perceived brightness* is modified by surroundings, condition of eye adaptation, and other factors. *Measured brightness,* or luminance ($\angle$), is the amount of light reflected from or transmitted through an object, expressed in footlamberts. The percentage of incident light which is reradiated from a surface is its reflectance (ρ). Shown below are rooms with low- and high-reflectance surfaces.

Low-Reflectance Room Surfaces

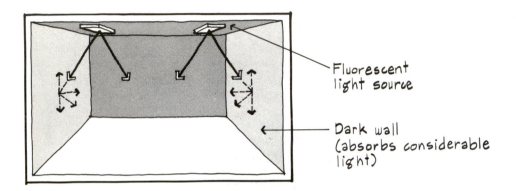

Note: With low brightness, room shown above appears dark or gloomy for office activities, but may be intimate or relaxing for dining.

High-Reflectance Room Surfaces

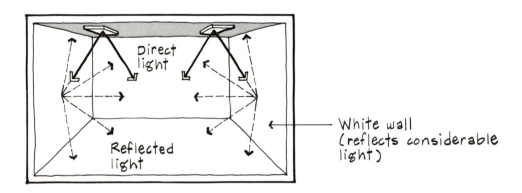

Note: With high brightness, room shown above appears bright or cheerful. Be careful, as walls can dominate visual field in small rooms. Under certain conditions, cool colors tend to increase apparent size of rooms.

BRIGHTNESS ADAPTATION

When eyes are adapted to 100 fL, a surface with a measured brightness of 100 fL should have a perceived brightness of 100 fL to an observer (see dashed lines on graph). However, if the observer's eyes are adapted to only 1 fL (e.g., under dark shadow conditions), this surface could have a perceived brightness of 400 fL. Although measured brightness (or luminance) would be the same in both of these situations, the surface could appear 4 times as bright due to brightness adaptation.

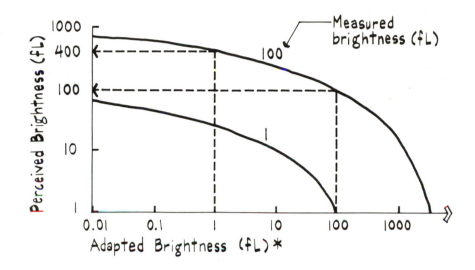

*Brightness to which eye is adapted. Influenced by all areas in the field of view.

Reference

R. G. Hopkinson and J. D. Kay, *The Lighting of Buildings,* Praeger, New York, 1969, p. 46.

In the examples below, various combinations of dark (flat black) and bright (matte white) surfaces are placed opposite a window wall and are presented in order of increasing illumination level on desk top work surfaces. As shown below, the ceiling is the most effective surface for projecting daylight into a room, whereas the floor is the least effective.

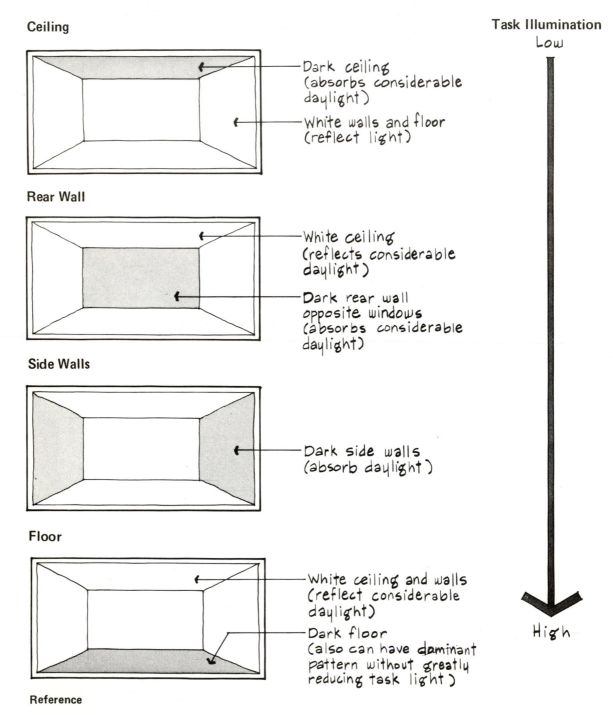

Ceiling

Dark ceiling (absorbs considerable daylight)

White walls and floor (reflect light)

Rear Wall

White ceiling (reflects considerable daylight)

Dark rear wall opposite windows (absorbs considerable daylight)

Side Walls

Dark side walls (absorb daylight)

Floor

White ceiling and walls (reflect considerable daylight)

Dark floor (also can have dominant pattern without greatly reducing task light)

Task Illumination
Low

High

Reference

B. H. Evans, *Daylight in Architecture,* McGraw-Hill, New York, 1981, pp. 74-75.

REFLECTANCE OF MATERIALS

Reflectance (ρ) is the percentage of incident light that is reflected from a surface, with the remainder absorbed, transmitted, or both. Value in the Munsell color system can be used to identify the property of light reflectance. To find the approximate reflectance of a surface of known Munsell *value* (*V*), use the following formula:

$$\rho \simeq V(V - 1)$$

where ρ = reflectance (%)
V = value (no units)

For example, a value of 9 will have a $\rho \simeq 9(9 - 1) = 72\%$. Luminance (*L*) of a diffuse reflecting surface is the incident illumination level times the reflectance.

$$L = E \times \rho$$

where L = luminance (fL)
E = illumination level or illuminance (fc)
ρ = reflectance (%)

Typical reflectances for finish materials are given below.

Material	Reflectance (%)	Material	Reflectance (%)
Metals:		Glass:	
Aluminum, brushed	55-58	Clear or tinted	5-10
Aluminum, etched	70-85	Reflective	20-30
Aluminum, polished	60-70	Ground cover:	
Stainless steel	50-60	Asphalt	5-10
Tin	67-72	Concrete	40
		Grass and other vegetation	5-30
		Snow	60-75
Masonry:			
Brick, dark buff	35-40	Paint:*	
Brick, light buff	40-45	White	70-90
Brick, red	10-20	White porcelain enamel	60-83
Cement, gray	20-30		
Granite	20-25	Wood:	
Limestone	35-60	Light birch	35-50
Marble, polished	30-70	Mahogany	6-12
Plaster, white	90-92	Oak, dark	10-15
Sandstone	20-40	Oak, light	25-35
Terra-cotta, white	65-80	Walnut	5-10

*Refer to manufacturers' brochures or to *Light and Interior Finishes*, General Electric Technical Publication TP-129, Cleveland, February 1969.

References

J. E. Flynn and S. M. Mills, *Architectural Lighting Graphics,* Van Nostrand Reinhold, New York, 1962, pp. 121, 155.

J. E. Kaufman (ed.), *IES Lighting Handbook* (1981 Reference Volume), p. 7-10.

RECOMMENDED REFLECTANCES

The following recommended reflectances of the Illuminating Engineering Society of North America (IES) apply to general lighting systems for working areas in offices and educational facilities. The preferred ranges apply to matte or diffuse reflecting surfaces and finishes.

	Reflectance (%)	
	Classroom	Office
Ceilings	70-90	> 80
Walls*	40-60	50-70
Partitions (e.g., partial-height barriers)	—	40-70
Floors†	30-50	20-40
Furniture and machines	—	25-45
Desk and bench tops	35-50	35-50

*Walls containing windows should have high reflectance (> 80%) to decrease contrast between bright glazing and surround. Window frame, sash, and glazing bars also should have a light-colored matte finish.

†Use surfaces having reflectances > 25% for rooms where visual efficiency is a major concern (e.g., kitchens, bathrooms, etc.). Light-colored floors can help illuminate lower shelves of storage racks, bookcases, etc. Do not exceed 40% where reflected glare conditions would be critical.

Note: Small areas (<10% of observer's visual field) can have reflectances outside ranges given in the table. For example, glass, sculpture, and hardware can be used to provide accent and interest.

EXAMPLE REFLECTIVE SURFACES

Matte reflective surfaces reradiate incident light in a diffuse pattern; specular or glossy surfaces reflect light like a mirror when angle of incidence ($\angle i$) equals angle of reflectance ($\angle r$). Avoid specular finishes for surfaces surrounding reading tasks (e.g., desk tops, partitions for task-ambient lighting layouts in open-plan offices). Example matte and glossy materials are listed below.

Matte (or diffuse)	Glossy (or specular)
Brick, rough	Aluminum, polished
Concrete	Enamel paint
Flat paint, low gloss	Glass
Limestone	Marble, polished
Plaster, white	Plastics, polished
Plastics, low gloss (ABS, MF, PVC)	Stainless steel
Sandstone	Terrazzo
Wood, unfinished	Tin
	Wood, oiled

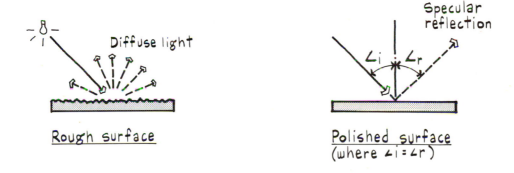

Note: Specular materials can have high reflectance (e.g., polished aluminum) or low reflectance (black tinted glass), and matte materials can also have high reflectance (flat white paint) or low reflectance (flat black paint).

TRANSMITTANCE OF MATERIALS

Transmittance (τ) is the percentage of incident light that is transmitted through a material. Luminance (L) of a diffuse transmitting material is the incident illumination level times the transmittance.

$$L = E \times \tau$$

where L = luminance (fL)

E = illumination level or illuminance (fc)

τ = transmittance (%)

Typical transmittances are given below.

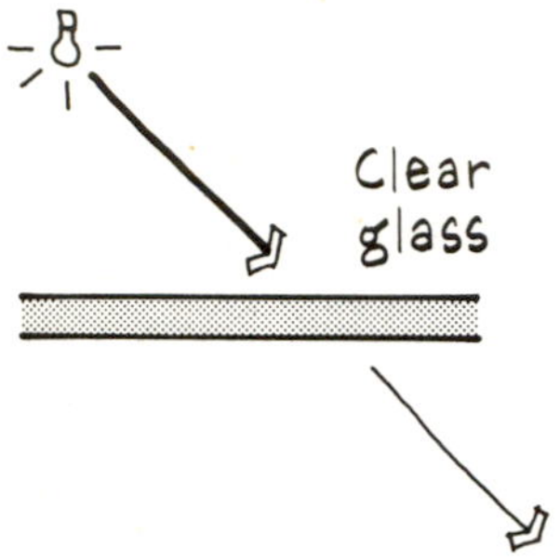

Clear glass

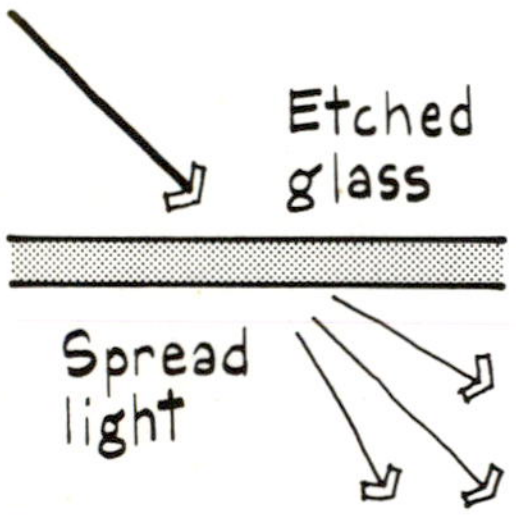

Etched glass

Spread light

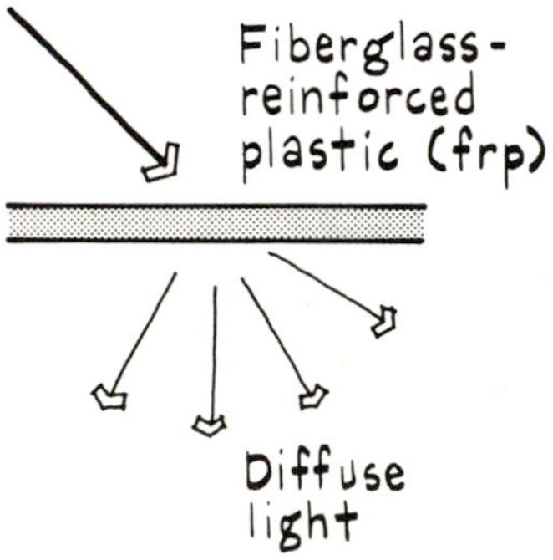

Fiberglass-reinforced plastic (frp)

Diffuse light

Material	Transmittance (%)
Direct transmission:	
Clear glass or plastic	80-94
Transparent colored glass or plastic	
blue	3-5
red	8-17
green	10-17
amber	30-50
Spread transmission:	
Etched glass, toward source	82-88
Etched glass, away from source	63-78
Diffuse transmission:	
Alabaster	20-50
Glass block	40-75
Marble	5-40
Plastics (acrylic, vinyl, fiberglass-reinforced plastic)	30-65

References

J. E. Flynn and S. M. Mills, *Architectural Lighting Graphics,* Van Nostrand Reinhold, New York, 1962, p. 133.

J. E. Kaufman (ed.), *IES Lighting Handbook* (1981 Reference Volume), pp. 6-7 and 7-10.

TYPES OF GLARE

Glare is bright light which can interfere with visual perception. Old persons are more sensitive to glare than young persons. Discomfort glare can be uncomfortable, and even painful, but does not significantly reduce ability to perform visual tasks. It is influenced by brightness conditions within the entire field of vision. Disability glare reduces the ability to perceive visual information needed for task performance. It is influenced by object brightness (e.g., direct sunlight on a desk top, or the dangerous condition of high-beam headlights from oncoming automobiles at night). Shown below are examples of glare caused by a bright source directly in the field of vision, called *direct glare,* and glare from a glossy or polished surface, which reflects the image of light source, called *reflected glare.* Discomfort and disability glare can be caused by either direct light or reflected light. Veiling reflections occur when small areas of the visual task reflect light, reducing contrast between task and immediate surround. Pencil handwriting is highly susceptible to veiling reflections, as pencil graphite can act as tiny mirrors.

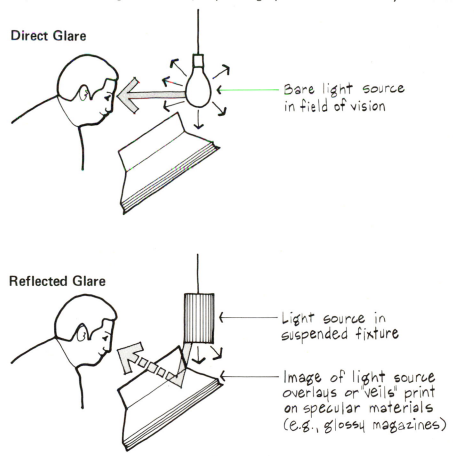

Direct Glare

Bare light source in field of vision

Reflected Glare

Light source in suspended fixture

Image of light source overlays or "veils" print on specular materials (e.g., glossy magazines)

Note: Glossy surfaces and light sources at the mirror angle can create *veiling reflections,* where contrast between task and surround will be greatly reduced. Position of the human eye offers poor shielding from reflected glare off desk top or floor surfaces.

REFLECTED GLARE AND VEILING REFLECTIONS

Veiling reflections can occur when the angles of incidence for light on the horizontal work surface are within the observer's viewing zone. A light source is at the *mirror angle* when the angle of incidence equals the viewing angle (e.g., the offending zone for a viewing direction is seen in a mirror substituted for the reading task). The most frequent viewing angle for reading and writing tasks on flat desk surfaces is 25° (cf., C. L. Crouch and L. J. Buttolph, "Visual Relationships in Office Tasks," *Lighting Design & Application,* May 1973).

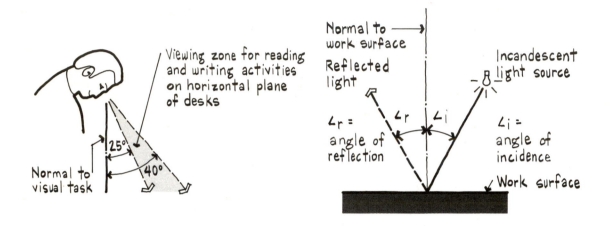

To reduce veiling reflections:

1. Locate light source away from mirror angle (e.g., daylight from side can provide visual performance conditions equivalent to electric light sources in ceilings at 3 times the illumination level).

2. Use light fixtures with low surface luminance (e.g., by dimming, with lenses to reduce light output at offending angles).

3. Provide relatively uniform illumination throughout room (e.g., by indirect light sources).

4. Use matte work surface finish with reflectance of 35 to 50%. (Avoid white desk surfaces with 85% or more reflectance, as paper with pencil or typing will be less bright and too contrasting.)

5. Tilt task or work surface away from mirror angle (e.g., drafting tables with adjustable drawing surface).

Lighting fixture (or luminaire) at position 2 shown below produces more reflected glare than at position 1. Light from the offending zone will cause low contrast, as visibility of pencil writing on paper is reduced due to specular reflections from pencil graphite.

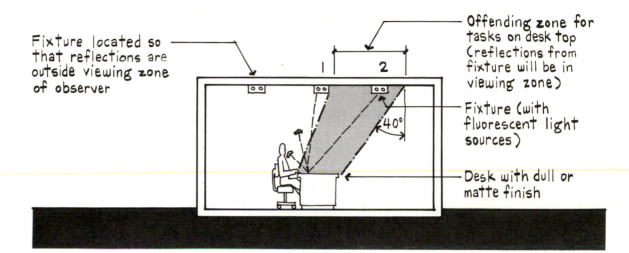

Fixture located so that reflections are outside viewing zone of observer

Offending zone for tasks on desk top (reflections from fixture will be in viewing zone)

Fixture (with fluorescent light sources)

Desk with dull or matte finish

HOW TO FIND LIGHT SOURCES IN OFFENDING ZONE

Check for light sources in offending locations by moving a small mirror or 8 × 10 glossy photo over the entire work surface (e.g., desk tops, position of CRT screens). Bright images of lighting fixtures or lamps reflected in the mirror indicate that they should be relocated, removed, or shielded (e.g., satin bottom finish diffuser laid on top of parabolic louvers). If reflected images are due to bright room surfaces, refinish them with low-reflectance, matte surfaces. As shown below, tilted work surfaces can reduce size of *offending zone* (i.e., location where light sources cause reflected glare) and move it toward person seated at desk.

Flat Work Surface

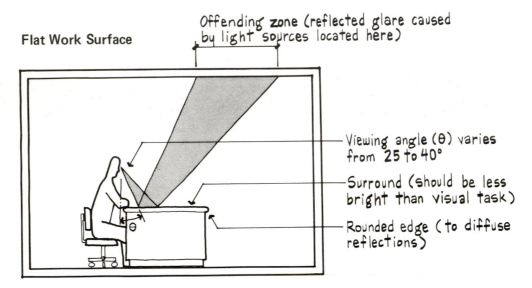

Offending **zone** (reflected glare caused by light sources located here)

Viewing angle (θ) varies from 25 to 40°

Surround (should be less bright than visual task)

Rounded edge (to diffuse reflections)

Tilted Work Surface

Offending **zone** (closer to observer and reduced in size due to tilted work surface)

Note: To help identify surface irregularities or defects in materials, scratches in paint, and so on, light source should be located at mirror angle. Defects will then be emphasized by shadows created by the directional light.

SURROUNDING BRIGHTNESS AND VISION

For constant task brightness, visual efficiency increases as surrounding brightness is raised, up to a point where efficiency begins to rapidly diminish. High levels of surrounding brightness in field of view cause eyes to adapt by reducing amount of light on retina, and sensitivity to contrast decreases.

Immediate surround or background (chalkboard surface)

Task object (chalk letters on board)

Surround (wall, ceiling, and floor surfaces)

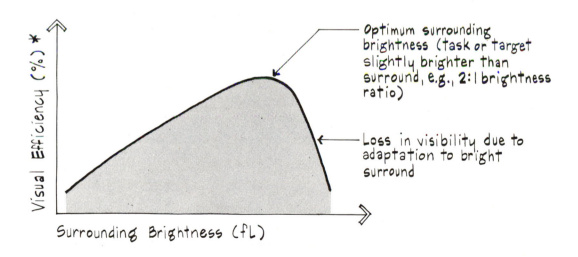

Optimum surrounding brightness (task or target slightly brighter than surround, e.g., 2:1 brightness ratio)

Loss in visibility due to adaptation to bright surround

*Visual efficiency is quantitative assessment of task performance based on speed, accuracy, etc.

Note: Do not set lighting levels at optimum for most difficult, infrequently occurring task, as visual efficiency will then be low for other, less demanding tasks (i.e., too much light will be provided).

SURROUNDING BRIGHTNESS AND CONTRAST

Contrast is desired between the object to be viewed and its immediate surround, but not with the background or overall field of view. Visibility increases as contrast increases. Contrast between the ink letters you are now reading and the white paper they are printed on (i.e., immediate surround) is a vital element of efficient visual perception. The size of the letters, the sharpness of detail, and the time it takes to read them are also extremely important. Contrast (C) can be expressed as:

$$C = \frac{L_t - L_s}{L_s}$$

where L_t = luminance (or measured brightness) of task (fL)

L_s = luminance (or measured brightness) of surround (fL)

For example, a task which consists of white paper with black print having a task luminance of 150 fL and a surround luminance of 50 fL will have C = (150 − 50)/50 = 2.

The human eye is more sensitive to contrast at high brightness levels than at low levels. For example, brightness differences as low as 1% can be detected when eyes are completely adapted to daylight. As shown by the curves of equal conspicuity (i.e., how well details stand out from their background), contrast must be extremely high for visibility at low brightness levels. This is an important consideration in the illumination of exit signs for visibility under emergency conditions in smoke-filled rooms.

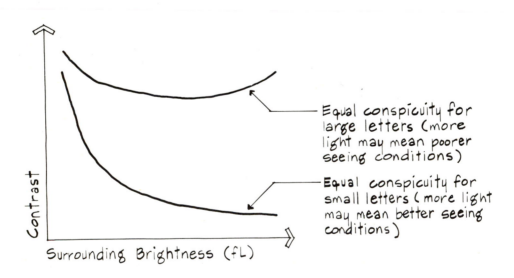

Equal conspicuity for large letters (more light may mean poorer seeing conditions)

Equal conspicuity for small letters (more light may mean better seeing conditions)

Reference

G. T. Yonemura, "Criteria for Recommending Lighting Levels," U.S. National Bureau of Standards, NBSIR 81-2231, March 1981, p. 23.

TASK BRIGHTNESS

For task background brightness above 20 to 30 fL, significant increases in brightness only slightly improve visibility. For many situations, therefore, visibility may be improved by increasing object size, decreasing viewing distance, and providing high-quality lighting (e.g., low reflected glare and minimum veiling reflections). As shown by the curves below, more light above 20 fL did not improve performance for older persons (50- to 60-year-old group) any more than it did for younger persons (20-year-old group). However, below 20 fL, older persons had greater benefit than younger persons did from more light.

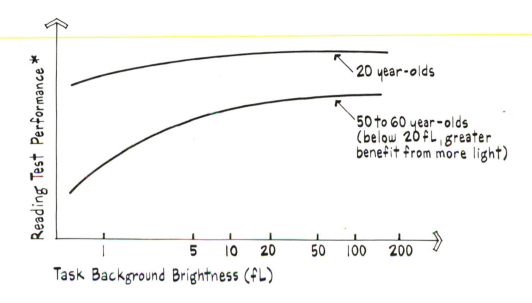

*Numerical recognition (i.e., proofreading) of dark and gray ink printed and handwritten materials.

Note: Tests for numerical recognition showed no significant performance differences when conducted under fluorescent, high-pressure sodium, or metal halide light sources.

Reference

D. K. Ross, "Task Lighting — Yet Another View," *Lighting Design & Application,* May 1978.

Several conceptual approaches to controlling brightness of light sources and room surfaces are given below:

1. Reduce brightness of light sources. Brightness of windows and their shape influence glare more than the size of the opening. Low-transmittance glass or low-gloss films can be used to reduce brightness of window openings. Sky glare can be controlled in tall buildings by restricting window height or by selectively screening upper portion of the window as shown below.

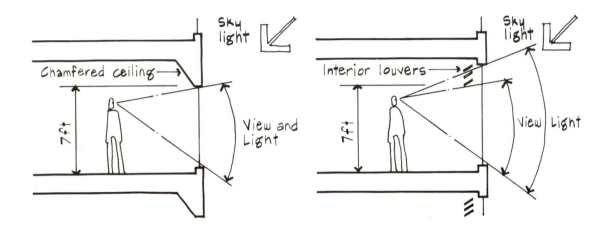

2. Position electric light sources so that specular reflections are not normally viewed (e.g., light sources located below or away from specular surfaces).

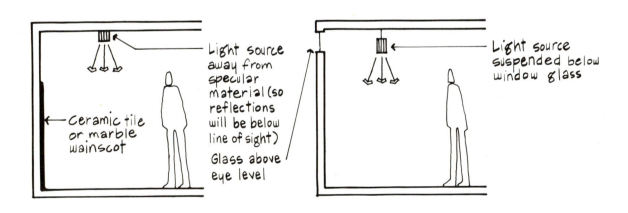

3. Increase brightness of area surrounding potential objectionable image (e.g., with high-reflectance finish). Avoid dark backgrounds which increase perceived brightness of light sources in field of view.

4. Shield daylight sources with baffles, screens, drapes, etc. Use large-scale elements for solar shading (e.g., horizontal overhangs, deep reveals) or use fine-mesh screens, drapes, or narrow-slat blinds, which also can avoid figure-background conflicts. Be careful, as sloped glass can reflect bright image of adjacent concrete or white pavers.

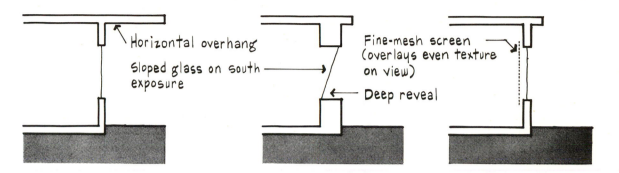

Horizontal overhang

Sloped glass on south exposure

Fine-mesh screen (overlays even texture on view)

Deep reveal

5. Use large area at lower brightness or smaller areas at same brightness. For example, in the reflected ceiling plans below, the four identical light sources on the left will be perceived as brighter than the four smaller sources of identical total area on the right. Large source areas can be less comfortable than the same sources arranged in smaller areas away from the normal line of sight.

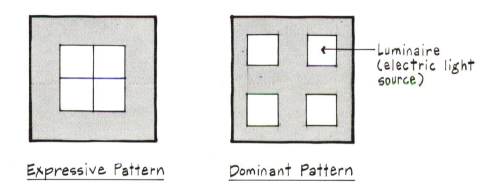

Luminaire (electric light source)

Expressive Pattern   Dominant Pattern

The table below presents basic human biological (or psychological) needs for visual information along with example lighting objectives.

Visual information for	Examples and lighting conditions
Physical orientation and location	1. Level horizontal lines of reference (e.g., moldings, wainscots, expansion joints) 2. Emphasis on dangerous edges in stairs and corridors 3. Clear definition of circulation intersections
Physical security	1. Light gradients to complement structure (e.g., scallops of light coordinated with wall panels) 2. Clearly visible egress routes with well-lighted exit signs
Relaxation	1. Nonuniform lighting layouts with control of glare 2. Emphasis on walls rather than overhead lighting 3. Interesting visual rest centers (e.g., illuminated sculpture, paintings, plants) as occupants periodically scan environment
Time orientation	Awareness of day-night cycle through clear windows and skylights
Contact with nature and people	1. Openings to allow daylight penetration (and distant views to relax eye muscles) 2. Avoidance of visual noise from solar-shading devices
Definition of personal territory	1. Task-ambient lighting such as torchères and furniture-integrated fixtures 2. Large ceiling coffers or columns in open plans

Note: For a comprehensive table of biological (or psychological) needs for visual information and their implications for the luminous environment, see W. M. C. Lam, *Perception and Lighting as Formgivers for Architecture,* McGraw-Hill, New York, 1977, p. 20.

CHECKLIST FOR GOOD LIGHTING

The goal of architectural lighting is to create the visual environment that best accommodates the functions intended (such as work or relaxation). Visual comfort results when we are able to receive the clear visual information that we instinctively or consciously want to know. Some general guidelines for achieving good lighting are presented below:

1. Visual conditions improve with increasing illumination up to a point where diminishing returns are quickly reached (e.g., at task background luminance of 20 to 30 fL).

2. Light must be free from disability glare (e.g., an oncoming car's high-beam headlights at night) or discomfort glare (e.g., one or two burning candles in a small room at night).

3. Visual conditions are improved if the visual task can be distinguished from its surroundings by being brighter, more contrasting, more colorful, strongly patterned, or a combination of two or more of these factors.

4. Visual conditions are also better if the visual task is seen in an unobtrusive and unconfusing setting. The surroundings should not be so bright or so colorful that attention is drawn away, or so dark that the task appears excessively bright and glaring or the setting monotonous.

5. Sufficient overall light should be provided in rooms, with focal light on the visual task. Avoid creating conditions where the eyes must adapt too quickly over too great a range of brightnesses.

6. Light sources must not be a source of discomfort glare. Consequently, building openings should have shading devices such as overhangs, fine-mesh screens, etc.

7. Dull uniformity should be avoided. For example, small points of light from low-wattage light sources can contribute "sparkle" without glare. Sparkle or glitter occurs when a pleasant composition of luminous brilliance is achieved.

8. Flat surfaces should not be unevenly lit unless focus is to be placed on art, entries, panels, etc.

9. Enough light must reach ceilings in order to avoid gloomy conditions which occur when desired visual information on structure is missing.

10. Light sources should be selected with regard to color-rendering needs of people, finishes, and furnishings.

11. Surroundings should be moderately bright. This light should be provided by reflection from wall and ceiling surfaces or by openings for daylight.

12. Daylight should be provided through openings to achieve contact with nature and people and to induce feelings of well-being and freshness. Variety of light is the dominant daily characteristic of natural light. (See Chap. 6.)

Electric light sources and daylight cannot be applied like a coat of paint to buildings after design and functional decisions have been made. Consequently, lighting objectives and desired concepts should be established from the very earliest design stages of projects.

Reference

R. G. Hopkinson, *Architectural Physics: Lighting,* Her Majesty's Stationery Office, London, 1963, p. 125.

Chapter 2
Light Sources

INCANDESCENT LAMPS

The basic elements of an incandescent lamp are shown below. Incandescent lamps emit light when an electric current heats their filaments to incandescence. Tungsten filaments are either straight (S), coil (C, as shown below), or coiled-coil (CC). Incandescent lamps are relatively compact point sources of light. As such, they can be used by designers to direct beams of light where desired.

Basic Elements

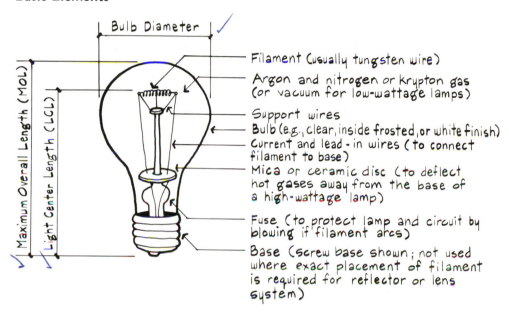

Bulb Diameter

Maximum Overall Length (MOL)

Light Center Length (LCL)

Filament (usually tungsten wire)

Argon and nitrogen or krypton gas (or vacuum for low-wattage lamps)

Support wires

Bulb (e.g., clear, inside frosted, or white finish)

Current and lead-in wires (to connect filament to base)

Mica or ceramic disc (to deflect hot gases away from the base of a high-wattage lamp)

Fuse (to protect lamp and circuit by blowing if filament arcs)

Base (screw base shown; not used where exact placement of filament is required for reflector or lens system)

Note: Tungsten-halogen incandescent lamps (also called "quartz" lamps) have a halogen gas additive in the bulb which reacts with the tungsten evaporated from the filament in order to redeposit it on the filament.

Example Shapes

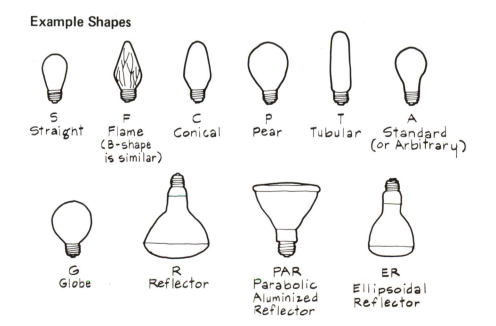

S
Straight

F
Flame
(B-shape
is similar)

C
Conical

P
Pear

T
Tubular

A
Standard
(or Arbitrary)

G
Globe

R
Reflector

PAR
Parabolic
Aluminized
Reflector

ER
Ellipsoidal
Reflector

VOLTAGE EFFECTS ON INCANDESCENT LAMP OUTPUT AND LIFE

Operating incandescent lamps above their rated voltage will reduce lamp life and increase lumen output as shown by the graphs below. For example, operating a 120-V rated lamp at 125 V (i.e., 4% increase) will reduce life by nearly 40% while producing 16% more lumens. If the same lamp has its voltage reduced by 4% below 120 V, life will be extended by over 60% while producing 13% less lumens.

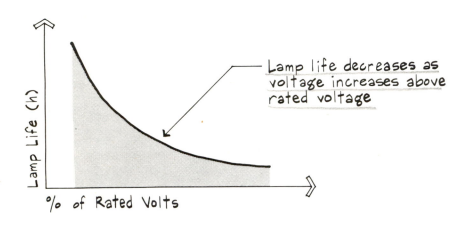

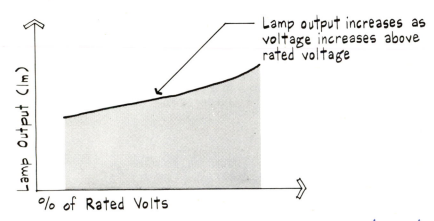

Dimming incandescent will make it last long time
Increase voltage burns it out

Reference

R. N. Helms, *Illumination Engineering for Energy Efficient Luminous Environments*, Prentice-Hall, Englewood Cliffs, N.J., 1980, pp. 72-74.

FIXTURES AND LAMP BEAM SPREAD

Reflector lamps (e.g., R or PAR lamp designations) project light in a conical beam pattern. This characteristic allows more light to be directed out of a grooved, downlight fixture than is possible with standard lamps. Ellipsoidal reflector (ER) lamps project light toward a focal point about 2 in ahead of the lamp, therefore less light is trapped in the fixture.

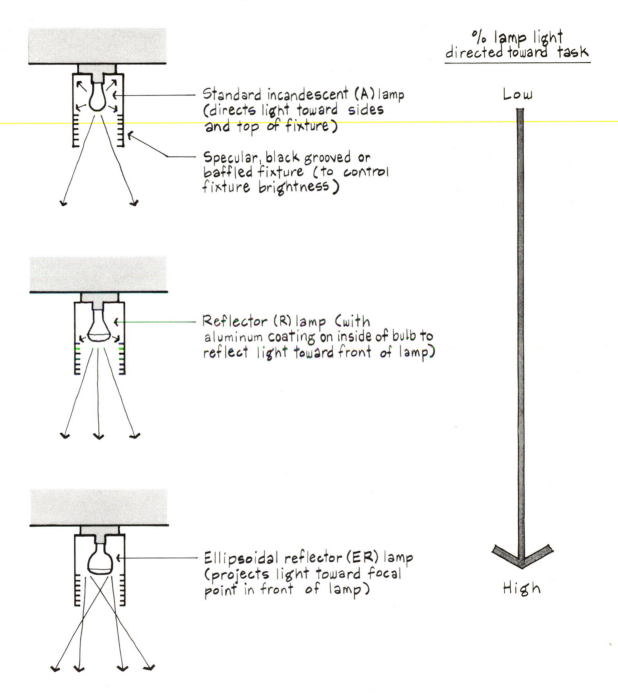

% lamp light directed toward task

Standard incandescent (A) lamp (directs light toward sides and top of fixture)

Specular, black grooved or baffled fixture (to control fixture brightness)

Low

Reflector (R) lamp (with aluminum coating on inside of bulb to reflect light toward front of lamp)

Ellipsoidal reflector (ER) lamp (projects light toward focal point in front of lamp)

High

Note: Fixtures with ellipsoidal reflector lamps will have lower surface luminance than those with flood or A lamps.

INCANDESCENT LAMP DATA

The table below presents light output data for typical incandescent lamps. For comprehensive listings, refer to current catalogs by lamp manufacturers or to Chap. 8 in *IES Lighting Handbook* (1981 Reference Volume), which presents several tables of data based on industry averages.

Lamp designation*	Lamp (W)	Average rated life (h)	Initial output (lm)	Efficacy (lm/W)
S-11	7 1/2	1400	45	6.0
A-15	15	2500	126	8.4
A-17	15	1000	120	8.0
A-19	25	1000	357	14.3
A-19	40	1500	455	11.4
A-21	50	1000	830	16.6
A-19	60	1000	890	14.8
A-19	75	750	1180	15.7
A-21	100	750	1690	16.9
A-19	100	2500	1460	14.6
A-21	150	750	2810	18.7
PS-25	150	750	2660	17.7
A-23	200	750	4000	20.0
PS-30 (SBIF)†	200	1000	3320	16.6
PS-30	300	750	6000	20.0
PS-30	300	1000	6000	20.0
PS-40	500	1000	10,140	20.3

*Designation indicates bulb shape (e.g., S for straight side, A for standard, and PS for pear-straight neck) and largest bulb diameter in eighths of an inch.

†"SBIF" indicates silver bowl, inside frosted.

Note: For general service incandescent lamps, lamp lumen depreciation (LLD) at 70% lamp life is about 0.90 for less than 500 W, 0.85 for 500 to 1500 W.

FLUORESCENT LAMPS

The basic elements of a fluorescent lamp are shown below. Fluorescent lamps produce light by emitting electrons from cathodes at their ends. This electron arc stream activates the phosphor coating (i.e., "fluorescent" material) on the inside of the bulb. Bipin or single-pin bases are used to connect lamp to the electric circuit. Reflector and aperture lamps can be used when directional control of light output from bare fluorescent lamps is desired.

Basic Elements

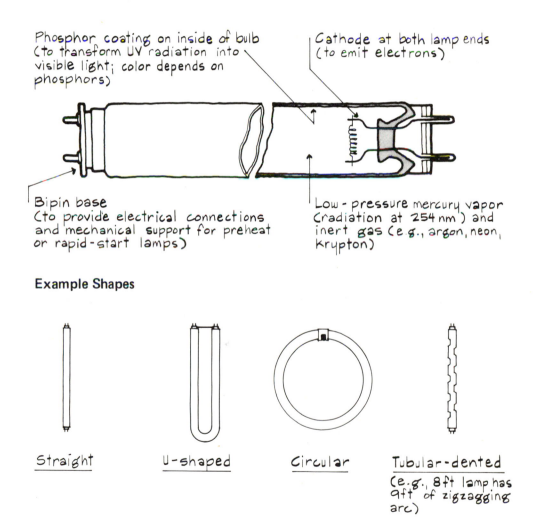

Phosphor coating on inside of bulb (to transform UV radiation into visible light; color depends on phosphors)

Cathode at both lamp ends (to emit electrons)

Bipin base (to provide electrical connections and mechanical support for preheat or rapid-start lamps)

Low-pressure mercury vapor (radiation at 254 nm) and inert gas (e.g., argon, neon, krypton)

Example Shapes

Straight

U-shaped

Circular

Tubular-dented (e.g., 8ft lamp has 9ft of zigzagging arc)

Note: Daylight (D), white (W), and warm white (WW) fluorescent lamps can provide fair color rendition; cool white (CW), soft white, and warm white deluxe (WWX) fluorescent lamps can provide good color rendition; and cool white deluxe (CWX) and natural white fluorescent lamps can provide excellent color rendition.

FLUORESCENT LAMPS AND TEMPERATURE

The effect of temperature on fluorescent lamp output is shown below. Temperature scale on graph is lamp's bare bulb wall temperature at its coolest point. Output (in lm) depends on lamp, ballast, fixture, and actual installation. At temperatures of about 105°F, the optimum amount of mercury is contained in the arc stream.

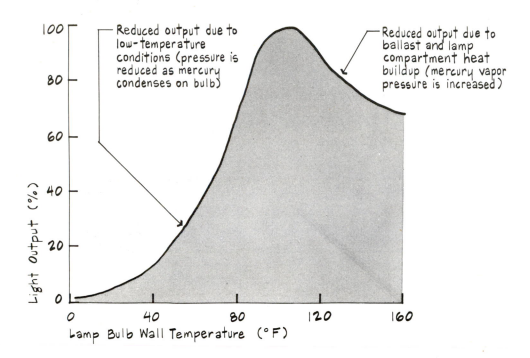

To improve lamp output and efficacy (in lm/W), use chain-suspended or pendant-supported open fixtures, or water-cooled or return-air systems for recessed fixtures (see page 49).

Note: Outdoors in cold weather, use high-output or 1500-mA lamps in tightly enclosed, gasketed fixtures or jacketed lamps.

HEAT FROM LIGHT SOURCES

Return-Air Fixtures

Air is drawn through the lighting fixture to lower the temperature of the lamps and to remove a significant percentage of lamp and ballast heat before it enters the occupied zone in rooms. Light output of standard lamps in return-air fixtures can be about 10% greater than in static fixtures.

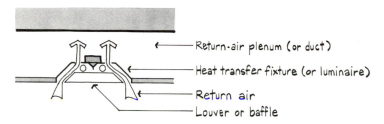

- ← Return-air plenum (or duct)
- ← Heat transfer fixture (or luminaire)
- ← Return air
- Louver or baffle

Note: Supply-air fixtures are also available. Be sure to isolate lamps from low supply air temperatures which will reduce light output and cause unstable operation of fluorescent lamps.

Return-Air Plenum

Lamp heat is removed by flow of return air around lamps into plenum. Plenum air can be used to heat perimeter zones in underheated season or can be exhausted to outdoors in overheated season.

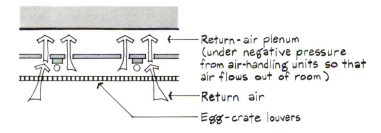

- ← Return-air plenum (under negative pressure from air-handling units so that air flows out of room)
- ← Return air
- Egg-crate louvers

Water-Cooled Fixtures

Lamp heat is removed by flow of water through tubing which can be connected to cooling unit (or heat is rejected by evaporative cooling of ground water). Tubing also can be connected to louvers at window openings to improve radiant temperature conditions in underheated season or connected to fire protection sprinkler system piping.

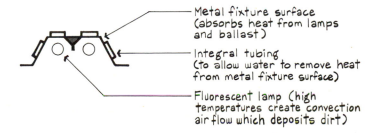

- Metal fixture surface (absorbs heat from lamps and ballast)
- Integral tubing (to allow water to remove heat from metal fixture surface)
- Fluorescent lamp (high temperatures create convection air flow which deposits dirt)

TYPICAL FLUORESCENT LAMP OUTPUT DEPRECIATION

Shown below is the typical loss in light output for fluorescent lamps at various burning times (in h). Loss of light output (or lamp lumen depreciation, LLD) depends on the phosphor type, ballast, and lamp current loading. Mean output (in lm) represents the average light output of a lamp over its rated life.

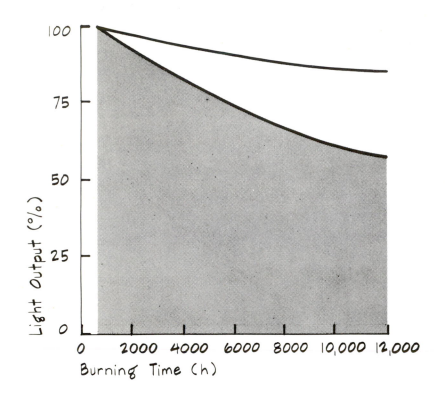

FLUORESCENT LAMP USE AND LIFE

The electron-emissive coating on the electrodes of fluorescent lamps evaporates slowly during normal operation and more rapidly during start-up, which knocks material off cathodes. Lamps operated continuously will have the longest lamp life (e.g., see curve for preheat and instant-start lamps shown below), but generally will require more frequent replacement than those operated with on-off interval use. Fluorescent lamps are less sensitive to frequent starting than in the past. For example, the 4-ft rapid-start fluorescent lamp has the same rated life at 3 and 12 hours per start-up.

Lamps should only be operated if light is needed for visual tasks. For example, reduce illumination by switching controls off at night or when daylight is sufficient.

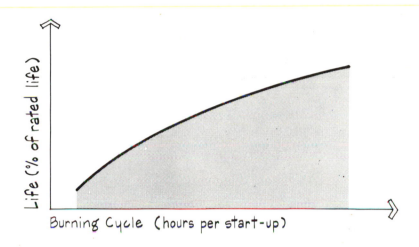

Fluorescent and HID lamps use ballasts to limit current to their operational requirements. In addition, ballasts provide starting voltage "kick" (i.e., initial current surge), and ballast design determines power factor correction. Ballasts labeled CBM indicate laboratory-tested performance which meets the standards of the Certified Ballast Manufacturers Association.

Fluorescent Lamp Wiring Diagram

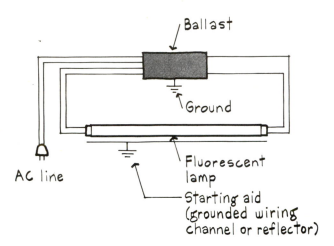

HID Lamp Wiring Diagram

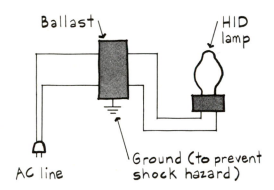

Be careful as internal ballast vibrations can produce loud humming or buzzing sounds. Manufacturers rate fluorescent ballasts from A to F according to the noise levels generated by the ballasts. The A rating is the lowest noise rating and F the highest or loudest ballast under test conditions. For rating of HID lamp noise, see "H-I-D Lighting System Noise Criterion (LS-NC) Ratings," National Electrical Manufacturers Association (NEMA), 2101 L Street, N.W., Washington, DC 20037.

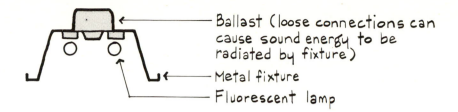

Ballast (loose connections can cause sound energy to be radiated by fixture)

Metal fixture

Fluorescent lamp

At locations where extremely low levels of sound are essential (e.g., hearing testing and research laboratories, music practice facilities), use A-rated ballasts for fluorescent lamps or consider remote mounting of ballasts. For example, ballasts can be mounted in the plenum or in rooms remote from sensitive areas, with wiring connecting ballasts to light sources. Be sure to consider voltage-drop conditions for remote-mounted applications. For example, the maximum distance for remote mounting of an enclosed ballast for high-pressure sodium lamps is about 35 ft.

Note: For a comprehensive discussion of noise control techniques, see M. D. Egan, *Concepts in Architectural Acoustics,* McGraw-Hill, New York, 1972.

FLUORESCENT LAMP DATA

The table below presents light output data for typical fluorescent lamps. For comprehensive listings, refer to current catalogs by lamp manufacturers or to Chap. 8 in *IES Lighting Handbook* (1981 Reference Volume), which presents several tables of data based on industry averages.

Lamp designation*	Lamp (W)	Diameter (in)	Length (in)	Lamp life at 3 hours per start (h)	Initial output (lm)	Initial output (lm/ft) ‡	LLD† (%)
Rapid start (about 1 s delay):							
F30 T12 CW	30	12/8	36	18,000	2210	737	0.81
F40 T12 CW	40	12/8	48	20,000	3150	788	0.84
F40 T12 WW	40	12/8	48	20,000	3175	794	0.84
F40 T12 CWX	40	12/8	48	20,000	2200	550	0.84
F48 T12 CW/HO	63	12/8	48	12,000	4300	1075	0.82
F60 T12 CW/HO	75	12/8	60	12,000	5400	1080	0.82
F72 T12 CW/HO	87	12/8	72	12,000	6650	1108	0.82
F96 T12 CW/HO	113	12/8	96	12,000	9150	1144	0.82
F48 T12 CW/VHO	116	12/8	48	9000	6900	1725	0.69
F72 T12 CW/VHO	168	12/8	72	9000	10,640	1773	0.72
F96 T12 CW/VHO	215	12/8	96	9000	15,250	1906	0.72
Slimline (instant start):							
F42 T6 CW	25	6/8	42	7500	1835	524	0.76
F42 T6 WW	25	6/8	42	7500	1875	536	0.76
F64 T6 CW	38	6/8	64	7500	3000	563	0.77
F24 T12 CW	21	12/8	24	7500-9000	1065	533	0.81
F48 T12 CW (or WW)	39	12/8	48	7500-12,000	3000	750	0.82
F72 T12 CW	57	12/8	72	7500-12,000	4585	764	0.89
F96 T12 CW	75	12/8	96	12,000	6300	788	0.89
Energy-saving:							
F40 CW/RS	35	12/8	48	20,000	2830	708	—
F96 CW	60	12/8	96	12,000	5600	700	—

*Designation indicates overall length including lampholders, bulb type (e.g., T for tubular, with the number indicating tube diameter in eighths of an inch), and color classification. Approximate operating current (in mA) and base type are also available from lamp manufacturers' catalogs.

†LLD is lamp lumen depreciation (in decimal %). LLD depends on statistically determined lamp life and relamping schedule.

‡Initial output data (in lm/ft of lamp) are useful for the design of cove lighting systems.

Note: Cool white deluxe and warm white deluxe lamps have about 30% lower efficacy than that of cool white and warm white lamps.

HIGH-INTENSITY DISCHARGE LAMPS

The basic elements of mercury and high-pressure sodium high-intensity discharge (HID) lamps are shown below. HID lamps produce light by passing a high-pressure electron arc stream through a gas vapor. They require about 5 min to warm up to full brightness. When power to HID lamps is interrupted, additional time is needed to cool lamps down prior to restriking. HID fixtures can contribute to thermal discomfort due to radiated heat from extremely high surface temperatures (e.g., 300 to 400°F).

Mercury

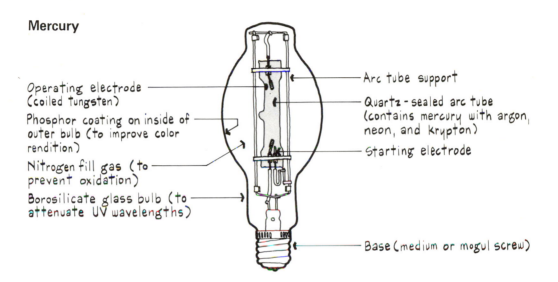

Operating electrode (coiled tungsten)

Phosphor coating on inside of outer bulb (to improve color rendition)

Nitrogen fill gas (to prevent oxidation)

Borosilicate glass bulb (to attenuate UV wavelengths)

Arc tube support

Quartz-sealed arc tube (contains mercury with argon, neon, and krypton)

Starting electrode

Base (medium or mogul screw)

Note: Metal halide lamps are very similar in construction to mercury lamps. The metal halide arc tube contains various halides (e.g., sodium and scandium iodides) to improve color rendition.

High-Pressure Sodium

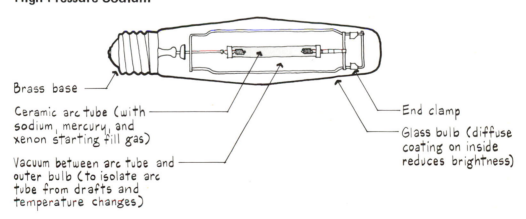

Brass base

Ceramic arc tube (with sodium, mercury, and xenon starting fill gas)

Vacuum between arc tube and outer bulb (to isolate arc tube from drafts and temperature changes)

End clamp

Glass bulb (diffuse coating on inside reduces brightness)

Note: Mercury lamps are available that are "self-ballasted." These lamps have an internal ballast circuit which allows them to directly replace incandescent lamps if used in adequately wired porcelain sockets.

HIGH-INTENSITY DISCHARGE LAMP DATA

The table below presents light output data for typical HID lamps. The first letter in the lamp designation indicates type: mercury (H), metal halide (M), high-pressure sodium (S), and self-ballasted mercury (B). For comprehensive listings, refer to current catalogs by lamp manufacturers or to Chap. 8 in *IES Lighting Handbook* (1981 Reference Volume), which presents several tables of data based on industry averages.

Lamp designation*	Description	Rated average life (h)	Initial output (lm)	Mean output (lm)	LLD† (%)
Mercury (3- to 5-min warm-up and restrike delay):					
H45AY-50/DX	deluxe white	16,000	1575	1260	—
H43AY-75/DX	deluxe white	24,000	3000	2430	—
H38MP-100/DX	deluxe white	24,000+	4275	3500	0.69
H39KC-175/WDX	warm deluxe white	24,000+	7650	6600	0.77
H39KB-175	clear	24,000+	7975	7430	0.88
H39KC-175/DX	deluxe white	24,000+	8600	7640	0.71
H33GL-400/DX	deluxe white	24,000+	23,125	19,840	0.78
H33GL-400/WDX	warm deluxe white	24,000+	21,500	18,000	0.74
H36GW-1000/DX	deluxe white	24,000+	63,000	48,380	0.63
Metal halide (5- to 10-min warm-up and restrike delay):					
MV400/BD, BU/I	clear, vertical burning	15,000	34,000	26,500	0.70
M47PA-1000/BD, BU/I	clear, vertical burning	10,000	115,000	92,000	0.75
M48PC-1500/BD, BU	clear, vertical burning	3000	155,000	140,700	—
High-pressure sodium (about 1-min delay):					
S54SB-100	clear	24,000	9500	8550	0.84
S55SC-150	clear	24,000	16,000	14,400	0.84
S50VA-250	clear	24,000	27,500	24,750	0.88
S51WA-400	clear‡	24,000	50,000	45,000	0.88
S52XB-1000	clear‡	24,000	140,000	126,000	0.83

*Designation by American National Standards Institute (ANSI) indicates lamp type by first letter (H for mercury, M for metal halide, S for high-pressure sodium); ballast by first numerals; nominal wattage by last numerals; and color by DX for deluxe white, WDX for warm deluxe white. HT indicates mercury lamp with internal safety switch to shut off lamp if outer bulb breaks.

†LLD is lamp lumen depreciation (in decimal %).

‡High-pressure sodium lamps especially suited for pole-mounted outdoor applications.

LAMP COLOR SPECTRUM

The graph of relative energy emitted at wavelengths by a light source is called a *spectral energy distribution* curve (or *lamp spectrum*). For spectral energy distribution of daylight, see page 14.

Incandescent Lamp

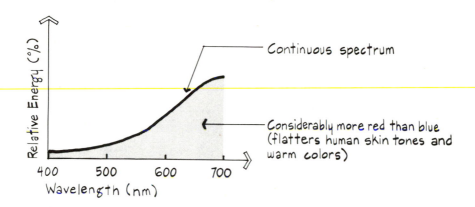

Fluorescent Lamp

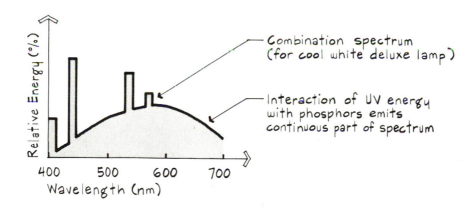

Mercury Lamp (Clear Bulb)

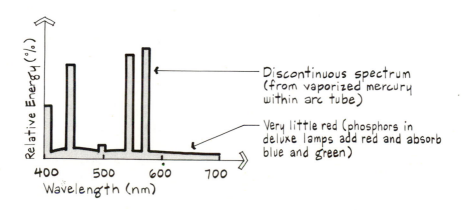

LAMP COLOR RENDITION

Finishes should be evaluated using the type of lamp (or combinations of lamps and daylight) which will actually be used in the building, as color rendition depends on lamp color spectrum, reflective property of surfaces, and context. For example, as the perception of skin color is important in health care occupancies, select light sources which do not distort red hues. Be careful, as the color of HID lamps tends to vary and shift with life or burning time. The color-rendering situations shown below are typical for most observers, however, judgment of apparent surface color also depends on the experience and expectations of an individual with normal color vision.

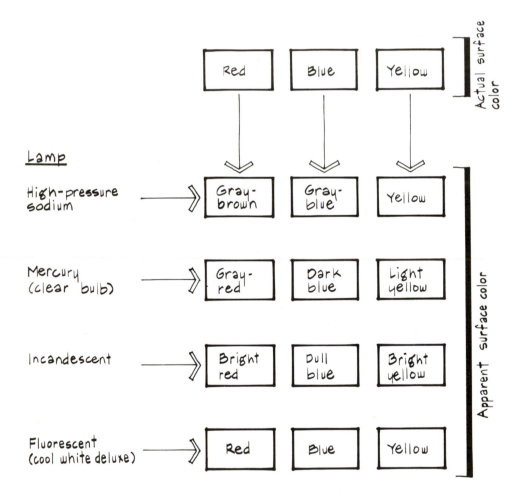

Note: Reflected light from cool white or cool white deluxe fluorescent lamps on neutral surface colors generally appears white; from warm white or warm white deluxe fluorescent and high-pressure sodium lamps, it generally appears yellowish white.

In many situations, color constancy can compensate for color distortion by lamps. For example, a white surface illuminated by an incandescent lamp will appear correctly as white if the yellow sensations are perceived by an observer as belonging to the incandescent light source.

COLOR RENDERING INDEX

The color rendering index (CRI) is a measure of how well light sources render color. In the CRI method, the performance of a test source is compared to a standard reference source on eight color samples. A CRI of 100 means an exact color match with the reference source. The index is an average value, which means poor performance at one color may be concealed by better performance at another color. Therefore, two lamps having identical CRIs can have widely varying color-rendering abilities. To compare lamps, they must have nearly the same chromaticity or color temperature. For example, cool white fluorescent lamps at a CRI of 67 can be compared to cool white deluxe fluorescent lamps at a CRI of 90, but cannot be compared to high-pressure sodium lamps.

Schematic of Color Rendering Test

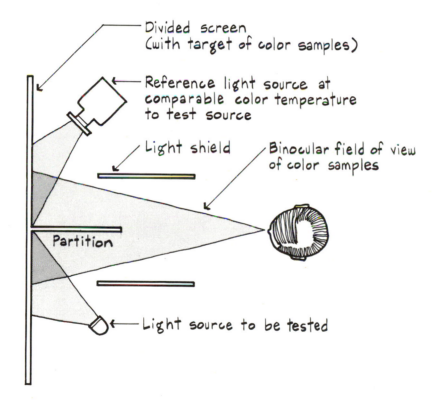

Divided screen
(with target of color samples)

Reference light source at
comparable color temperature
to test source

Light shield

Binocular field of view
of color samples

Partition

Light source to be tested

Note: For most color judgment work, illumination levels of about 30 fc are sufficient (cf., P. R. Boyce, *Human Factors in Lighting*, Macmillan Publishing Co., New York, 1981, p. 144).

The curves below depict lamp failures over time for lamps having identical life ratings. Rated lamp life is the point in time when 50% of a statistical sample of lamps have failed (see dashed lines on graph below). A lighting system with curve 2 lamps would have more early failures than one with curve 1 lamps.

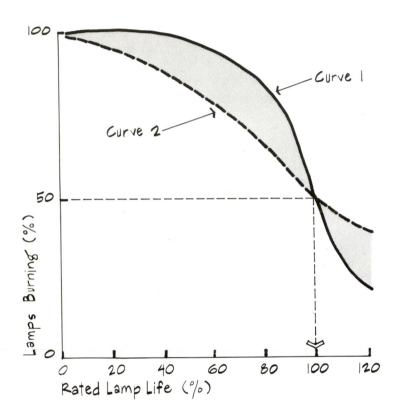

Note: Spot relamping is the replacement of lamps on a one-by-one basis; group relamping is the replacement of all lamps in a room or zone. The most economical group relamping time usually is about 60 to 80% of rated lamp life. Consider retaining the better used lamps for spot replacements between group relampings.

COLOR TEMPERATURE

Color temperature (K) of an electric light source expresses its warmth or "coolth" (e.g., yellowish white, bluish white, or neutral in appearance), not the spectral energy distribution or the physical temperature. On the scale below, color temperatures are given for electric light sources and daylight.

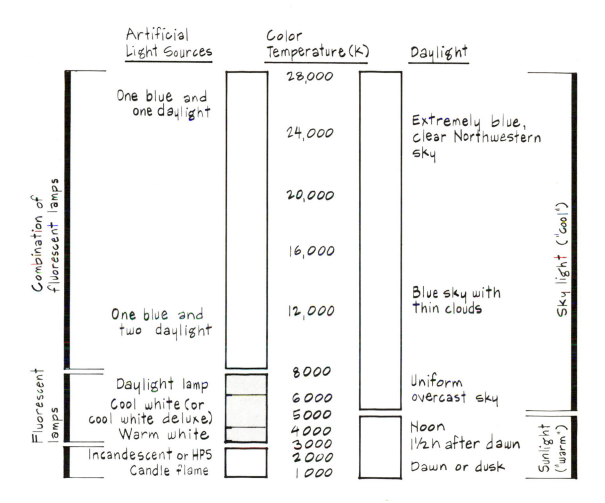

Note: Studies at Kansas State University on the effects of lighting and color on thermal comfort indicate that under cool white fluorescent lamps, warmer temperatures are preferred; and under warm white fluorescent lamps, cooler temperatures are preferred. In addition, thermal comfort is greater in orange than in blue work stations (cf., F. H. Rohles et al., "The Effects of Lighting, Color, and Room Decor on Thermal Comfort," *ASHRAE Transactions*, Vol. 87, Part 2, January 1982).

INCANDESCENT LAMP EFFICACY AND COLOR TEMPERATURE

The graph below shows lamp efficacy (in lm/W) for incandescent lamps at a wide variety of wattages (i.e., 40 to 1500 W).

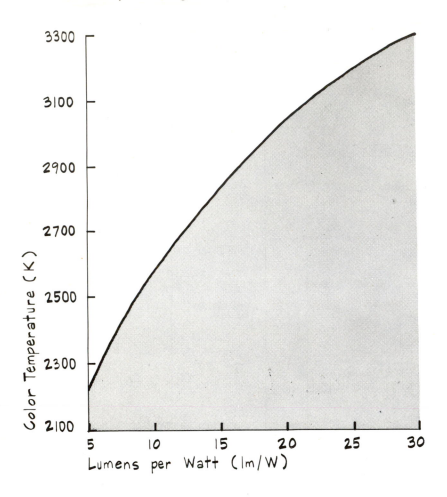

HEAT AND LIGHT FROM LIGHTING FIXTURES

Heat emitted by lighting fixtures is due to energy produced by the lamp and ballast. Heat emitted (in Btuh) is 3.4 times the wattage supplied to the lighting fixture for all lamp types and their associated ballasts (cf., M. D. Egan, *Concepts in Thermal Comfort,* Prentice-Hall, Englewood Cliffs, N.J., 1975, p. 78). The table below gives the nominal value (in %) of the total wattage consumed by fixtures that is converted to heat and visible light.

Lamp	Lighting system energy for lamps (%)*			
	Ballast losses	Infrared heat	Conducted and convected heat	Converted to light
Incandescent	—	72	18	10
Fluorescent	9	32	36	23
Mercury	11	48	27	14
Metal halide	13	35	31	21
High-pressure sodium	14	38	22	26

*For a specific lighting system, the energy distribution percentage depends on lamp size, ballast arrangement, and other factors.

SHIELDING OF LAMPS

Baffles and louvers, as shown below, can provide textured patterns and shielding for lamps to prevent direct glare. The shielding angle (in degrees) is the maximum angle between the horizontal and an observer's line of sight to the shielding materials when the lamps first can be seen. Eggcrate louvers can provide shielding for most viewing directions, whereas baffles provide shielding in only one direction. Be careful, as white or aluminum louvers can become the brightest elements in the visual field. Parabolic-wedge louvers can provide dark surface at higher efficiency than black flat-blade baffles.

Flat Baffles

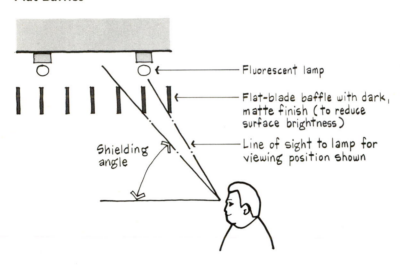

Fluorescent lamp

Flat-blade baffle with dark, matte finish (to reduce surface brightness)

Line of sight to lamp for viewing position shown

Shielding angle

Parabolic Louvers

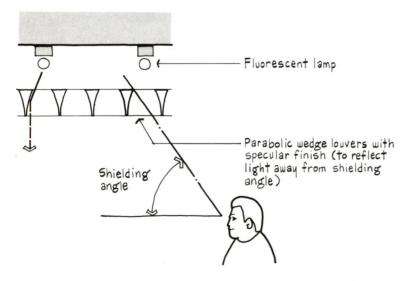

Fluorescent lamp

Parabolic wedge louvers with specular finish (to reflect light away from shielding angle)

Shielding angle

Note: Work surfaces under lamps shielded by louvers or baffles may have "heads-down" viewing angles at the mirror angle of the lamps.

REFLECTORS AND DIFFUSERS

Reflectors, lenses, and diffusing elements can be used to achieve a wide variety of light distribution and brightness characteristics.

Specular Reflector

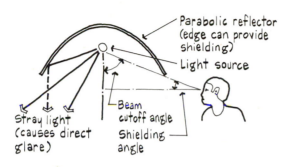

Parabolic reflector (edge can provide shielding)

Light source

Stray light (causes direct glare)

Beam cutoff angle

Shielding angle

Louvers (or Baffles)

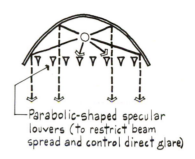

Parabolic-shaped specular louvers (to restrict beam spread and control direct glare)

Lens (Clear, Prismatic, or Fresnel)

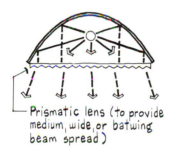

Prismatic lens (to provide medium, wide, or batwing beam spread)

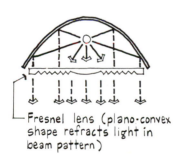

Fresnel lens (plano-convex shape refracts light in beam pattern)

Shield

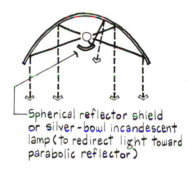

Spherical reflector shield or silver-bowl incandescent lamp (to redirect light toward parabolic reflector)

Note: Parabolic-shaped reflectors reflect considerably less sound energy than flat or prismatic lenses. This characteristic is important in open-plan offices, where flat-lens luminaires can reduce acoustical isolation between work stations by as much as 10 dB at high sound frequencies. The decibel (dB) is a unit used to express the intensity level of sound energy (e.g., 0 dB represents the level at the threshold of hearing and 130 dB, the threshold of pain).

Lenses are the shielding or diffusing portions of light fixtures which control brightness and direct light. Shown below are sections of lenses along with example beam spread patterns which they can create. The prismatic and fluted lenses control transmitted light by refraction (i.e., bending of light according to Snell's law). Snell's law predicts the amount of bending, as the ratio of indices of refraction of glass (or plastic) and air is inversely proportional to the sine of their respective angles of incidence ($\angle i$) and refraction ($\angle r$), which is (sin $\angle i$/sin $\angle r$) $\simeq$ 1.5 for air and clear plate glass.

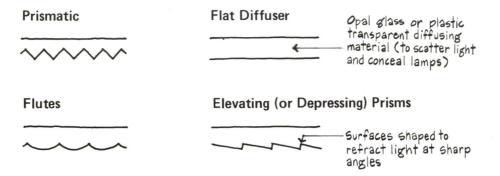

Prismatic

Flat Diffuser

Opal glass or plastic transparent diffusing material (to scatter light and conceal lamps)

Flutes

Elevating (or Depressing) Prisms

Surfaces shaped to refract light at sharp angles

Beam Spread Patterns

Beam spread patterns (or candlepower distribution curves) illustrate the relative distribution of light rays for bare lamps or, as shown below, for a fixture with lens. For a detailed discussion of how to use candlepower distribution curves, see page 138.

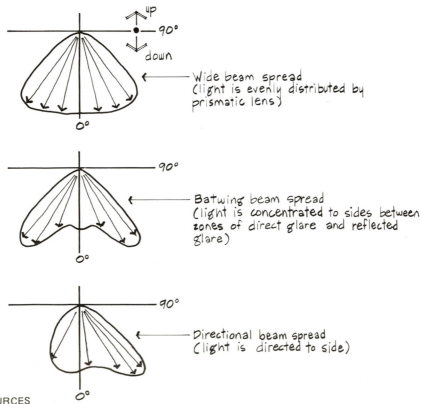

up

down

90°

Wide beam spread (light is evenly distributed by prismatic lens)

0°

90°

Batwing beam spread (light is concentrated to sides between zones of direct glare and reflected glare)

0°

90°

Directional beam spread (light is directed to side)

0°

BRIGHTNESS AND GLARE

Visual comfort limits for glare depend on the relationship of brightness and size of the source, the position of the object in the visual field, and the eye adaptation of the viewer. For example, the greater the angle ($\angle\beta$, in degrees), between the source of glare and the horizontal line of sight, the less the discomfort. The sketch below shows generally acceptable average luminance levels for different angles of incidence.

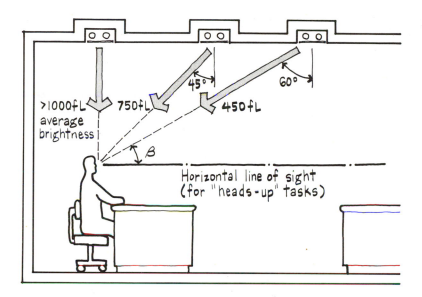

Note: Brightness of surround determines eye adaptation, which in turn influences the perception of glare. For example, when eyes are adapted to low levels of light in a building, windows at the end of a corridor can cause discomfort or even disability glare.

Discomfort glare from luminaires can be controlled by limiting brightness as shown on the graph below. The limit lines on the graph pivot about point *A* and are referred to as a *scissors curve* due to their resemblance to a pair of scissors. To control direct glare, values of measured fixture brightness should fall below the limit lines.

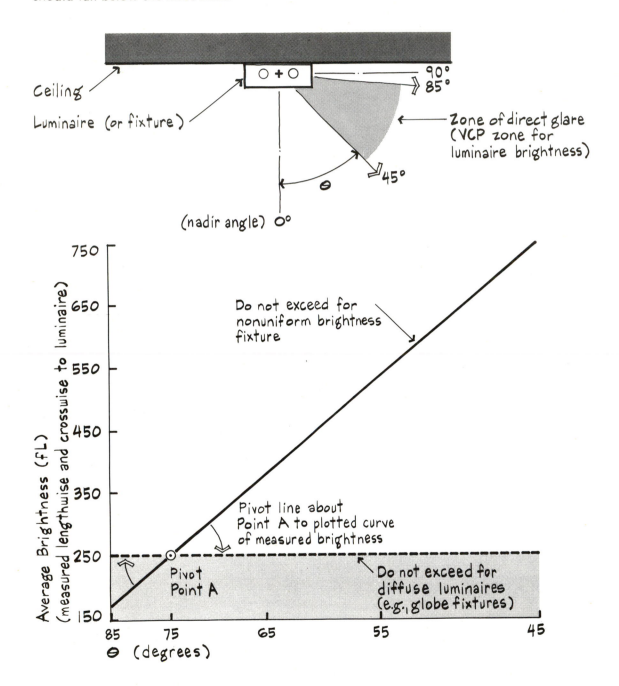

VISUAL COMFORT PROBABILITY (VCP) INDEX

The *visual comfort probability* (VCP) index method for rating visual comfort evaluates the probability (in %) that a person looking straight ahead while seated at the center rear of a room (i.e., usually the worst position for direct glare) will find the degree of direct glare just acceptable (or tolerable). The VCP rating for lighting systems, arranged in a regular, or uniform, layout producing 100 fc, is determined by the subjective reactions of test participants. VCP ratings are affected by luminaire brightness in the 45 to 85° zone (see sketch on page 68), luminaire position and arrangement, brightness of room surfaces and furnishings, and average brightness of luminaire. Luminaire brightness is more important than number and size (e.g., halving the number of lamps in fixtures lowers luminaire brightness and results in a higher VCP, whereas halving the number of fixtures results in about the same VCP).

Bright luminaires can cause discomfort glare, as extremely high levels of luminaire brightness may require unpleasant eye adaptation. Occupants will look into a bright visual field with their heads up and on tasks at lower brightness with their heads down. In offices this continual long-term eye adaptation process can contribute to annoyance, frustration, and irritation.

The VCP does not rate overall acceptance of the visual environment in rooms. For example, a room with a lighting system having a high VCP can be dull and uninteresting. Conversely, a room with a low VCP may have illuminated crystal chandeliers and accent lights which add sparkle, drama, and interest.

For most observers with normal glare sensitivity, the following table describes the glare sensation corresponding to the VCP rating.

VCP (%)	Direct glare conditions
95-100	Unnoticeable
75-94	Acceptable
64-74	Distracting, but not uncomfortable
50-63	Threshold of discomfort
34-49	Uncomfortable
20-33	Perceptibly uncomfortable

FIXTURE GLARE CONTROL

The table below presents example direct glare conditions and efficiencies for a variety of shielding materials (e.g., louver, lens, diffuser) used in typical 2 X 4 ft fluorescent troffer light fixtures. Luminaire efficiency is the ratio of the lumens emitted by the luminaire to the lumens emitted by the lamps alone.

Shielding material	Direct glare conditions	Luminaire efficiency
Parabolic louver	Unnoticeable	Low
Dark metal louver	Acceptable	Low
Toned lens (i.e., pigmented)	Acceptable to distracting	Medium
White metal louver	Distracting (but not uncomfortable)	Low
Polarizer	Distracting (but not uncomfortable)	High
Clear lens	Can be uncomfortable	High
Plastic louver	Can be uncomfortable	Medium
Diffuser (i.e., translucent panel)	Uncomfortable	Medium

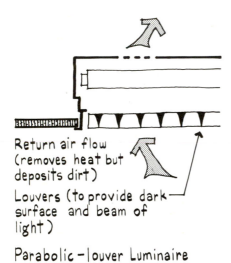

Return air flow (removes heat but deposits dirt)

Louvers (to provide dark surface and beam of light)

Parabolic-louver Luminaire

Note: Parabolic louvers and large-cell aluminum troffers with parabolic wedge-shaped baffles can be used near cathode ray tube (CRT) screens to reduce reflected glare. However, indirect lighting systems, which provide diffuse light by reflection from ceiling surfaces, do not cause images of light sources to be reflected by CRT screens.

EFFICACY OF LIGHT SOURCES

Efficacy is the light source output expressed in lumens per watt. The scale below represents lamp efficacy alone. HID lamp sources include high-pressure sodium, metal halide, and mercury. For energy consumption analyses, ballast losses should be included in the efficacy rating of HID and fluorescent lamps.

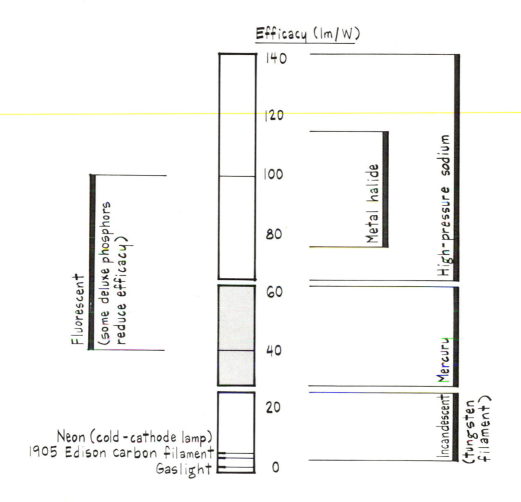

Reference

J. P. Frier and M. E. G. Frier, *Industrial Lighting Systems,* McGraw-Hill, New York, 1980, p. 26.

LAMP EFFICACY AND WATTAGE

The higher the wattage, the higher the output (in lm/W) of fluorescent and incandescent lamps. Lower-amperage fluorescent lamps provide higher output. The graph below shows fluorescent lamp current in milliampere (mA). Amperage is equal to wattage divided by voltage.

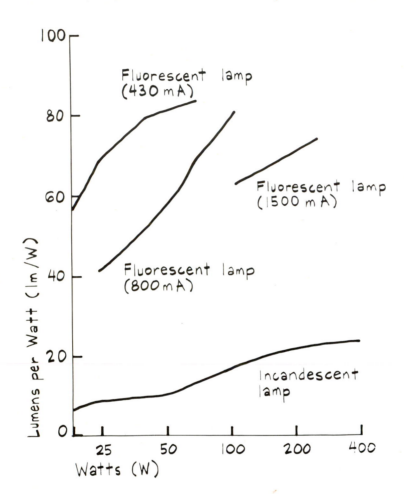

LIGHTING LOAD

To conserve energy, lighting loads (in W/ft^2) in buildings should be low. The graph below shows example relationships of illumination level (in fc) to lighting load for HID (high-pressure sodium, metal halide, and mercury), fluorescent, and incandescent lamps. At a given illumination level, HID and fluorescent sources will achieve lower lighting loads than incandescent lamps.

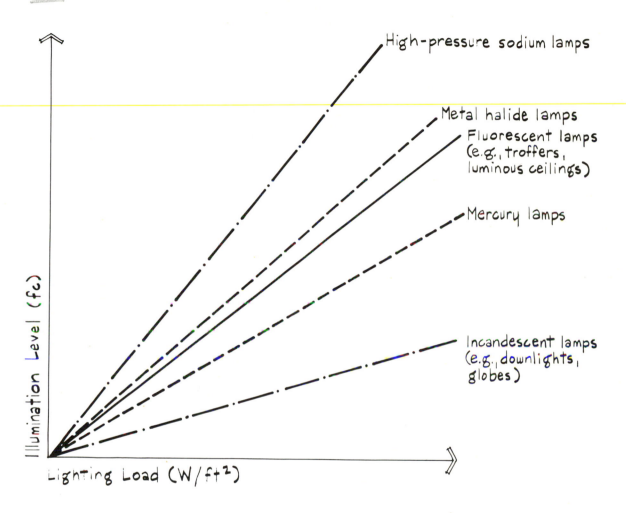

Reference

J. E. Kaufman, "Optimizing the Uses of Energy for Lighting," *Lighting Design & Application,* October 1973, p. 10.

CHARACTERISTICS OF ELECTRIC LIGHT SOURCES

	Incandescent (including tungsten-halogen)	Fluorescent	Low-pressure sodium
Basic description	High-intensity point source, compact size with one socket	Low-intensity line source, bulky size with two bases plus ballast, temperature sensitive	Low-pressure long line source, bulky ballast with one socket
Length (in)	$\frac{3}{16}$-18	6-96	12-44
Watts (W)	1-10,000	5-215	35-180
Visible energy (%)	10	23	35
Efficacy (lm/W)	10-25	25-100	130-180
Typical average life (h)	750-4000 (varies with applied voltage)	10-20,000	18,000
Start and restart times (min)	Instantly	Immediately	7-9 (start) 0-3 (restart)
Dimmability	Full range adjustability	Possible with rapid start dimming ballast plus dimming device	Not at present
Color rendition	Excellent (continuous spectrum)	Good (combination spectrum)	Poor (spectrum predominantly monochrome yellow)

	High-intensity discharge	
Mercury	**Metal halide**	**High-pressure sodium**
High-pressure point or short line source, moderately compact size with one socket plus ballast	High-pressure point or short line source, moderately compact size with one socket plus ballast	High-pressure point or short line source, moderately compact size with one socket plus ballast
5-16	8-15	7-15
40-1500	175-1500	35-1000
14	21	26
20-65	80-115	85-140
24,000+	7500-20,000	24,000+
3-6 3-8	2-3 5-10	3-4 1-2
Possible with special circuit plus auxiliary equipment	Possible with special circuit plus auxiliary equipment	Possible with special circuit plus auxiliary equipment
Very good (discontinuous spectrum) low in red	Excellent (discontinuous spectrum)	Good (discontinuous spectrum) yellow cast, low in blue-green

Illumination from the sky is constantly changing due to the earth's revolution about the sun and conditions of the sky (i.e., clouds, dust, pollution). The three basic sky conditions are clear (<30% cloud cover), partly cloudy (30 to 70% cloud cover), and overcast (100% cloud cover, with sun not visible). For further information on daylight in design, see Chap. 6.

Clear Sky (Produces intense, direct light from sun and diffuse light from sky)

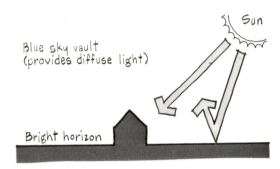

Partly Cloudy Sky (Constantly changing, intense, diffuse light)

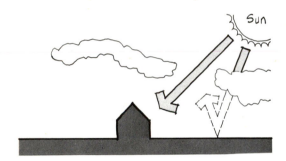

Overcast Sky (Produces diffuse light)

Note: Data on sunrise-to-sunset sky conditions are available for many locations in the United States from the National Oceanic and Atmospheric Administration (NOAA), National Climatic Center, Federal Building, Asheville, NC 28801.

Chapter 3
Light Measurement

Four singers are not 4 times as loud as one. The perception of sound is a logarithmic process, and the quantity or level of sound energy is expressed as the decibel. In this example, four singers would be 6 dB louder than one. To be perceived as twice as loud, a sound must increase by about 10 dB. Above the threshold level of sound needed for intelligibility, the quality of sound is more important than the quantity. For example, perception of speech requires room conditions that are free from echoes, hot spots, excessive reverberation (i.e., persistence of sound after source has stopped), intruding noises, and so on.

Similar factors also apply to light. Above task background illumination levels of 30 to 40 fc, large increases in quantity of light will be needed to produce only small increases in visibility. An important characteristic of good lighting is its freedom from *visual noise*; that is, freedom from discomfort glare, disability glare, and distracting or irrelevant patterns of light.

The "signal-to-noise" ratio for light must be high enough to allow the desired task or other visual information to be clearly perceived. Visual signals which confuse, cover (e.g., by veiling reflections), compete with desired task (e.g., disability glare), or interfere with other important visual information (e.g., discomfort glare) are unwanted. Therefore, good lighting designs must avoid visual noise.

In this chapter, information on how to measure illumination levels with light meters is presented. Light meters also can be used to establish lighting gradients and contours, and to measure brightness, reflectance, transmittance, and the like. In addition, information on visual task performance studies is presented.

LUMEN AND FOOTCANDLE UNITS

The lumen is a unit of light-producing power of a light source. It can be defined as the rate at which light falls on one square foot of surface area one foot from a source of one candlepower, or one candela. A candela is 1/60 the intensity of a square centimeter of a blackbody radiator operated at 2047 K, which is the freezing point of platinum. A footcandle, as shown on the sketch below, is the quantity of light (or illumination level) on one square foot of surface area one foot away from the light source. In the metric system, a lux is the quantity of light on one square meter of surface area one meter away from the light source (1 lux equals 0.09 fc).

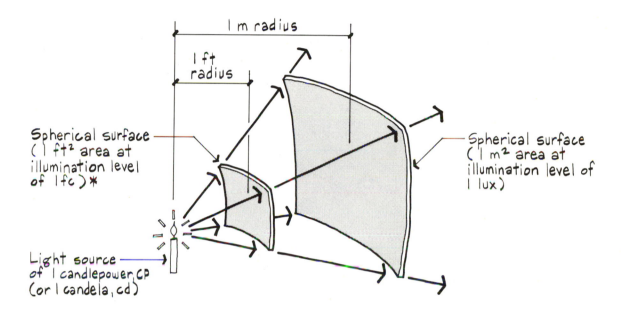

*One footcandle is equal to one lumen per square foot (lm/ft²). One lumen (lm) is equal to 12.57 candela (cd), i.e., 4π which is the surface area of a sphere.

Reference

"Light Measurement and Control," General Electric Technical Publication TP-118, Cleveland, March 1965, p. 5.

COLOR TEMPERATURE AND ILLUMINATION LEVEL

The graph below, often referred to as the *amenity curve* for light, indicates that warm light, at low color temperature, is more acceptable for lower illumination levels (e.g., by evoking red-gold light of flame sources and sunlight at dawn or dusk). Cool light, at high color temperature, is preferred at higher illumination levels because people may relate it to daylight.

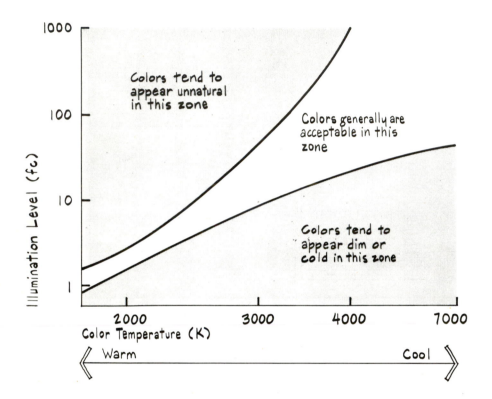

Note: According to the amenity curve shown above, warm white fluorescent lamps at 3000 K would be acceptable at 10 to 50 fc, whereas cool white fluorescent lamps at 4200 K would be acceptable at 30 fc and above.

Reference

A. A. Kruithof, "Tubular Luminescence Lamps for General Illumination," *Philips Technical Review*, March 1941, p. 69.

INVERSE-SQUARE AND COSINE LAWS FOR LIGHT

Inverse-Square Law

As the distance from a point source of light increases, the same light energy is distributed over a greater spherical surface area. As a consequence, the illumination level will be reduced. The inverse-square law for light is

$$E = \frac{cp}{r^2}$$

where E = illumination level (fc)
       cp = candlepower of source of light (cd)
        r = distance from point source (ft)

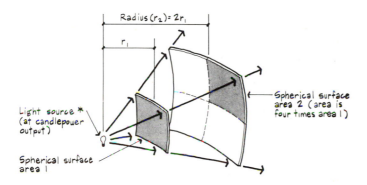

*Point source of light as distance r is more than 5 times the largest dimension of the light source.

Cosine Law

Light energy impinging on a surface at $\angle\,\alpha$ other than normal is distributed over a greater area. For example, area E_2 is greater than area E_1 as shown in the sketch below. The cosine law for light is

$$E_2 = E_1 \cos\alpha$$

where E = illumination level (fc)
        α = angle between ray of light and the normal to surface (degrees)

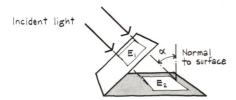

Reference

J. E. Kaufman (ed.), *IES Lighting Handbook* (1981 Reference Volume), p. 9-40.

Visibility improves by increasing object size, contrast, time for viewing, and illumination level (particularly when lighting is poor). As shown by the curves below, the best performance for large test objects occurs at a lower illumination level than that for the smaller sizes. For small test objects, even significant increases in illumination level (footcandle scale is logarithmic) do not achieve performance equivalent to viewing the larger, more visible test objects. For many situations, an increase from 1 to 2 fc is roughly equal to the visual improvement of an increase from 100 to 200 fc.

The direction of light is also important. For example, light on textiles at grazing angles can show defects as well as general diffuse sources, which produce 20 times the illumination level of the grazing light.

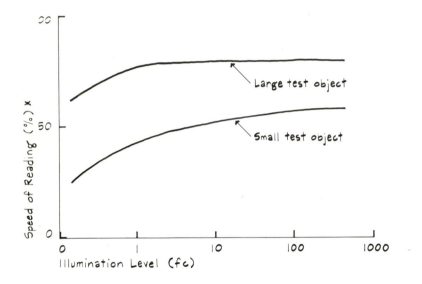

*Percentage of maximum possible speed of reading as determined by accuracy of responses.

Example test objects used to determine speed of reading in visual task performance studies are given below.

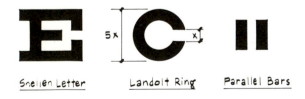

Snellen Letter   Landolt Ring   Parallel Bars

VISUAL TASK PERFORMANCE STUDIES

Visual task performance generally involves detection (I see something), recognition (it is a man), and identification (the man is Figley E. Whitesides). Threshold studies examine the minimum light level needed to detect, recognize, or identify visual tasks under various conditions of contrast, brightness, and time. In real-world situations, acceptable conditions for ease of seeing often involve detection or search well above threshold levels (e.g., proof-reading printed materials).

Search Chart Task (Subject asked to find specific numbers on chart.)

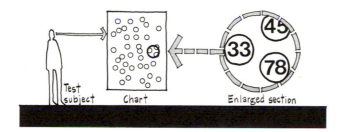

Luminous Disc (Subject asked to adjust target until "barely visible.")

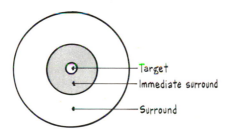

Landolt Ring Chart (Subject asked to count gap, or cancel gap with pencil, in every ring in a specific direction.)

During the 1920s to 1930s, a series of studies of lighting levels and work performance was conducted at the Hawthorne Works of the Western Electric Company by Professor Elton Mayo of Harvard University. Work performance can be measured by productivity (e.g., number of errors, speed, quantity of output).

At Hawthorne, the work consisted of inspecting parts, assembling relays, and winding coils. Lighting levels were varied from 3 to 44 fc. For control purposes, the same tasks were performed under uniform existing lighting conditions.

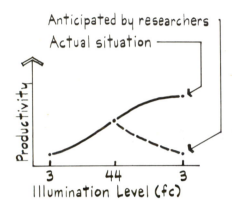

In two out of three departments tested, production seemed to increase with increased lighting levels. However, constant lighting levels maintained in one department resulted in as much increased production as did the increased lighting levels. Finally, when levels were reduced to as low as 3 fc, workers still maintained their usual productivity.

A follow-up study at Hawthorne concluded that productivity increases were due to increased motivation and a more positive attitude toward the job (e.g., participation by workers in a study of their working conditions) — not due to increased or decreased lighting levels. The term *Hawthorne effect* is used today to caution behavioral researchers about the difficulties of finding simple cause-effect relationships in real-world field studies.

References

W. M. C. Lam, *Perception and Lighting as Formgivers for Architecture*, McGraw-Hill, New York, 1977, p. 79.

H. M. Parsons, "What Happened at Hawthorne?," *Science*, 1974, pp. 922-932.

G. T. Yonemura, "Criteria for Recommending Lighting Levels," U.S. National Bureau of Standards, NBSIR 81-2231, March 1981.

LIGHT MEASUREMENTS WITH LIGHT METERS

Light meters are available (e.g., General Electric, Tektronix, Simpson Electric) that are color- and cosine-corrected and suitable for measuring both indoor and outdoor lighting conditions. It is important that a light meter be color-corrected to respond to color in much the same way the human eye does and be cosine-corrected to represent the true illumination level on the meter regardless of the angle of incidence of light. Light meters can be used to measure illumination levels, brightness, reflectance, transmittance, and approximate candlepower distribution.

Illumination Levels

To measure illumination levels, take readings (in lm/ft^2 or fc) with light cell parallel to and on the plane of interest. Illumination gradients (and contours) can be measured with a light meter (see page 92). These gradients provide a method of analyzing the relationships between light sources and room shapes and reflectances.

Brightness

To measure brightness (i.e., luminance in fL) of a diffuse reflecting surface, hold the meter's light cell close to the surface of interest and then draw it back 2 to 4 in until the reading remains constant. Avoid shadows on the area being measured from the meter or user. Luminance is equal to the meter reading (in fc).

To measure the brightness of a luminous source, place the light cell directly against the surface being measured and read the luminance directly.

Reflectance

The *reflected-incident light method* is used to determine reflectance (in %) of diffuse, or nonglossy, reflecting surfaces. For example, the meter is placed against a surface and then drawn back about 2 to 4 in until no shadow falls on the surface. The meter reading at this position is divided by the incident light reading when the base of the meter is against the surface. Be careful to avoid shadows and always keep the meter dial face up.

The *known-sample comparison method* is a more accurate method of measuring diffuse reflecting surfaces. A card of known reflectance measuring at least 8 × 10 in (e.g., Kodak test card) is placed against a surface, and the reflected light is read from the meter held about 3 in away from the card. The card is then removed so that the reflected light now comes from the surface of unknown reflectance. A second reading is taken with the meter at the same position as before. The reading of reflected light from the unknown surface is divided by the reading from the known sample, and the result is multiplied by the reflectance of the test card. For reasonably accurate results, be sure the test card is clean.

Transmittance

To measure transmittance (in %) of a transparent or translucent material, hold the meter's light cell flush on the sample. Using a constant light source on the opposite side, measure the footcandles from the source with and without the sample in place. Transmittance is the ratio (in %) of these two readings.

Approximate Candlepower Distribution

In the laboratory, a photometer (i.e., light-sensitive cell which measures footcandles at known distances from the source) is used to determine the candlepower distribution of light sources or luminaires. If a point source is measured, the candlepower (in cd) is the footcandle reading at a given position times the square of the distance from the source. The distance should be at least 5 times the maximum dimension of the source. A graphic record of the intensity of light emitted at various angles from a light source is called a *candlepower (or candela) distribution curve* (see sketch below).

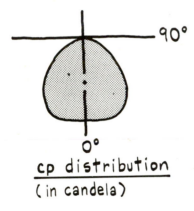

cp distribution
(in candela)

Note: The lumen rating of light sources and the published "photometric characteristics" are based on assuming the source to be the center of a standard 1-ft sphere. Since candlepower is usually not equal in all directions, the surface of the standard sphere is subdivided into zones of smaller area, each zone illuminated by the average candlepower directed toward its center. As the areas of the zones are unequal, lumens for each zone are found by multiplying midzone candlepower times its respective area or zonal constant. The total is the lumen rating for a light source or luminaire.

The light meter also can be used to estimate an approximate curve for in-place luminaires (see page 91). Nevertheless, manufacturer's performance data should only come from certified photometric tests with calibrated equipment in light-absorbing test spaces.

Illumination Level Measurements

To determine room illumination, a number of footcandle readings are taken at regular intervals, and the average is computed. Hold the meter's light cell parallel to the plane of interest, usually the work surface. Do not cast shadows on meter or hold it close to your body where bright clothing would add reflected light to the reading.

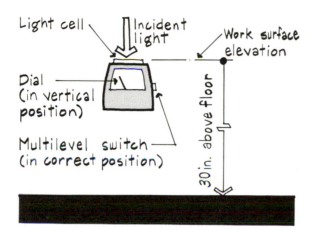

Brightness Measurements

To measure brightness (i.e., luminance), position the meter's light cell against the surface being measured and slowly retract meter to a position 2 to 4 in away until a constant reading is obtained. Luminance (in fL) is equal to the meter reading (in fc). (Multiply meter reading by 1.25 if meter is not cosine corrected.)

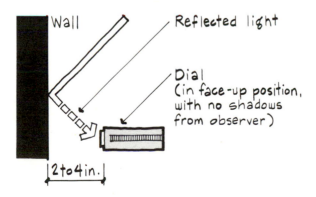

Brightness Measurements of Luminous Source

For a luminous source, place the light cell directly against the surface being measured. The meter reading is equal to the luminance level (in fL).

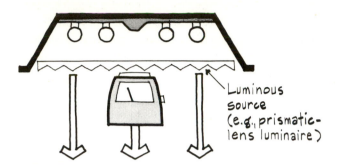

Luminous source (e.g., prismatic-lens luminaire)

Warning: Light meters are extremely fragile. Do not bump or drop them.

REFLECTANCE MEASUREMENTS

Reflected-Incident Light Method

Step 1: Measure incident light. For example, meter reading with base against wall is 70 fc.

Step 2: Measure reflected light. For example, meter reading with light cell facing wall is 45 fc.

Step 3: Calculate reflectance of surface. For example, ρ of wall will be

$$\rho = \frac{45}{70} \simeq \boxed{64\%}$$

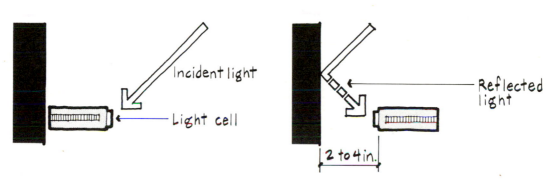

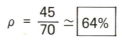

Known-Sample Comparison Method

Step 1: Measure reflected light from known reflectance test card. For example, ρ of test card is 90% and meter reading is 60 fc.

Step 2: Measure reflected light from wall at same meter position. For example, meter reading is 43 fc with card removed.

Step 3: Calculate reflectance of surface. For example, ρ of wall will be

$$\rho = \frac{43}{60} \times 90 \simeq \boxed{65\%}$$

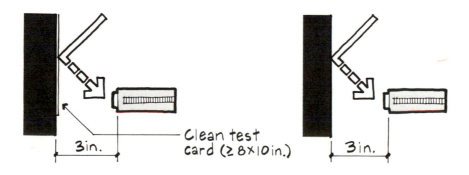

Note: Test cards are available from Kodak (Eastman Kodak Co., 343 State St., Rochester, NY 14650). Test card has a gray side of 18% reflectance and a white side of 90% reflectance.

TRANSMITTANCE AND CANDLEPOWER MEASUREMENTS

Transmittance Measurements

Step 1: Measure light through material. For example, meter reading with sample completely covering light cell is 80 fc.

Step 2: Measure incident light with sample removed. For example, meter reading with sample removed is 150 fc. Be careful to maintain same distance from light source.

Step 3: Calculate transmittance of sample. For example, τ of sample will be

$$\tau = \frac{80}{150} \simeq \boxed{53\%}$$

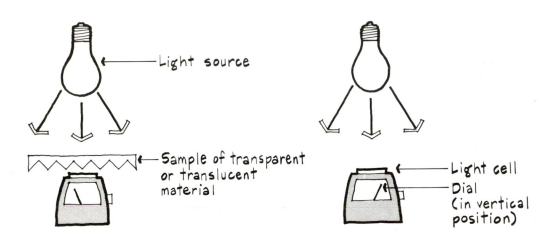

Note: An opaque shoe box can be used to measure transmittance. Using a light meter with a remote light cell probe, place probe in box opposite an opening approximately 2 in square. Position a constant, diffuse light source about 1 ft away from the box and measure transmitted light with and without the sample covering the opening. Transmittance is the ratio of the reading with the sample in place to the reading with the sample removed.

Approximate Candlepower Measurements

Step 1: Measure light at distance r greater than $5x$ away from light source at $\angle\ \theta$, where x is the maximum source dimension. For example, meter reading at 5 ft away and normal to 30° angle is 100 fc.

Step 2: Calculate approximate candlepower for light source at 30°. For example, approximate candlepower will be

$$\text{cp} = 100 \times 5^2 \simeq \boxed{2500 \text{ cd}}$$

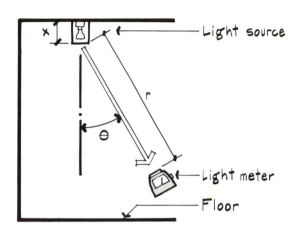

ILLUMINATION LEVEL WORKSHEET

Shown below are plan and section views of a room with suggested positions for illumination level measurements to establish light distribution patterns. Superimposed on the section drawing is a grid to facilitate plotting of illumination gradients (i.e., graphic plot of illumination level variations). *Isofootcandle contours* (i.e., plots of equal illumination levels in footcandles) can be plotted on plan views.

Plan View

Contours connecting points of equal footcandle values are called *isofootcandle lines.* A plot of equal illumination levels in lux is an *isolux contour.*

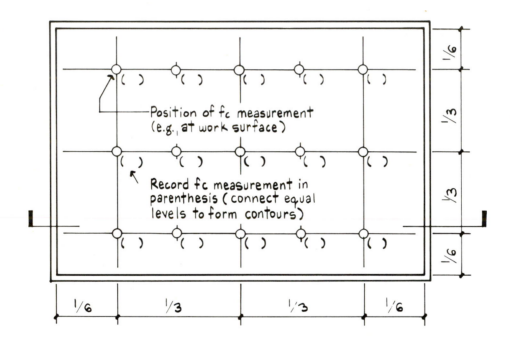

Section View

The grid overlay can be used to plot footcandle values at the position of measurement. When connected, the values establish an illumination gradient as shown by the examples on pages 94 and 95. Vertical illumination level scale can be linear or logarithmic to emphasize perceived brightness differences.

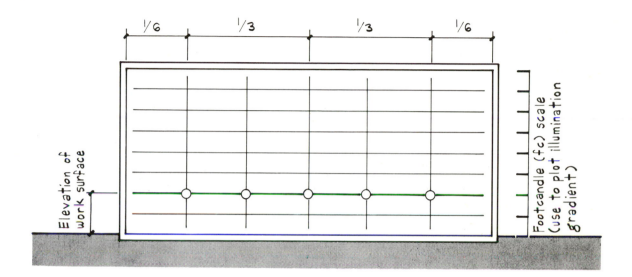

Note: For a description of uniform survey procedures to measure illumination levels and luminance in rooms, see J. E. Kaufman (ed.), *IES Lighting Handbook* (1981 Reference Volume), pp. 4-33 to 4-36.

ILLUMINATION GRADIENT MEASUREMENTS

Illumination gradients are the graphic representation of the increase or decrease of illumination levels along an axis of measurement. Shown below are section views depicting illumination gradients for different lighting situations.

Directional Downlighting

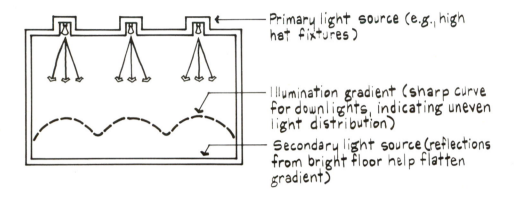

Primary light source (e.g., high hat fixtures)

Illumination gradient (sharp curve for downlights, indicating uneven light distribution)

Secondary light source (reflections from bright floor help flatten gradient)

General Diffuse Lighting

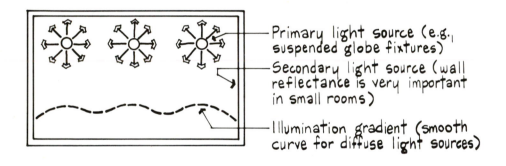

Primary light source (e.g., suspended globe fixtures)

Secondary light source (wall reflectance is very important in small rooms)

Illumination gradient (smooth curve for diffuse light sources)

Large Area Lighting (e.g., Luminous or Illuminated Ceiling)

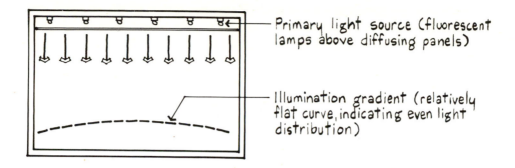

Primary light source (fluorescent lamps above diffusing panels)

Illumination gradient (relatively flat curve, indicating even light distribution)

Note: For uniform illumination levels, maximum and minimum values of illumination gradient should not differ more than about 15% from the average value.

Reference

R. E. Fischer (ed.), *Architectural Engineering—Environmental Control*, McGraw-Hill, New York, 1965, pp. 118-180.

Chapter 4
Light and Form

LIGHTING DESIGN AND FORM

Lighting can be used to define form, shape, and scale of spaces. Below is a checklist of essential elements of lighting design which provide appropriate quantity and quality of light in buildings.

1. Establish the desired composition in the space (e.g., appropriate brightness ratios, texture, etc.). Light on room surfaces should reveal the design intent and can create spatial interest, as shapes can be modified through the illusion created by light.

2. Identify the appropriate illumination levels needed for the task activities (e.g., reading handwriting in hard pencil on poor quality paper, typing, reading specular CRT screens, drafting). Refer to guidelines which take into account the effect of contrast and size of task on visibility as well as the age of observers, level of speed and accuracy of task performance, and reflectance of background on which details are to be viewed. (See page 122, Chap. 5.)

3. Determine the desired appearance of objects (e.g., color rendition, sparkle, shadows and modeling to reveal form clearly). Illuminated model studies can be used to help define and evaluate these objectives. (See Chap. 7.)

4. Select appropriate luminaires and lamps for various elements of the lighting system. (See Chaps. 2 and 5.) A luminaire is a complete lighting unit consisting of a lamp (or lamps); parts to position, protect, and direct the light; and a connection to a power supply. Usually more than one lighting technique will be needed (e.g., illuminated ceiling with task or accent light). Lamps integrated into the structure of buildings can be used to help articulate surfaces and form.

5. Plan daylighting to complement electrical lighting. When daylighting is sufficient, luminaires should be operated at lower illumination levels or turned off. (See Chap. 6.) Lighting controls should be coordinated with furniture placement, space use schedules, and work zones.

6. Lay out luminaires and lamps to enhance form and evaluate the lighting system so that visual clutter is avoided and glare is controlled.

Reference

R. T. Dorsey, "Design Approach: The New Thrust in Lighting Practice," *Lighting Design & Application,* July 1971.

General Lighting

General lighting provides uniform illumination over the entire area of a room, allowing flexibility in the placement of work stations. "Localized-general" lighting also provides approximately uniform illumination, but luminaires are located in a pattern that responds to the specific arrangement of work stations.

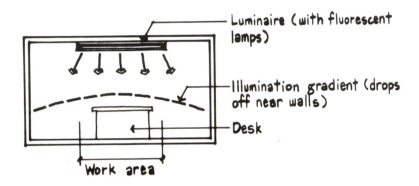

Local Lighting

Local lighting provides high illumination on relatively small areas. It can be too bright and uncomfortable unless surrounding surfaces are also illuminated as shown below. Local lighting used with general lighting is called *supplementary lighting*.

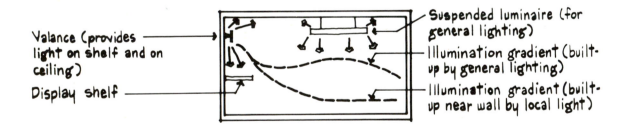

Task-Ambient Lighting

Task-ambient lighting provides high illumination on the "task" from light sources located close to the work area, supplemented by "ambient" illumination, usually from indirect light sources (e.g., furniture-integrated fixtures which direct light toward the ceiling).

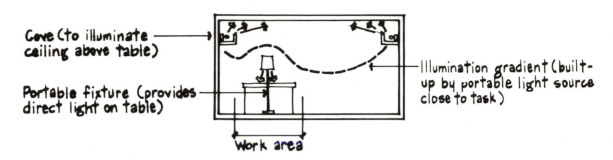

Cove (to illuminate ceiling above table)

Illumination gradient (built-up by portable light source close to task)

Portable fixture (provides direct light on table)

Work area

Reference

R. E. Fischer (ed.), *Architectural Engineering—Environmental Control,* McGraw-Hill, New York, 1965, p. 146.

LOCATION OF LIGHT SOURCES

Glossy surfaces can act like a mirror by reflecting light sources or bright objects into the view of observers. Consequently, light sources should be located away from mirror angle in concealment zone as shown below. The mirror angle is the angle equal to (and opposite) the viewing angle between line of sight and plane of surface under observation.

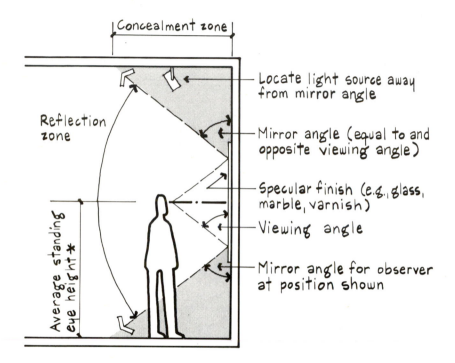

*Average standing eye height can vary from 56 to 69 inches. It depends on sex, ethnicity, age, and shoes worn.

Note: To reduce veiling reflections, minimize bright sources, objects, and surfaces at mirror angle.

ACCENT LIGHT

Accent or focal light is used to emphasize objects such as paintings, graphics, etc., or to draw attention to a part of the visual field. Most recessed adjustable and "eyeball" fixtures have aiming angles of 0 to 35°. At aiming angles > 50°, hot spots or streaks of light will occur on ceilings. Damage to sensitive objects from light depends on the illumination level and duration of the exposure to light. UV filters can be used on glazing to mitigate the damage from daylight.

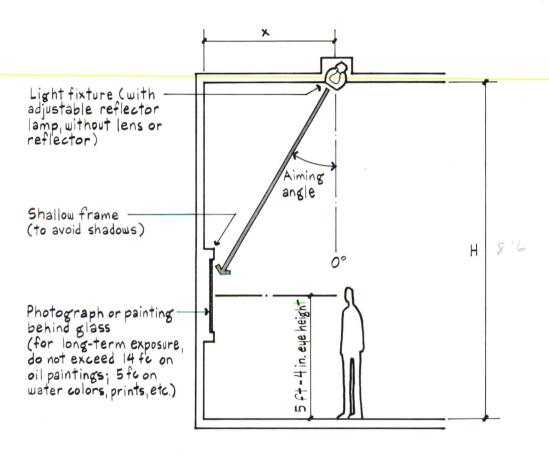

Light fixture (with adjustable reflector lamp, without lens or reflector)

Shallow frame (to avoid shadows)

Photograph or painting behind glass (for long-term exposure, do not exceed 14 fc on oil paintings; 5 fc on water colors, prints, etc.)

Aiming angle

0°

H   8'6

5 ft - 4 in. eye height

To prevent specular reflections at the mirror angle, accent light should be positioned away from walls as suggested by the following formula.

$$x = 0.6H - 3$$

where x = distance from wall (ft)

H = floor-to-ceiling height (ft)

$$x = 0.6(8.5) - 3$$
$$x = 5.10 - 3$$
$$x = 2.10'$$

A scallop pattern of light occurs when a conical beam of light encounters room surfaces. As shown by the sketch below, room surfaces can "slice" through the cone of light, creating scallops.

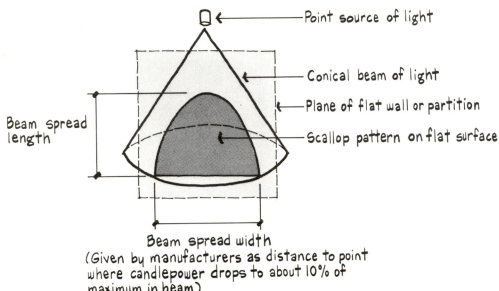

Point source of light

Conical beam of light

Plane of flat wall or partition

Scallop pattern on flat surface

Beam spread length

Beam spread width
(Given by manufacturers as distance to point where candlepower drops to about 10% of maximum in beam)

Continuous, flat surfaces normally should be perceived as having even illumination. The scallop patterns on the planar form of the wall surface shown on the left below distort its form. On the example wall on the right, distinct scallop patterns of light are coordinated with individual panel elements to emphasize their repetitive pattern. Distinct patterns of light also can be used to define entrances and to highlight paintings, sculpture, or plants.

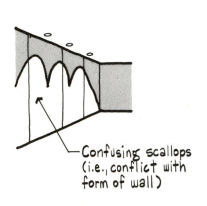

Confusing scallops (i.e., conflict with form of wall)

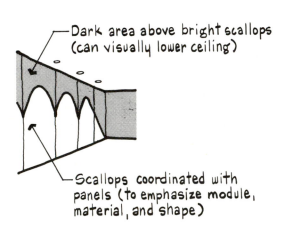

Dark area above bright scallops (can visually lower ceiling)

Scallops coordinated with panels (to emphasize module, material, and shape)

HOW TO PLOT SCALLOP PATTERNS OF LIGHT

Step 1: Draw the beam spread on a section drawing of a room. The beam spread of a fixture or lamp is the angle (in degrees) within which most of its light is produced. Candlepower distribution curves and beam spread angles are available from fixture manufacturers.

Step 2: On an elevation drawing, draw the intersection of the light ray with the wall at vertical distance h down from ceiling (or light source position). Measure h from step 1.

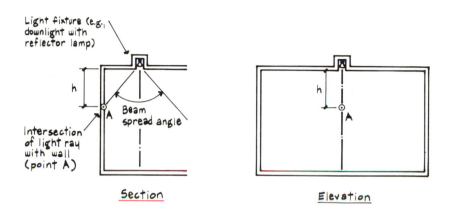

Light fixture (e.g., downlight with reflector lamp)

Beam spread angle

Intersection of light ray with wall (point A)

Section

Elevation

Step 3: Draw two rays, one from the light fixture at the beam spread angle and the second line parallel to this ray, intersecting point A from step 2.

Step 4: Draw a line between the parallel lines from step 3. Curve the line to point A. This plotted shape approximates the actual shape of the scallop pattern.

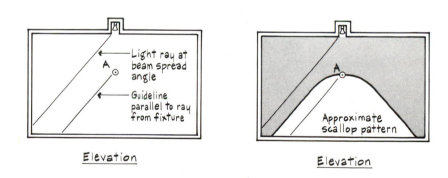

Light ray at beam spread angle

Guideline parallel to ray from fixture

Elevation

Approximate scallop pattern

Elevation

Note: As condition of beam edge, interreflected light, and other factors will affect scallop pattern, an illuminated model or full-scale mock-up can be used if precision is critical. (See Chap. 7.)

Reference

G. Zekowski, "The Art of Lighting is a Science/The Science of Lighting is an Art," *Lighting Design & Application,* March 1981.

Wall washers can provide relatively uniform illumination on vertical surfaces to give the visual impression of enlarged space, emphasize texture, accentuate entrances and exits, and so on. The eye perceives vertical surface brightness more readily than horizontal surface brightness. Use matte wall finishes to avoid specular reflections. Do not place light sources opposite doors or windows or at corridor intersections where they can become sources of direct glare. As shown below, grazing light can emphasize texture, joints, and the like. To avoid highlighting construction joints, orient the joints parallel to the direction of incident light.

Incandescent   Fluorescent (or HID)

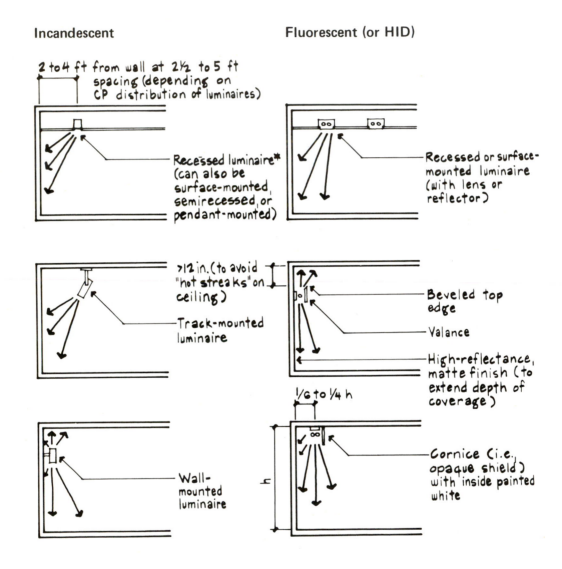

*For grazing light (to accent unfinished wood, rough brick, concrete, or stucco), wall washers should be approximately 1 ft from wall.

Reference

S. R. Shemitz, "Lighting: Tools that Suit Architectural Objectives," *Architectural Record,* March 1968.

Reflected ceiling plans are views of ceilings projected downward to appear on drawings as if viewed in a mirror held underneath. A reflected ceiling plan can be used to show how fixture patterns relate to form and space. For example, striped or checkerboard ceiling fixture layouts can create undesirable figure-background conflicts as shown below. Keep in mind that fixture patterns are often visible even when unlit.

Dominant Checkerboard

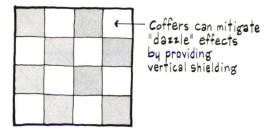

Coffers can mitigate "dazzle" effects by providing vertical shielding

Dominant checkerboard pattern can create "dazzle" effects from the high-contrast pattern of identical figure (bright lighting fixtures) and background (dark, flat ceiling surface) shapes.

Expressive

Perimeter bands of light (e.g., coves, cornices, or valances) can contribute to the creation of an intimate or private atmosphere in rooms by emphasizing the surroundings rather than the occupants.

Dominant Diagonal

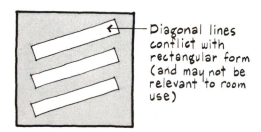

Diagonal lines conflict with rectangular form (and may not be relevant to room use)

Lines of fluorescent fixtures arranged in rectangular or square patterns, or used to fill a large central coffered area, also can be dominant by attracting attention to the bold patterns they create.

Neutral

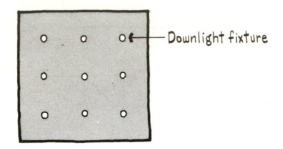

Downlight fixtures can be spaced evenly or unevenly without conflicting with form. However, at night or on overcast days, downlights can produce patterns of irrelevant dots of light on building form when viewed from outdoors. Surface-mounted downlight fixtures also may create an unwanted "pimpled" appearance.

Note: Nonuniform layouts can often be arranged to achieve low energy use. However, uncoordinated, nonuniform layouts can be dominant by attracting the eye to areas of little relevance to the architectural form and intent.

LUMINOUS CEILINGS

Luminous ceilings provide even illumination at low luminance (e.g., less than 250 fL). Many applications of luminous ceilings are oppressive and monotonous, appearing visually as an overcast sky at low elevation. In nature clouds are generally pleasing as they constantly change, providing visual interest. Luminous ceilings, on the other hand, are static and therefore can be dull and gloomy. In classrooms, conference rooms, and the like, be careful, as luminous ceilings can be soporific due to eyes being attracted upward to their normal sleep position. In addition, even illumination will provide poor modeling conditions. Luminous ceilings often emphasize maintenance problems by showing dirt and uneven joints. However, they can be used to conceal mechanical services (pipes and ducts) and structural elements. Signage and information overlays can add interest to luminous panels (e.g., see D. E. Spencer and V. E. Spencer, "Narrative Luminous Ceilings," *Lighting Design & Application*, April 1977). An example suspended luminous ceiling and panel element detail are shown below.

Luminous Ceiling

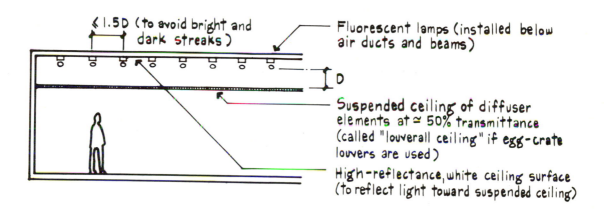

‹ 1.5 D (to avoid bright and dark streaks)

Fluorescent lamps (installed below air ducts and beams)

D

Suspended ceiling of diffuser elements at ≃ 50% transmittance (called "louverall ceiling" if egg-crate louvers are used)

High-reflectance, white ceiling surface (to reflect light toward suspended ceiling)

Panel Element Detail

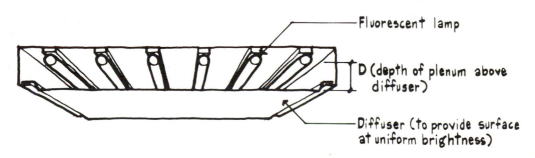

Fluorescent lamp

D (depth of plenum above diffuser)

Diffuser (to provide surface at uniform brightness)

ILLUMINATED CEILINGS

   Illuminated ceilings can be used to achieve spaciousness, eliminate visual impressions of gloomy conditions during the day, and serve as a light source. For acceptable visual comfort in most situations, ceiling luminance should be < 500 fL. Be careful, however, as indirect lighting at high levels of even brightness can create many of the undesirable characteristics of luminous ceilings. Indirect sources, which provide light by diffuse reflection from the ceiling surface, can be located in walls, in suspended fixtures, or in room furniture. Room dividers, high cabinets, etc. can reduce ambient light at work stations by blocking the spread of indirect light. In the furniture-integrated lighting system shown below, light from fixtures is directed laterally toward the ceiling to achieve a wide spread so that brightness on the ceiling above the fixtures will not be too high.

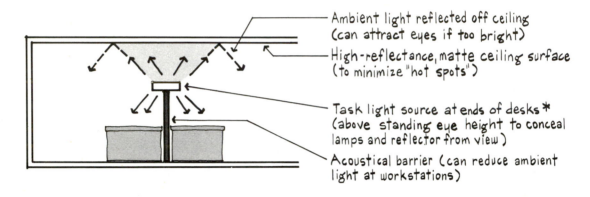

Ambient light reflected off ceiling (can attract eyes if too bright)

High-reflectance, matte ceiling surface (to minimize "hot spots")

Task light source at ends of desks * (above standing eye height to conceal lamps and reflector from view)

Acoustical barrier (can reduce ambient light at workstations)

*Ceiling surface should be at least 3 ft above HID lamps and at least 2 ft above fluorescent luminaires.

   When partial-height room dividers extend above eye level in open-plan spaces, visually neutral ceilings can be used to avoid unfavorable contrast of regular fixture layouts with random configuration of dividers. (Standing eye height is roughly 56 to 69 in above floor, depending on age, sex, shoes worn, and other factors.)

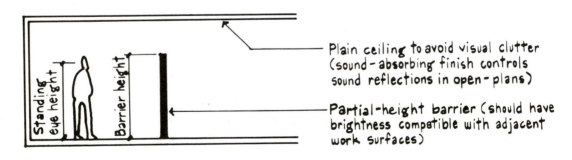

Plain ceiling to avoid visual clutter (sound-absorbing finish controls sound reflections in open-plans)

Partial-height barrier (should have brightness compatible with adjacent work surfaces)

Standing eye height

Barrier height

Reference

J. Panero and M. Zelnik, *Human Dimension & Interior Space,* Whitney Library of Design, Watson-Guptill Publications, Inc., New York, 1979.

Task and ambient lighting should be integrated into a coherent and compatible lighting concept. Task light is light on a seeing task (i.e., visual information an observer is attempting to see and comprehend). Ambient light is light which surrounds a "seeing" task. Ambient light can be provided by fixtures (e.g., a furniture-integrated uplight source as shown below, floor-mounted torchères) or by daylight (e.g., light shelves, clerestories).

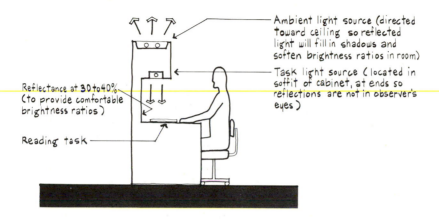

Ambient light source (directed toward ceiling so reflected light will fill in shadows and soften brightness ratios in room)

Task light source (located in soffit of cabinet, at ends so reflections are not in observer's eyes)

Reflectance at 30 to 40% (to provide comfortable brightness ratios)

Reading task

The plan view below of task lighting shows light-source positions where veiling reflections are created and where conditions are improved for the viewing position shown. Light-source positions behind the observer will produce undesirable hand and body shadows on reading and writing tasks. As indicated on the sketch below, a compromise solution locates sources at left and right sides of task (see shaded areas) and vertically close to task so that the brightness of the source will be shielded from view. Batwing linear prism and polarized lensed luminaires can provide acceptable visibility when positioned in the "veiling reflections zone" shown by the sketch.

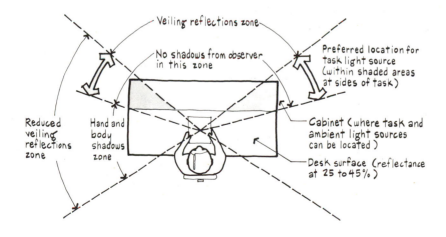

Veiling reflections zone

No shadows from observer in this zone

Preferred location for task light source (within shaded areas at sides of task)

Reduced veiling reflections zone

Hand and body shadows zone

Cabinet (where task and ambient light sources can be located)

Desk surface (reflectance at 25 to 45%)

Reference

P. L. Shellko and H. G. Williams, "The Integration of Task and Ambient Lighting in Office Furniture," *Lighting Design & Application,* September 1976.

Coves can be used to direct light toward ceilings, providing overall diffuse illumination (called *ambient luminescence*). Often bright ceiling surfaces will seem to recede, giving occupants a sense of place or orientation in large spaces. In addition, reflected light from ceilings can soften hot spots from direct light sources in rooms. The sketch below presents cove placement distance D from ceiling in terms of ceiling span S to be illuminated. As D increases, the uniformity of ceiling brightness increases.

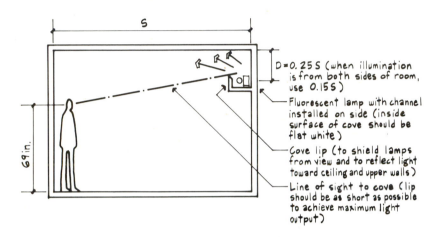

Reference

J. E. Flynn and S. M. Mills, *Architectural Lighting Graphics,* Van Nostrand Reinhold, New York, 1962, p. 182.

Cove details at various placement distances are shown below. (For additional information, see Chap. 11 in *Lighting Handbook*, Westinghouse Electric Corporation, Bloomfield, N.J., January 1978.) To avoid shadows from fluorescent lamp bases and lampholders, stagger lamps so that they overlap or use two rows with their bases offset.

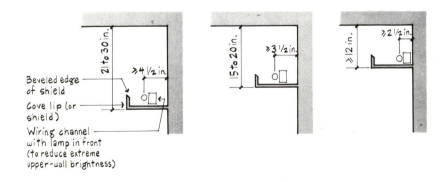

Note: For valance or wall bracket lighting, light shield should not extend above top of wiring channel.

LIGHTING OF STAIRS

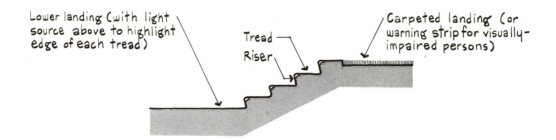

Lower landing (with light source above to highlight edge of each tread)

Tread

Riser

Carpeted landing (or warning strip for visually-impaired persons)

Bad stair lighting can be hazardous. For example, any abrupt change in brightness or any sources of glare, conflicting shadow patterns, or insufficient illumination can cause confusion and intensify other hazards, such as low surface traction. The true image of stairs should be conspicuously revealed by lighting conditions so that users can discriminate tread edges when viewing them from above. Illumination levels on stair treads should exceed levels on surrounding surfaces.

Avoid   **Better (Light from Above)**

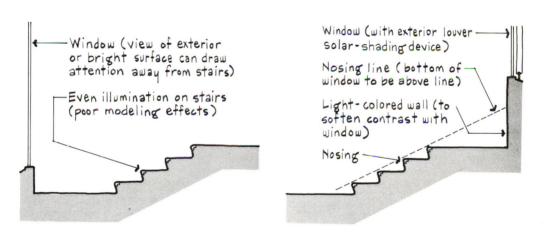

Window (view of exterior or bright surface can draw attention away from stairs)

Even illumination on stairs (poor modeling effects)

Window (with exterior louver solar-shading device)

Nosing line (bottom of window to be above line)

Light-colored wall (to soften contrast with window)

Nosing

Even illumination on stairs may *not* provide the essential contrast needed to highlight tread edges. In addition, glazing at the end of stairs or corridors can be a source of glare and distraction. (See example on left above.)

Lighting stairs from above, which creates shadows directly below rounded tread nosings, emphasizes form by highlighting the edge of each tread. However, sharp shadows parallel to stair width can create confusing patterns which distort the perception of tread depth when viewed from above. Be sure to shield the light source to avoid direct glare.

Note: Avoid sources of uplight which could momentarily blind users in stair areas. Outdoor spotlights which illuminate steps should be oriented downward to prevent the creation of blinding glare for persons approaching the stairs. Illuminated vertical surfaces (e.g., by sources concealed in handrails) can provide emphasis on stairs without glare.

SENSORY CUES AND STAIRS

Dangerous edges in stairs (and corridors) should be emphasized by changes in color and materials. Use markings, extending the full width of the stair, which contrast with remainder of riser and tread. Contrast nosing strips should be nonskid, secured to prevent loosening, and flush with tread, and should not extend more than 1½-in onto tread from nosing edge.

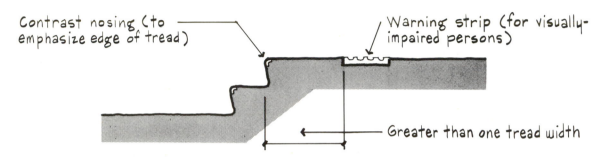

The table below indicates a perceived change in hardness between floor-covering materials and warning strip materials. Black dots in the table identify warning strips that can be detected by a cane. To be effective, warning strips must have different hardness than the normal floor-covering material.

Warning Strip

Floor Covering	Carpet	Rubber	Wood	Sheet vinyl	Resilient tile
Smooth concrete	●	●	●	●	●
Terrazzo	●	●	●	●	●
Brick	●	●	●	●	●
Quarry tile	●	●	●	●	●
Resilient tile	●	●	●		
Sheet vinyl	●	●	●		
Wood	●	●			
Rubber	●				

Reference

B. M. Johnson, ''Accessible Pedestrian Systems for Those with Physical Disabilities,'' Division of Building Research, National Research Council of Canada, BP Note No. 14, December 1979.

STAIR AND HANDRAIL VISIBILITY

In the example flight of stairs shown below, illumination is provided on the lower landing by directional lighting from a fixture on the ceiling or from window openings at the sides. The luminance of the stair treads should be at least 3 fL. Slightly rounded stair nosings are preferred, as they create a sharp edge on each tread to reveal their form when viewed from the upper landing. Handrails (located on both sides of stairs wider than 40 in) should provide cues to the location of the top and bottom of the flight of stairs and should have a finish that contrasts with adjacent surfaces. In addition, users should be able to maintain their grasp for the entire length (i.e., no breaks for brackets, spindles, etc.).

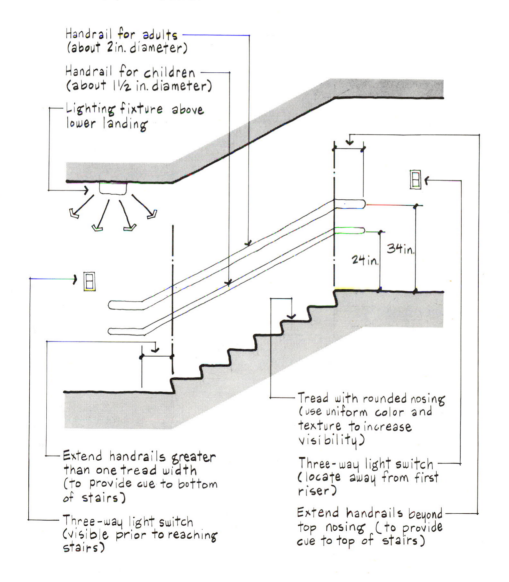

Handrail for adults (about 2 in. diameter)

Handrail for children (about 1½ in. diameter)

Lighting fixture above lower landing

24 in.

34 in.

Tread with rounded nosing (use uniform color and texture to increase visibility)

Extend handrails greater than one tread width (to provide cue to bottom of stairs)

Three-way light switch (visible prior to reaching stairs)

Three-way light switch (locate away from first riser)

Extend handrails beyond top nosing (to provide cue to top of stairs)

Reference

J. Archea et al., "Guidelines for Stair Safety," U.S. National Bureau of Standards, NBS BSS 120, May 1979.

Brightness

To clearly present figure images on illuminated signs, figure elements should be brighter than their background or surround. In general, figures will be clearly perceived when they can be distinguished from their surround by being brighter, more contrasting, more colorful, or a combination of these characteristics. The backlighted exit sign shown below has letters which are brighter than the surrounding area of opaque plastic. Where back-lighted signs have opaque lettering on a bright luminous surround, the intended message normally is overpowered by the surrounding visual noise.

Letters brighter than immediate surround for maximum visibility

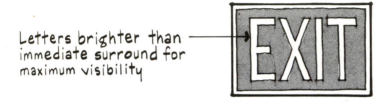

Note: Studies under simulated smoke conditions indicate that yellow and orange may be the most visible colors for illuminated exit signs. See M. D. Egan, *Concepts in Building Firesafety,* Wiley, New York, 1978, p. 200.

Location of Light Sources

Do not place distracting light sources near directional graphics such as exit signs. As shown below, bright surfaces above coves can compete with important visual information needed for safety. Also shown below is an example in which scallop patterns from point sources of light create shadows which cover essential signage.

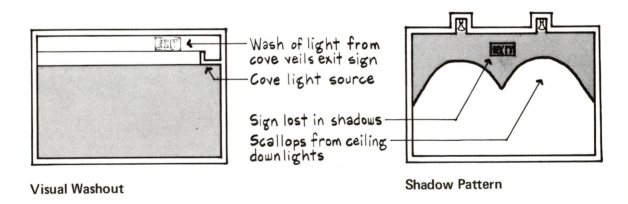

Wash of light from cove veils exit sign

Cove light source

Sign lost in shadows

Scallops from ceiling downlights

Visual Washout

Shadow Pattern

Note: For required illumination of means of egress and emergency lighting, refer to local building codes and the authority having jurisdiction.

OPENINGS AND BRIGHTNESS

Pyramidal light wells can be used to increase the apparent size of energy-efficient skylights. This technique, as shown below, also reduces the sharp transition or edge of brightness at the boundary of the view of the sky and the room.

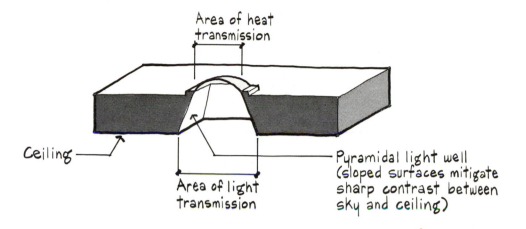

Skylight at Mormon Tabernacle, Salt Lake City, Utah

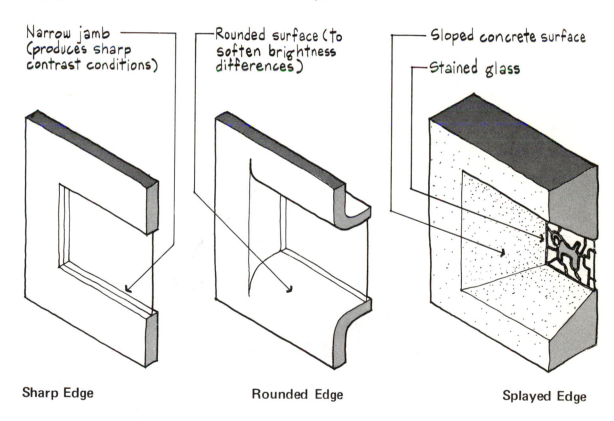

Sharp Edge   **Rounded Edge**   **Splayed Edge**

Note: Rounded sills shown above are similar to jambs at the Rotunda, University of Virginia, Charlottesville, Va., by Thomas Jefferson. The deep-splayed concrete opening is similar to windows at the Chapel of Notre Dame, Ronchamp, France, by Le Corbusier.

Edges of ceilings and beams, as shown below, can be used to shield light sources from view. Light sources also can be concealed in recessed slots, handrails, and so on. Be careful, however, as indirect lighting by itself does not enhance modeling effects or provide sparkle.

Indirect Lighting

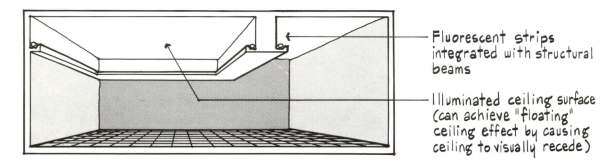

Fluorescent strips integrated with structural beams

Illuminated ceiling surface (can achieve "floating" ceiling effect by causing ceiling to visually recede)

Light Shelves

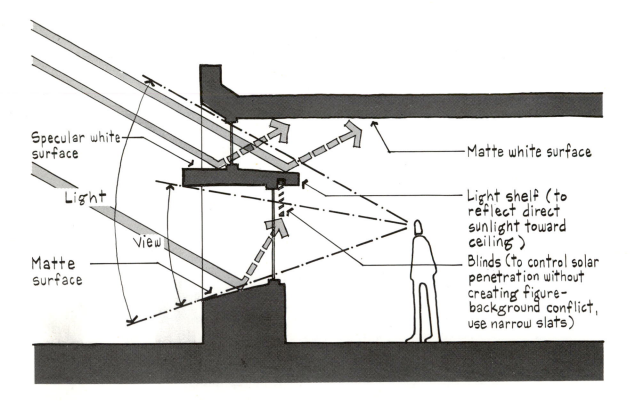

Specular white surface

Light

View

Matte surface

Matte white surface

Light shelf (to reflect direct sunlight toward ceiling)

Blinds (to control solar penetration without creating figure-background conflict, use narrow slats)

Note: Where windows are recessed as shown above, noise isolation provided by glass can be reduced below performance measured in acoustical testing laboratory. This phenomenon, called the *deep niche effect*, is due to interreflections of sound energy at window openings (and other factors), which reduce isolation by as much as 9 dB.

BLACK HOLE EFFECT

At night, bright reflections from lighting fixtures, superimposed on the black hole void at window openings, can be perceived as visual noise. Glazed interior partitions also can reflect bright sources in a distracting pattern that is unrelated to form or activities.

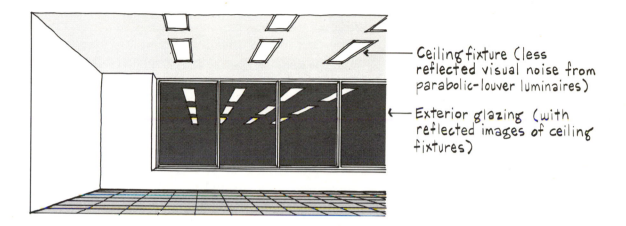

Ceiling fixture (less reflected visual noise from parabolic-louver luminaires)

Exterior glazing (with reflected images of ceiling fixtures)

Window Wall (with Reflected Fixtures)

Visual noise (i.e., distracting stimuli which interfere or compete with desired signals) from reflections off glass can be controlled by using recessed light sources in coffers or vaults; parabolic louvers with low surface brightness; sloped glazing; or the techniques to eliminate black hole effects illustrated below.

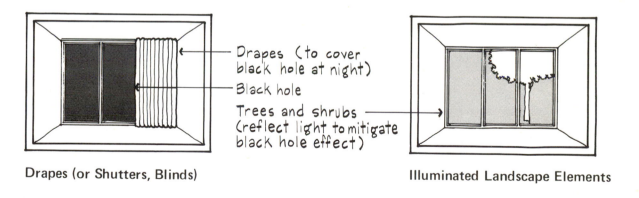

Drapes (to cover black hole at night)

Black hole

Trees and shrubs (reflect light to mitigate black hole effect)

Drapes (or Shutters, Blinds)   **Illuminated Landscape Elements**

Note: Lighting can be used to connect indoors and outdoors by extending fixture array beyond window walls. For outdoor lighting of landscape elements, mercury lamps can be used to complement evergreens and evoke feeling of moonlight.

The patterns of brightness in a room can alter the subjective impressions of the occupants. The table on the next page presents lighting conditions which tend to reinforce the subjective visual impressions of clarity (e.g., test subjects were asked if conditions were clear or hazy, distinct or vague), spaciousness, relaxation, privacy, and pleasantness. The table can be used to assist in establishing design goals for lighting systems. For example, if "clarity" and "spaciousness" are appropriate visual impressions for users of a research laboratory space, the following conditions would be desirable: bright and uniform light on horizontal work surfaces, perimeter emphasis, cool color temperature light, and brightness as a reinforcing factor. To meet these goals, a lighting system consisting of luminaires evenly spaced on the ceiling could provide relatively uniform illumination on the horizontal surface of work benches. Cool white or cool white deluxe fluorescent lamps would provide the desired cool color temperature in the room. Finally, a uniform wash of light on high-reflectance, matte wall surfaces (e.g., by fluorescent lamps behind cornices or recessed luminaires in ceiling) or window openings for daylighting (with glare controls) would contribute brightness at the perimeter of the room, which would reinforce the impression of spaciousness.

References

J. E. Flynn, "A Study of Subjective Responses to Low Energy and Nonuniform Lighting Systems," *Lighting Design & Application*, February 1977, p. 8.

G. R. Steffy, "Lighting by Design," *Consulting Engineer*, August 1981.

Subjective Visual Impression

Lighting Conditions	Clarity (or public)	Spaciousness	Relaxation	Private or intimate (emphasis on background)	Pleasantness
Brightness as reinforcement			●		
Low illuminance in area of occupancy				●	
Warm color temperature light sources				●	●
Cool color temperature light sources	●				
Perimeter emphasis (e.g., wall wash, accent lights)	●	●	●	●	●
	(Some)	(Uniform)	(Nonuniform)	(High brightness)	
Nonuniform layouts			●	●	●
Bright, uniform light on horizontal work surface *	●	●			
		(Central)			

*Or nonuniform overhead lighting layouts emphasizing center of room.

Note: The above table is based primarily on studies of a limited range of lighting conditions conducted in conference room, classroom, and dining spaces. Further studies on a wider range of spaces and lighting conditions are needed to expand current knowledge of the effects of light on subjective impressions of space and form.

Chapter 5
Lighting Systems

FACTORS OF VISION AND LIGHTING CONDITIONS
AFFECTING DESIGN ILLUMINATION LEVELS

The quantity of light, or *illumination level*, is only one of several important characteristics of lighting systems. Nevertheless, recommendations for appropriate footcandle or lux target values for seeing tasks are published by the Illuminating Engineering Society of North America (IES), the Commission Internationale de l'Éclairage (CIE), and the General Services Administration (U.S.). For most situations, however, the designer should consult with the authority having jurisdiction on required illumination level criteria. Keep in mind that there is no generally accepted evidence that low illumination levels result in organic harm to the eyes any more than there is evidence that indistinct sounds damage the ears or faint smells damage the nose (cf., D. G. Cogan, "Popular Misconceptions Pertaining to Ophthalmology," *New England Journal of Medicine*, Vol. 242, 1941). Lighting conditions and visual task situations for which low illumination levels from electric light sources would be appropriate are listed below.

1. High task contrast (e.g., 8-point type and larger, typed originals, felt tip pen on matte paper). For example, in offices visual tasks can vary in difficulty from easy-to-read 8-point type and larger printed images to drafting, bookkeeping, and extremely difficult-to-read low-contrast carbon copies. Example point type sizes are shown below. For best speed of reading, use 8 to 11-point type.

6 ABCDEFGHIJKLMNOPQRSTUV
8 ABCDEFGHIJKLMNOPQ
10 ABCDEFGHIJKLMN
11 ABCDEFGHIJKL
14 ABCDEFGHIJ

Type Size (in points; 1 point = $1/72$")

2. Tasks at better viewing angles (e.g., tilted desk tops), where reflected glare and veiling reflections will be reduced, and use of optical aids (e.g., binocular loupes, magnifiers). Reorienting tasks away from the mirror angle or bringing tasks closer to the eyes can dramatically improve viewing conditions.

3. Provisions of daylight with good modeling conditions and few veiling reflections. Be sure work stations are arranged so that normal task sight lines are parallel to walls with openings for daylight (i.e., light on visual tasks coming from sides of tasks).

4. Tasks in which no serious consequences from mistakes in perception would result (e.g., no increased cost, reduction in productivity, or danger of injury).

5. Tasks of short duration or tasks where sufficient observation time is available.

Note: For minimum footcandle levels for life safety, refer to "Life Safety Code" and "National Electrical Code," published by the National Fire Protection Association (NFPA), Batterymarch Park, Quincy, MA 02269. Usually stair tread luminance of 3 fL will be sufficient (cf., A. T. Hattenburg et al., "Energy Budget Procedures and Performance Criteria for Energy Conserving Building Illumination Systems," U.S. National Bureau of Standards, NBSIR 80-2052, May 1980, p. 10).

To use the IES tables of recommended illumination levels (called *illuminance*) in fc or lx on horizontal surfaces, the following program characteristics must be established: (1) age of workers or occupants, (2) required speed and/or accuracy of task performance, and (3) reflectance of background on which task details are to be seen.

For example, to determine the recommended illumination levels for the performance of visual tasks involving medium contrast, such as "reading medium pencil handwriting" in a technical school lecture room, first establish the recommended category from the table on page 123. The categories reflect the influence of contrast and size of details on task visibility. Category E, with a range of 50-75-100 fc, fits this type of activity. Next, find the total weighting factor (see table on page 124) which determines if the low, medium, or high footcandle value for category E should be selected. The component weighting factors are selected as follows:

Task and observer characteristics	Weighting factor
1. Workers' ages* (in this example, students under age 40)	−1
2. Speed and/or accuracy (not important, as errors will not be costly or related to safety)	−1
3. Reflectance of task background (paper at 70%)	0
Total	−2

*Consider average age as well as variation in ages.

As total weighting factor is −2, select the low value of 50 fc to use as the recommended illuminance on the task. The IES illuminance values are only "target" values, so that deviations based on the experience and judgment of the designer are expected.

When visual tasks are similar throughout a room, design to meet the requirements of a representative task. When visual tasks vary considerably, use a variety of lighting layouts to provide appropriate illumination to those tasks in the room or use controls that vary the output of the light sources.

For a comprehensive listing of recommended task illuminance for a wide variety of activities, see pp. 2-3 to 2-24 in J. E. Kaufman (ed.), *IES Lighting Handbook* (1981 Application Volume). These values are often referred to as classical or "raw" footcandles to distinguish them from equivalent sphere illumination (ESI) footcandles (i.e., illuminance from an evenly illuminated sphere which would produce task visibility equivalent to that produced by a specific lighting system). For example, to achieve 50 ESI fc may require 45 to 250 raw fc on the task, depending on the amount of veiling reflections produced by the actual lighting situation.

ILLUMINANCE RECOMMENDED FOR USE IN SELECTING VALUES FOR INTERIOR LIGHTING DESIGN

Illuminance category	Ranges of illuminance maintained in service in lux (fc)	Type of activity
General illuminance throughout room:		
A	20-30-50 (2-3-5)	Public spaces with dark surroundings
B	50-75-100 (5-7.5-10)	Simple orientation for short temporary visits
C	100-150-200 (10-15-20)	Working spaces where visual tasks are only occasionally performed
Illuminance on task:		
D	200-300-500 (20-30-50)	Performance of visual tasks of high contrast or large size: reading printed material, typed originals, handwriting in ink, and good xerography; rough bench and machine work; ordinary inspection; rough assembly
E	500-750-1000 (50-75-100)	Performance of visual tasks of medium contrast or small size: reading medium pencil handwriting, poorly printed or reproduced material; medium bench and machine work; difficult inspection; medium assembly
F	1000-1500-2000 (100-150-200)	Performance of visual tasks of low contrast or very small size: reading handwriting in hard pencil on poor-quality paper and very poorly reproduced material; highly difficult inspection
Illuminance on task, obtained by a combination of general and local (supplementary) lighting:		
G	2000-3000-5000 (200-300-500)	Performance of visual tasks of low contrast and very small size over a prolonged period: fine assembly; very difficult inspection; fine bench and machine work
H	5000-7500-10,000 (500-750-1000)	Performance of very prolonged and exacting visual tasks: the most difficult inspection; extra-fine bench and machine work; extra-fine assembly
I	10,000-15,000-20,000 (1000-1500-2000)	Performance of very special visual tasks of extremely low contrast and small size: e.g., surgical procedures

Courtesy of Illuminating Engineering Society of North America.

Note: The IES recommended values are not used to determine appropriate illuminance in the architectural environment when design objectives involve focusing on merchandise, emphasizing room surfaces to attract attention, creating a relaxing mood, and so on.

WEIGHTING FACTORS TO BE CONSIDERED IN SELECTING SPECIFIC ILLUMINANCE VALUES

Weighting factors in the table below are determined on the basis of worker and task information. When the algebraic sum of the weighting factors is −3 or −2, use the lowest value in the illuminance ranges; when −1 to +1, use the middle value; and when +2 or +3, use the highest value.

For Illuminance Categories A through C

Room and occupant characteristics	Weighting factor		
	−1	0	+1
Occupants' ages	Under 40	40 to 55	Over 55
Room surface reflectances*	> 70%	30 to 70%	< 30%

For Illuminance Categories D through I

Task and worker characteristics	Weighting factor		
	−1	0	+1
Workers' ages	Under 40	40 to 55	Over 55
Speed and/or accuracy†	Not important	Important	Critical
Reflectance of task background‡	> 70%	30 to 70%	< 30%

*Average weighted surface reflectances, including wall, floor, and ceiling reflectances, if they encompass a large portion of the task area or visual surround. For instance, in an elevator lobby, where the ceiling height is 25 ft, neither the task nor the visual surround encompasses the ceiling, so only the floor and wall reflectances would be considered.

†In determining whether speed and/or accuracy is not important, important, or critical, the following questions need to be answered: What are the time limitations? How important is it to perform the task rapidly? Will errors produce an unsafe condition or product? Will errors reduce productivity and be costly? For example, in reading for leisure there are no time limitations and it is not important to read rapidly. Errors will not be costly and will not be related to safety; thus, speed and/or accuracy is not important. If, however, prescription notes are to be read by a pharmacist, accuracy is critical because errors could produce an unsafe condition and time is important for customer relations.

‡The task background is that portion of the task upon which the meaningful visual display is exhibited. For example, on this page the meaningful visual display includes each letter which combines with other letters to form words and phrases. The display medium, or task background, is the paper, which has a reflectance of approximately 85%.

Courtesy of Illuminating Engineering Society of North America.

The ESI method evaluates the degree to which actual lighting situations approach the effectiveness of the reference sphere lighting (where the percentage of light at the mirror angle is low, avoiding veiling reflections). When comparing lighting systems, ESI differences of 20% or less generally are not significant. The steps below describe, in general, how ESI can be measured in rooms.

Step 1: Under a hemispherical source, measure brightness of task L_t and background L_b. Contrast C is related to task detail (e.g., pencil marks) and background brightness as follows:

$$C = (L_t - L_b)/L_b$$

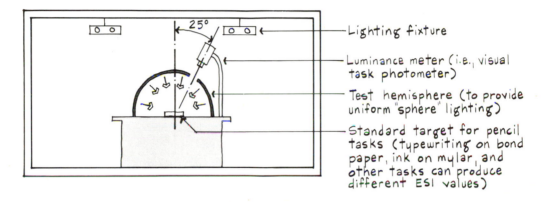

- Lighting fixture
- Luminance meter (i.e., visual task photometer)
- Test hemisphere (to provide uniform "sphere" lighting)
- Standard target for pencil tasks (typewriting on bond paper, ink on mylar, and other tasks can produce different ESI values)

Step 2: Under actual lighting conditions, again measure brightnesses of task and background to establish contrast.

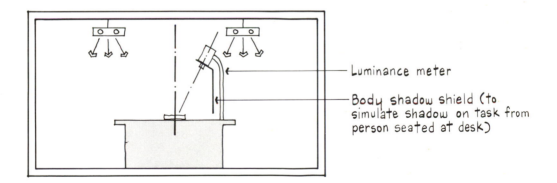

- Luminance meter
- Body shadow shield (to simulate shadow on task from person seated at desk)

Step 3: The contrast rendition factor (CRF) is the ratio of contrasts found by steps 1 and 2. The ESI for a position in a room is determined by the following: the CRF; the location, distribution, and size of light sources; the room dimensions and reflectances; and the light distribution characteristics of the fixtures.

Note: A small portable attachment to allow light meters to measure contrast and ESI levels in fc or lx is commercially available from Smith, Hinchman & Grylls Associates, Inc., 455 West Fort Street, Detroit, MI 48226.

ESI CONTOURS

   ESI contours can assist the designer by indicating the preferred locations for work stations. Contour plots of equal ESI footcandle values (for pencil tasks on flat surfaces) are shown in the plan view below. The section view shows illumination gradients for raw and ESI footcandle values from the luminaires. Notice that the locations of the highest raw footcandles from the luminaires do not correspond to the locations of the highest ESI footcandles (where there are fewer veiling reflections).

Section

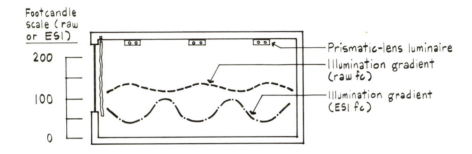

Plan

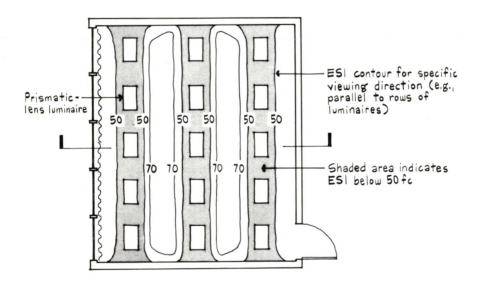

Reference

H. G. Williams, "ESI: The True Measure of a Lighting System," *Actual Specifying Engineer,* October 1974.

NONUNIFORM OVERHEAD LIGHTING LAYOUTS

Shown below are nonuniform overhead layouts of 2 X 4 ft fluorescent troffers (i.e., recessed lighting fixtures with housings hidden from view) in order of decreasing ESI footcandle values at the normal reading position on the desk top. The illuminance (in raw fc) of layout 3 is 15 fc more than that of layout 2, but ESI footcandle value is 35 fc less due to veiling reflections from fixtures located in front of the viewing position.

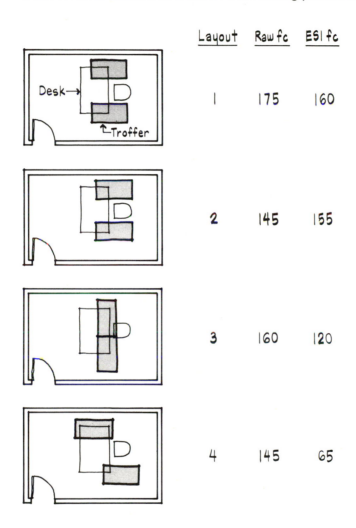

Layout	Raw fc	ESI fc
1	175	160
2	145	155
3	160	120
4	145	65

Note: To minimize veiling reflections in private offices, place lighting fixtures over edge of working side of desk so that light will be distributed like daylight from windows along side walls (see layouts 1 and 2 above). Do not use incandescent downlights over desks and conference tables, as they produce disturbing body shadows and reflected glare.

Reference

Office Lighting, General Electric Technical Publication TP-114R1, Cleveland, May 1979, p. 14.

Shown below are example lighting systems which provide relatively high ESI fc/W of energy consumption. Field measurements of ESI fc/W·ft² in classrooms varied from about 11 for luminous ceilings (where light on reading tasks is diffuse) to 22 for suspended fixtures (where task light comes primarily from ceiling and walls due to considerable uplight). Generally, 35 ESI fc will be sufficient for reading pencil on white paper.

Luminous Ceiling

Illumination Level (ESI fc/W·ft²)

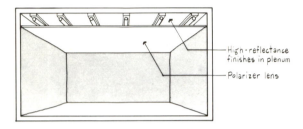

High-reflectance finishes in plenum

Polarizer lens

Cove

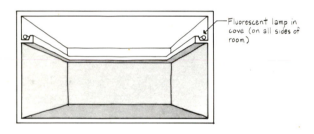

Fluorescent lamp in cove (on all sides of room)

Low

Higher

Note: Light on reading tasks is diffuse, but ESI fc/W value is relatively low.

Suspended Fixtures

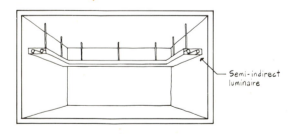

Semi-indirect luminaire

Reference

"Optimizing Usage of Energy: The Potential in Lighting Systems for Buildings," *The Construction Specifier,* April 1978, pp. 56-57.

GENERIC TYPES OF LUMINAIRES

Arrows adjacent to the sketches of luminaires and beam spread patterns below indicate the percentage of light output directed toward ceiling and floor. Luminaires for general lighting are classified according to these percentages by the CIE (Commission Internationale de l' Éclairage).

Indirect*

This type of luminaire can be used to create a feeling of height in large rooms with low ceilings. Light reflected from the ceiling and upper walls can complement structure; prevent gloomy, dark ceilings; and reduce or eliminate shadows.

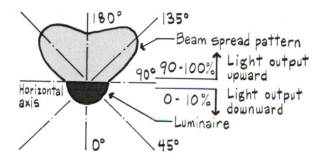

Semi-Indirect*

Light reflected from the ceiling tends to soften shadows and improve brightness ratios. Luminaire brightness can be approximately equal to the brightness of the ceiling because light is directed downward.

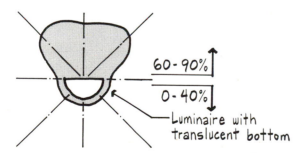

*To avoid excessive ceiling brightness immediately above luminaires, suspend them at least 12 to 18 in below ceiling.

Direct-Indirect*

These luminaires provide approximately equal light to the floor and ceiling and very little light to the sides. Consequently, brightness can be low in the zone of direct glare.

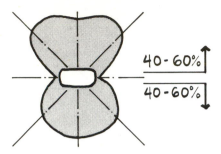

Diffuse*

These fixtures provide approximately equal light in all directions. To control direct glare, diffusing enclosures should be large and lamp wattage low.

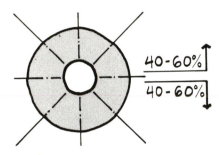

Semi-Direct

A small percentage of light directed upward tends to soften shadows caused by direct luminaires (e.g., downlights).

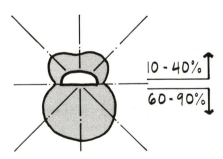

*To avoid excessive ceiling brightness immediately above luminaires, suspend them at least 12 to 18 in below ceiling.

Direct (Wide Beam Spread Luminaire)

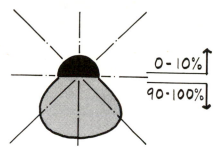

0 - 10%

90 - 100%

Direct (Highly Concentrated Beam Spread Downlight Luminaire)

Direct fixtures can be used for focus and emphasis. To prevent high brightness ratios, be sure sufficient illumination is provided on walls and other vertical surfaces.

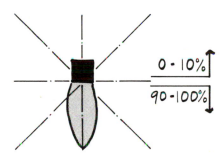

0 - 10%

90 - 100%

Note: Beam spread depends on reflector, lens, and position of lamp in luminaire.

SHAPE OF CANDLEPOWER DISTRIBUTION CURVES

The shape of a candlepower distribution curve provides information on the pattern of light output from a lamp or luminaire. For example, the shape of the curve can indicate where potential problems from direct and reflected glare might occur and where "hot spots" may be created on room surfaces. Example candlepower distribution curves for recessed and suspended luminaires are given below. See page 138 for a description of how to determine candlepower values.

Recessed Luminaire

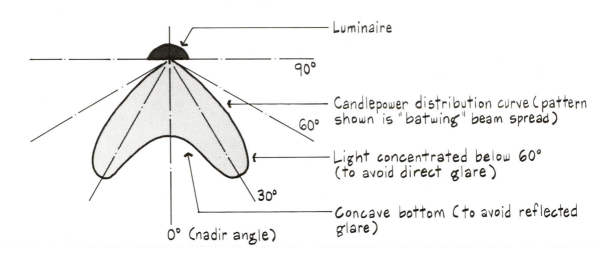

Luminaire

Candlepower distribution curve (pattern shown is "batwing" beam spread)

Light concentrated below 60° (to avoid direct glare)

Concave bottom (to avoid reflected glare)

90°

60°

30°

0° (nadir angle)

Suspended Luminaire

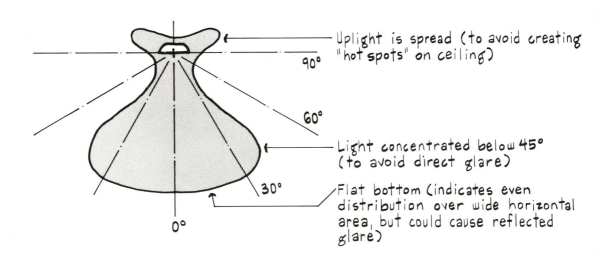

Uplight is spread (to avoid creating "hot spots" on ceiling)

Light concentrated below 45° (to avoid direct glare)

Flat bottom (indicates even distribution over wide horizontal area, but could cause reflected glare)

90°

60°

30°

0°

Suspended Luminaire

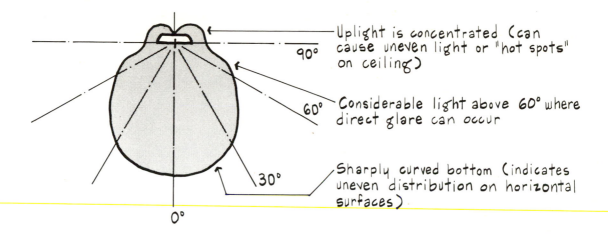

Uplight is concentrated (can cause uneven light or "hot spots" on ceiling)

Considerable light above 60° where direct glare can occur

Sharply curved bottom (indicates uneven distribution on horizontal surfaces)

90°

60°

30°

0°

Lighting fixtures can be considered point sources if the distance to the surface to be illuminated is more than 5 times the largest physical dimension of the fixture. Illumination levels for point sources vary directly with candlepower and inversely with distance from source squared. Point sources can be used to focus on objects and areas or to provide sparkle or glitter.

Light on Sloped Surface

To calculate illumination levels on a sloped surface, find $\angle \alpha$ between normal to surface and line connecting light source and point of interest. Next, find candlepower from photometric data curves or tables. Illumination level can be computed by:

$$E = \frac{cp}{r^2} \cos \alpha$$

where E = illumination level (fc)

        cp = candlepower of source of light, varies with angle from nadir (cd)

        r = distance from source of light to point of interest (ft)

        α = angle between ray of light and the normal to surface (degrees)

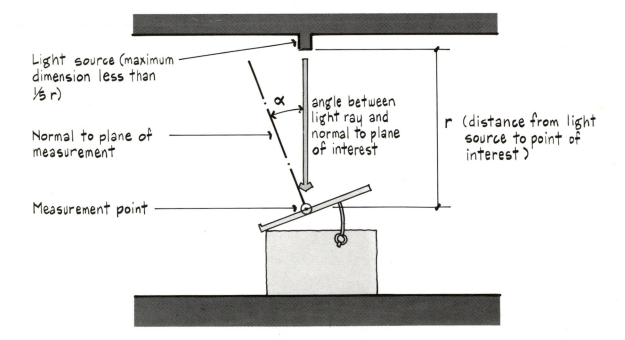

Light source (maximum dimension less than ⅕ r)

Normal to plane of measurement

α angle between light ray and normal to plane of interest

r (distance from light source to point of interest)

Measurement point

Light from Multiple Sources (Abney's Law)

Illumination level at any point (e.g., point *A* shown below) is the sum of the illumination levels from all sources contributing light at that point. Illumination level can be computed by:

$$E = \frac{cp}{r_1^2} \cos \alpha_1 + \frac{cp}{r_2^2} \cos \alpha_2 + \cdots$$

where   *E* = illumination level (fc)

cp = candlepower of source of light, varies with angle θ from nadir (cd)

r = distance from source of light to point of interest (ft)

α = angle between ray of light and the normal to surface (degrees)

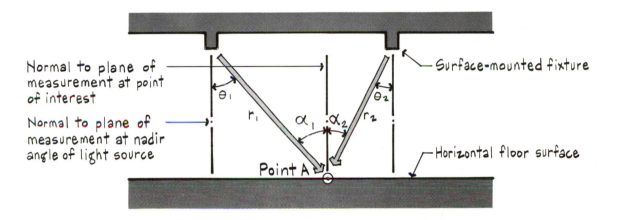

Note: Angle θ equals angle α when the normal to the plane of measurement at point of interest is parallel to the normal to the plane of measurement at the nadir angle of light source (see drawing above). For a review of the basics of trigonometric ratios and angles, see page 144.

To achieve an overlap of beam spreads from point sources, use narrow beam spread fixtures at high mounting heights and wide beam spread fixtures at low mounting heights. For preliminary layouts, spacing S for even illumination can be found by

$$S = SR \times MH$$

where   MH = mounting height, or height from work surface to light source (ft)

        SR = spacing ratio ($\leqslant$0.5 for narrow beam spread, 0.6 to 0.9 for medium, and $\geqslant$1.0 for wide)

Note: Check with fixture manufacturers for recommended S:MH ratios.

Avoid using point sources for general illumination in offices, classrooms, etc., as they can produce harsh shadows and uncomfortable reflections.

Highly Concentrated (or Narrow) Beam Spread (Uneven Illumination Shown)

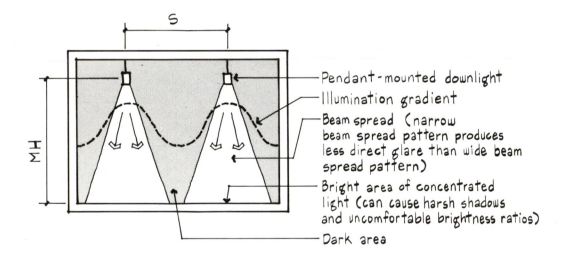

Pendant-mounted downlight

Illumination gradient

Beam spread (narrow beam spread pattern produces less direct glare than wide beam spread pattern)

Bright area of concentrated light (can cause harsh shadows and uncomfortable brightness ratios)

Dark area

Wide Beam Spread (*S*:MH ≃ 1.0, for Uniform Illumination)

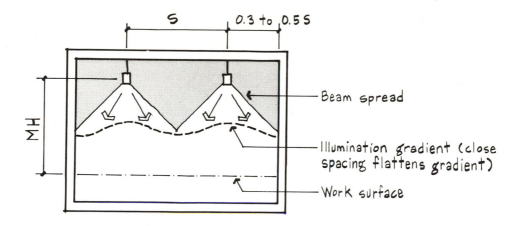

Note: For MH <20 ft, relamping can normally be performed from the floor by using a ladder or pole device. Above 20 ft, relamping usually requires scaffolding, elevating platforms, top-access luminaires, or luminaires with lowering devices (e.g., winch-operated cable). Consider using long-life lamps where access is especially difficult.

Candlepower distribution curves show light output produced by bare lamps or luminaires. Curves, plotted on polar coordinate graphs, can be used to represent the relative distribution of light. Candlepower values are found on the vertical scale of a graph which has degree lines radiating from the polar point. The *nadir* angle is 0° or the direction straight down. The horizontal plane containing the light source is 90°. For example, at 30° from the nadir, the luminaire represented by the graph below has a candlepower of 1750 cd (see dashed line on graph below).

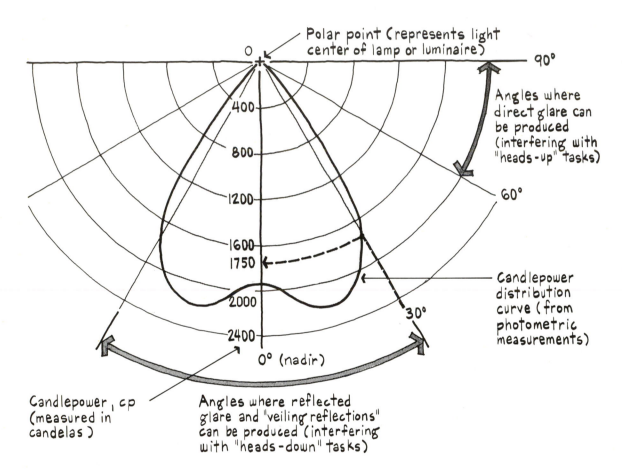

Polar point (represents light center of lamp or luminaire)

Angles where direct glare can be produced (interfering with "heads-up" tasks)

90°

60°

30°

0° (nadir)

400
800
1200
1600
1750
2000
2400

Candlepower distribution curve (from photometric measurements)

Candlepower, cp (measured in candelas)

Angles where reflected glare and "veiling reflections" can be produced (interfering with "heads-down" tasks)

Note: Rectilinear graphs are sometimes used to plot candlepower data when light intensity changes rapidly within a small, angular area. On these graphs, degrees from the beam axis are plotted against candelas.

LIGHT SOURCE (CONCENTRATED BEAM SPREAD)

Example Incandescent Downlight

Aperture diameter and recessed depth of fixture vary with lamp (e.g., wattage, beam characteristics) and fixture manufacturer's specifications.

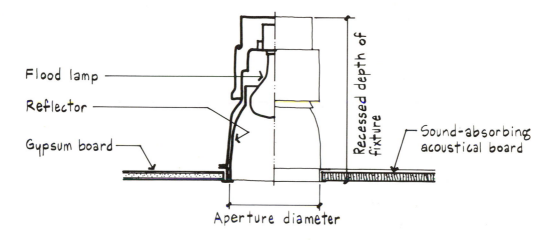

Photometric Data

When light output is symmetrical about the nadir angle (0°), only half the candlepower distribution curve is normally shown.

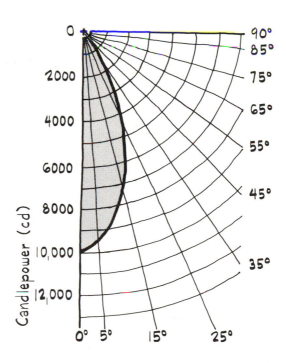

Example Incandescent Downlight

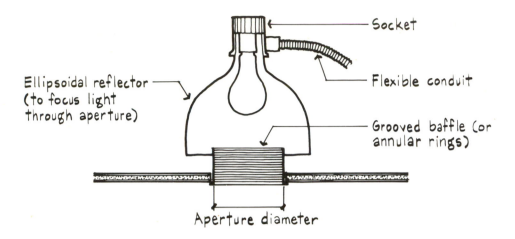

Socket

Ellipsoidal reflector
(to focus light
through aperture)

Flexible conduit

Grooved baffle (or
annular rings)

Aperture diameter

Photometric Data

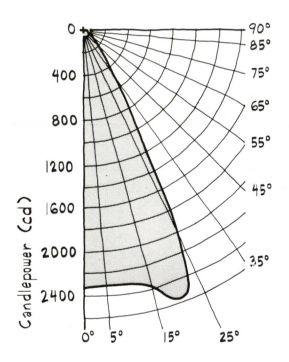

LIGHT SOURCE (WIDE BEAM SPREAD)

Example Incandescent Downlight

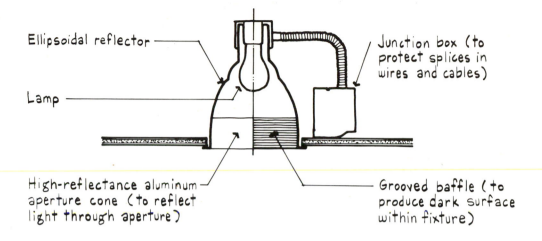

Ellipsoidal reflector

Lamp

Junction box (to protect splices in wires and cables)

High-reflectance aluminum aperture cone (to reflect light through aperture)

Grooved baffle (to produce dark surface within fixture)

Photometric Data

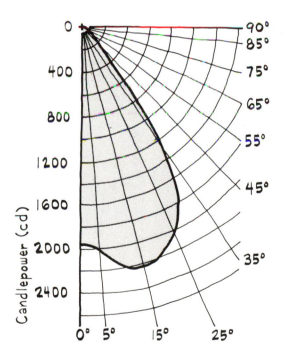

Candlepower (cd)

Example computations for a single downlight fixture are given below. Candlepower data, at a specific angle from the nadir for the point being computed, are obtained from the photometric graph on page 141.

1. Illumination level directly below fixture on work surface at point *A* is found as follows. Angle θ is $0°$ at the nadir, so $\cos\theta = 1$ and cp = 1950 cd. Distance (*r*) from light source to point of interest is $18 - 3 = 15$ ft.

$$E = \frac{cp}{r^2}\cos\theta = \frac{1950}{15^2}1 = \boxed{9 \text{ fc}}$$

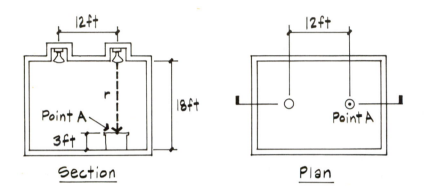

Section   Plan

2. Illumination level on horizontal plane of work surface 6 ft from fixture at point *B* is found as follows. Angle θ from $\tan\theta = x/y = 6/15 = 0.4$ and $\theta = 22°$ from table on page 145.

$$E = \frac{cp}{r^2}\cos\theta = \frac{2100}{15^2 + 6^2}0.9272 = \boxed{7 \text{ fc}}$$

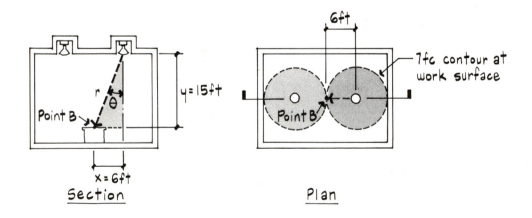

Section   Plan

If the adjacent downlight were switched on, illuminance at point *B* would be 14 fc (i.e., sum of angular components from two fixtures according to Abney's law).

3. Illumination level on vertical plane of end wall at point C is found as follows. Angle θ from $\tan \theta = x/y = 6/12 = 0.5$ and $\theta = 27°$ from table on page 145.

$$E = \frac{cp}{r^2} \sin \theta = \frac{1900}{12^2 + 6^2} \, 0.454 = \boxed{5 \text{ fc}}$$

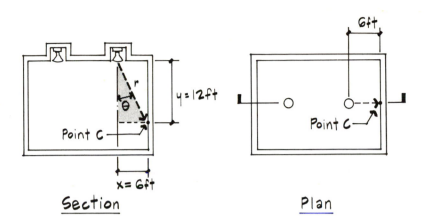

Section   Plan

Trigonometry is the relationships between sides and angles of triangles. In lighting systems, the geometry of a light ray from a point source can be "triangulated" to determine the illuminance on room surfaces.

The triangle shown below is a right triangle, as its two short sides, *x* and *y*, are perpendicular. The length ratios of the sides of right triangles are named *sine* (abbreviated *sin*), *cosine* (abbreviated *cos*), and *tangent* (abbreviated *tan*). These useful trigonometric ratios can be used to determine the size of angles. The sum of the three angles formed by a triangle equals 180°. The ratios are given below and values for $\angle\theta$ from 0° to 90° are presented by the table on page 145.

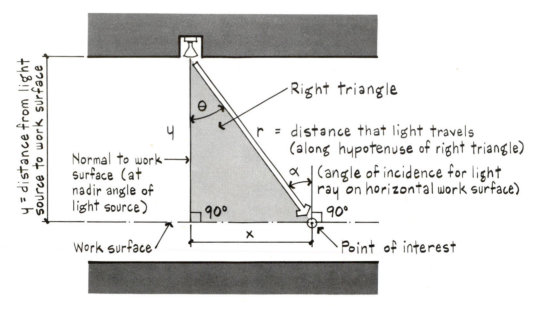

Side ratios	Pythagorean theorem
$\sin\theta = x/r$	$r^2 = x^2 + y^2$
$\cos\theta = y/r$	$r = \sqrt{x^2 + y^2}$
$\tan\theta = x/y$	

If one side and one angle of a right triangle are known, the unknown sides and angles can be computed. For example, if a work surface is 15 ft below a point source of light (distance *y*), the length of light travel (distance *r*) at $\angle\theta$ of 22° from the nadir can be found as follows: $\cos\theta = y/r$, cos 22 = 15/r, 0.9272r = 15, and r = 16.2 ft. In addition, the distance this ray is from the nadir (distance *x*) at the work surface can be found by the pythagorean theorem:

$$r^2 = x^2 + y^2 \text{ and } x = \sqrt{r^2 - y^2} = \sqrt{16.2^2 - 15^2} = \boxed{6 \text{ ft}}$$

TRIGONOMETRIC TABLE

Angle θ (degrees)	sin θ	cos θ	tan θ	Angle θ (degrees)	sin θ	cos θ	tan θ
0	0.0000	1.0000	0.0000				
1	0.0175	0.9998	0.0175	46	0.7193	0.6947	1.0355
2	0.0349	0.9994	0.0349	47	0.7314	0.6820	1.0724
3	0.0523	0.9986	0.0524	48	0.7431	0.6691	1.1106
4	0.0698	0.9976	0.0699	49	0.7547	0.6561	1.1504
5	0.0872	0.9962	0.0875	50	0.7660	0.6428	1.1918
6	0.1045	0.9945	0.1051	51	0.7771	0.6293	1.2349
7	0.1219	0.9925	0.1228	52	0.7880	0.6157	1.2799
8	0.1392	0.9903	0.1405	53	0.7986	0.6018	1.3270
9	0.1564	0.9877	0.1584	54	0.8090	0.5878	1.3764
10	0.1736	0.9848	0.1763	55	0.8192	0.5736	1.4281
11	0.1908	0.9816	0.1944	56	0.8290	0.5592	1.4826
12	0.2079	0.9781	0.2126	57	0.8387	0.5446	1.5399
13	0.2250	0.9744	0.2309	58	0.8480	0.5299	1.6003
14	0.2419	0.9703	0.2493	59	0.8572	0.5150	1.6643
15	0.2588	0.9659	0.2679	60	0.8660	0.5000	1.7321
16	0.2756	0.9613	0.2867	61	0.8746	0.4848	1.8040
17	0.2924	0.9563	0.3057	62	0.8829	0.4695	1.8807
18	0.3090	0.9511	0.3249	63	0.8910	0.4540	1.9626
19	0.3256	0.9455	0.3443	64	0.8988	0.4384	2.0503
20	0.3420	0.9397	0.3640	65	0.9063	0.4226	2.1445
21	0.3584	0.9336	0.3839	66	0.9135	0.4067	2.2460
22	0.3746	0.9272	0.4040	67	0.9205	0.3907	2.3559
23	0.3907	0.9205	0.4245	68	0.9272	0.3746	2.4751
24	0.4067	0.9135	0.4452	69	0.9336	0.3584	2.6051
25	0.4226	0.9063	0.4663	70	0.9397	0.3420	2.7475
26	0.4384	0.8988	0.4877	71	0.9455	0.3256	2.9042
27	0.4540	0.8910	0.5095	72	0.9511	0.3090	3.0777
28	0.4695	0.8829	0.5317	73	0.9563	0.2924	3.2709
29	0.4848	0.8746	0.5543	74	0.9613	0.2756	3.4874
30	0.5000	0.8660	0.5774	75	0.9659	0.2588	3.7321
31	0.5150	0.8572	0.6009	76	0.9703	0.2419	4.0108
32	0.5299	0.8480	0.6249	77	0.9744	0.2250	4.3315
33	0.5446	0.8387	0.6494	78	0.9781	0.2079	4.7046
34	0.5592	0.8290	0.6745	79	0.9816	0.1908	5.1446
35	0.5736	0.8192	0.7002	80	0.9848	0.1736	5.6713
36	0.5878	0.8090	0.7265	81	0.9877	0.1564	6.3138
37	0.6018	0.7986	0.7536	82	0.9903	0.1392	7.1154
38	0.6157	0.7880	0.7813	83	0.9925	0.1219	8.1443
39	0.6293	0.7771	0.8098	84	0.9945	0.1045	9.5144
40	0.6428	0.7660	0.8391	85	0.9962	0.0872	11.4301
41	0.6561	0.7547	0.8693	86	0.9976	0.0698	14.3007
42	0.6691	0.7431	0.9004	87	0.9986	0.0523	19.0811
43	0.6820	0.7314	0.9325	88	0.9994	0.0349	28.6363
44	0.6947	0.7193	0.9657	89	0.9998	0.0175	57.2900
45	0.7071	0.7071	1.0000	90	1.0000	0.0000	∞

EXAMPLE PROBLEM (POINT METHOD)

1. In the room shown below, downlight luminaires are arranged to highlight areas on the horizontal work surface.

Reflected Ceiling Plan

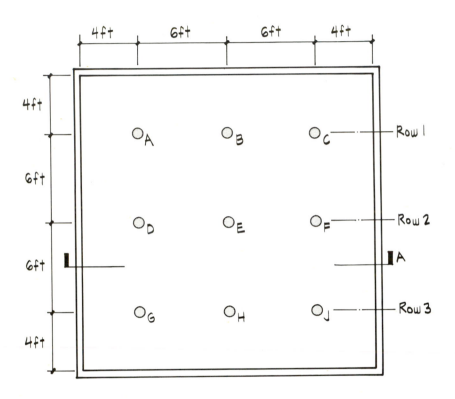

Section *A*

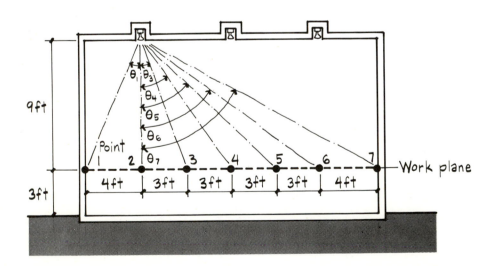

2. The table below is used to determine illumination at seven points on the work plane under row 2 from luminaire D by solving $(cp/r^2) \cos \theta$.

Point	Tan θ	θ	CP*	$x^2 + y^2$	r^2	$\frac{cp}{r^2} \times \cos \theta$	E (fc)
1	4/9 = 0.4444	24°	4500	$4^2 + 9^2$	97	$\frac{4500}{97} \times 0.9135$	42
2	–	0°	10,000	$0^2 + 9^2$	81	$\frac{10,000}{81} \times 1.0000$	123
3	3/9 = 0.3333	18°	6700	$3^2 + 9^2$	90	$\frac{6700}{90} \times 0.9511$	71
4	6/9 = 0.6667	34°	2000	$6^2 + 9^2$	117	$\frac{2000}{117} \times 0.8290$	14
5	9/9 = .0000	45°	500	$9^2 + 9^2$	162	$\frac{500}{162} \times 0.7071$	2
6	2/9 = .3333	53°	0	$12^2 + 9^2$	225	$\frac{0}{225} \times 0.6018$	0
7	6/9 = .7778	61°	0	$16^2 + 9^2$	337	$\frac{0}{337} \times 0.4848$	0

*Candlepower (cd) data from photometric curve on page 139.

3. The illumination at point 4 from luminaire A is found by determining the dimensions of the horizontal and vertical right triangles shown below. The bottom side of the vertical right triangle in the plane of luminaire A is $\sqrt{6^2 + 6^2}$ = 8.49 ft by the pythagorean theorem. Angle θ is found from tan $\theta = x/y$ = 8.49/9 = 0.9433. From the table on page 145, $\theta = 43°$ and cos 43 = 0.7314.

$$E = \frac{cp}{r^2} \cos \theta = \frac{800}{8.49^2 + 9^2} \, 0.7314 = \boxed{4 \text{ fc}}$$

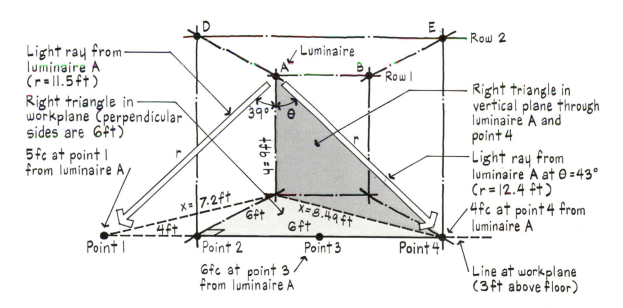

LIGHT ray from luminaire A (r = 11.5 ft)

Right triangle in workplane (perpendicular sides are 6 ft)

5 fc at point 1 from luminaire A

x = 7.2 ft

4 ft   6 ft

Point 1   Point 2

6 fc at point 3 from luminaire A

x = 8.49 ft   6 ft

Point 3   Point 4

D   E   Row 2

A   Luminaire   B   Row 1

39°   θ

y = 9 ft

r   r

Right triangle in vertical plane through luminaire A and point 4

Light ray from luminaire A at θ = 43° (r = 12.4 ft)

4 fc at point 4 from luminaire A

Line at workplane (3 ft above floor)

4. The table below is used to find the total footcandles at points 1 to 7 on the work plane under row 2. By symmetry, the illumination patterns from luminaires E and F are equal to D. Notice that luminaires located along rows 1 and 3 also contribute illumination at these points.

Luminaire	Illumination Level (E) at Points Under Row 2						
	1	2	3	4	5	6	7
D	42	123	71	14	2		
E		14	71	123	71	14	
F			2	14	71	123	42
A	5	14	6	4			
B		4	6	14	6	4	
C				4	6	14	5
G	5	14	6	4			
H		4	6	14	6	4	
J				4	6	14	5
Total (fc)	52	173	168	195	168	173	52

5. On section A, an illumination gradient is plotted, showing variations of direct light on the work plane from the nine luminaires. The point method does not account for interreflected light from room surfaces, as these components are usually negligible for downlights.

Section A

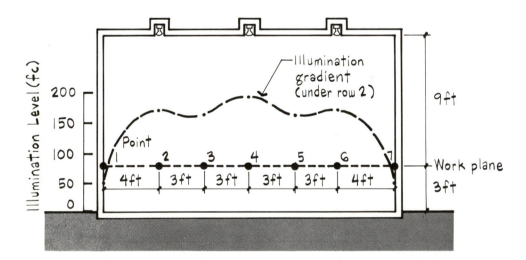

Note: To conserve energy, luminaires with low-wattage lamps can be used effectively to highlight areas in cafeterias, museums, etc. Focus can be achieved with peak footcandle values far below those represented by the above illumination gradient for the high-wattage lamps used in this example of point method computations. For comprehensive checklists of energy-conscious design strategies, see pages 165 and 166.

COEFFICIENT OF UTILIZATION

The coefficient of utilization (CU) is the ratio of lumens on the work surface to lumens emitted by the lamps of the luminaire. High CU values mean that more light reaches the work surface. The CU is influenced by room surface reflectances, size and shape of room, location of luminaires (i.e., mounting height), and luminaire design (e.g., pattern of candlepower distribution, lens efficiency). The size and shape of a room has the greatest effect on the CU. For example, in small rooms more light will be absorbed by the walls than in large rooms with low ceiling heights. As shown by the graph below, the CU decreases as the room cavity ratio (RCR) increases. (The RCR is $2.5h_c$ times the ratio of room perimeter to room area, where h_c is cavity height.) Rooms with greater ceiling height and correspondingly higher RCRs will provide less light on work surfaces due to the greater spread of light. The CU does not account for the effects of furniture and partial-height barriers, which extend above the work surface, or the effects of body shadows of room occupants on light distribution.

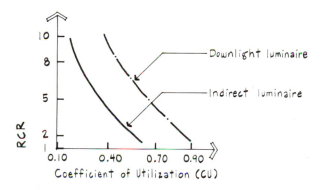

The CU can be used to determine the amount of lamp lumens required to achieve a uniform, maintained illumination level on a work surface by the formula.

$$F = \frac{E \times A}{CU \times LLD \times LDD}$$

where F = initial generated light from lamps of luminaire (lm)

E = illumination level or illuminance (fc)

A = area of work plane (ft^2)

CU = coefficient of utilization (decimal %)

LLD = lamp lumen depreciation (decimal %)

LDD = luminaire dirt depreciation (decimal %)

Note: The product of LLD and LDD was formerly called the *maintenance factor* (MF). In addition to the MF, rigorous computations account for additional causes of light loss such as temperature, voltage, and ballast effects; aging of luminaire finish; accumulation of dirt on room surfaces; and burned-out, unreplaced lamps. Procedures to determine these losses, called *light loss factors* (LLFs), are given in Section 9, IES *Lighting Handbook* (1981 Reference Volume).

The *cavity ratio,* which indicates cavity size and proportions, is calculated from room dimensions of length, width, and cavity height. Cavity ratios for rooms are found by evaluating the layer or cavity above suspended luminaires (called *ceiling cavity*), between the plane of the luminaires and the work surface (called *room cavity*), and below the plane of the work surface (called *floor cavity*). If the work surface is the floor, there will be no floor cavity and the floor cavity ratio (FCR) will be 0. Cavity ratios for rectangular or square plans can be computed by:

Know ✳

$$CR = 5h_c \left(\frac{L + W}{L \times W} \right)$$

where
CR = cavity ratio (no units)

h_c = height of cavity (ft)

W = width of cavity (ft)

L = length of cavity (ft)

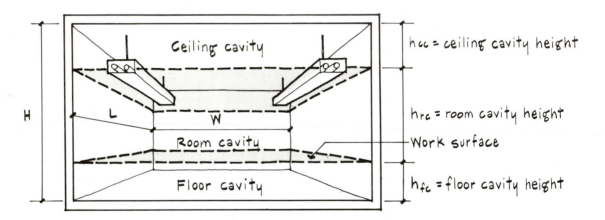

Note: To find cavity ratios for circular plans, use $5h_c/r$, where r is the radius of the cavity (in ft). For other irregular shapes, use $2.5h_c$ times cavity perimeter divided by area of cavity base.

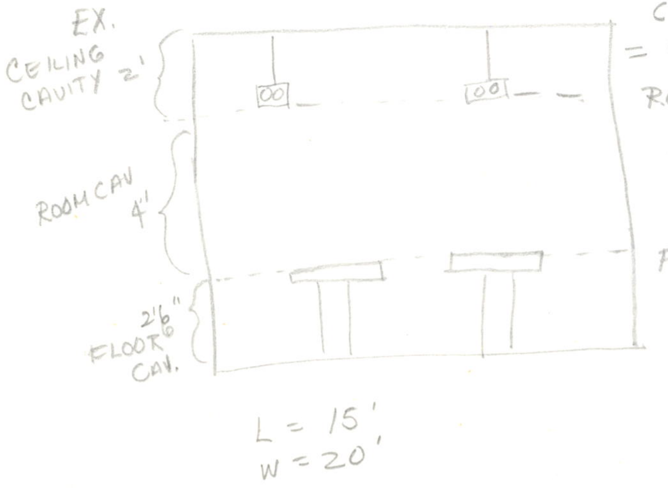

(handwritten annotations on diagram)

CEILING

$= CR = 5(2) \left(\frac{15 + 20}{15 \times 20} \right) = 10 \left(\frac{35}{300} \right) =$

ROOM CR $=$

$5(4') \left(\frac{15 + 20}{15 \times 20} \right) = 20 \left(\frac{35}{300} \right) =$

FLOOR

$5(2.5') \left(\frac{15 + 20}{15 \times 20} \right) = 12.5 \left(\frac{35}{300} \right) =$

EX.
CEILING CAVITY 2'
ROOM CAV 4'
FLOOR CAV. 2'6"

$L = 15'$
$W = 20'$

EFFECT OF REFLECTANCE ON COEFFICIENT OF UTILIZATION AND LOSS OF LIGHT FROM DIRT

Ceiling Reflectance

Reflectance (ρ) of ceilings has a greater effect on indirect luminaires (which bounce light off ceiling down to work surface) than on downlights, as shown by the graph below. The higher the reflectance of ceiling surfaces, the higher the CU. Wall reflectance has the least effect on CU, except when rooms are very small.

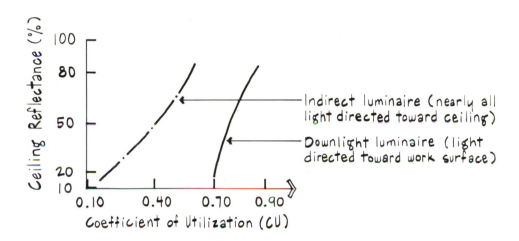

Dirt Depreciation

The luminaire dirt depreciation (LDD) factor is used in the lumen method to account for reduced illumination levels due to dirt accumulation on surfaces of luminaires. Enclosed luminaires with tightly gasketed lenses and ventilated luminaires will collect dirt much slower than open nonventilated or static luminaires. As shown by the graph below, the kind of environment (i.e., clean or dirty) and frequency of cleaning affect dirt depreciation.

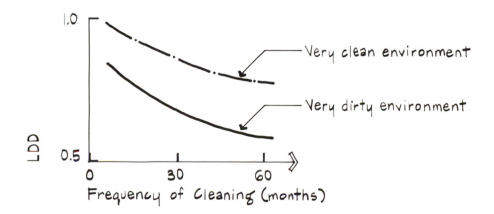

Note: When lamps are replaced, luminaires should be cleaned and plastic lenses replaced if their transmittance is low because of aging (called *yellowing*).

HOW TO FIND COEFFICIENT OF UTILIZATION

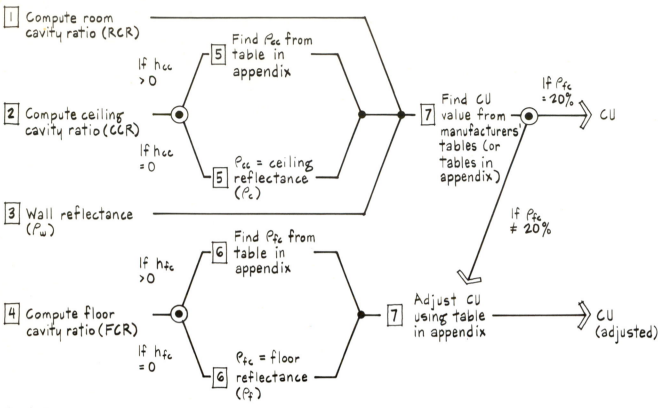

<u>Symbols</u>

☐ Steps

● All preceding steps to be evaluated

◉ Decision (i.e., must do one of the following steps)

COEFFICIENT OF UTILIZATION WORKSHEET

Room Identification: _____

Illuminance (in fc or lx): _____

Luminaire Data   **Lamp Data**

Designation: _____   Designation: _____

Lamps per Luminaire: _____   Initial Output (in lm): _____

LDD: _____   LLD: _____

Lumens per Luminaire: _____

Step 1: Fill in dimensions and reflectances on sketch.

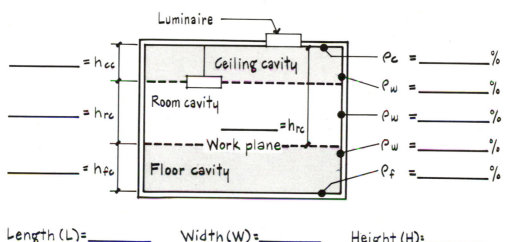

Length (L) = _____   Width (W) = _____   Height (H) = _____

Step 2: Using the formula $CR = 5h_c\left(\dfrac{L + W}{L \times W}\right)$

or tables, determine the following cavity ratios:

Ceiling cavity ratio,   CCR = _____

Room cavity ratio,   RCR = _____

Floor cavity ratio,   FCR = _____

Step 3: Obtain effective ceiling cavity reflectance (ρ_{cc}) from table on page 251. ρ_{CC} = _____%

Step 4: Obtain effective floor cavity reflectance (ρ_{FC}) from table on page 252. ρ_{FC} = _____%

Step 5: Obtain CU from luminaire CU tables.

CU = 0. _____

Note: If ρ_{FC} is other than 20%, adjust CU by factor from table on page 262.

Adjusted CU = 0. _____

In the lumen method for computing illuminance, the room is divided into three cavities (ceiling, room, and floor) and the effective cavity reflectances are determined for the ceiling and floor cavities. When the cavity ratios and reflectances are known, the CU can be found from tables. This method assumes that luminaires will be spaced in an array which provides uniform illumination. The procedure is outlined below using an example solution for the classroom described on page 156.

1. Divide the room into layers or cavities (see example worksheet on page 153). The work plane elevation for schools and offices is usually 30 in above the floor. In drafting and engineering rooms, the work plane elevation is usually 36 to 38 in above the floor; in retail shops and stores, 40 to 48 in; and in carpet stores, corridors, etc., the work plane is the floor level.

2. Determine the cavity ratios either by formulas or from tables.

$$\text{CCR} = 5h_{CC}\left(\frac{L+W}{L \times W}\right) = 5 \times 2.5\left(\frac{30+20}{30 \times 20}\right) = \boxed{1.0}$$

$$\text{RCR} = 5h_{RC}\left(\frac{L+W}{L \times W}\right) = 5 \times 7\left(\frac{30+20}{30 \times 20}\right) = \boxed{2.9}$$

$$\text{FCR} = 5h_{FC}\left(\frac{L+W}{L \times W}\right) = 5 \times 2.5\left(\frac{30+20}{30 \times 20}\right) = \boxed{1.0}$$

If fixtures are surface mounted or recessed, CCR will be zero.

3. Find the effective ceiling and floor cavity reflectances from the table on page 159. Use the actual ceiling reflectance value for ρ_{CC} when fixtures are surface-mounted or recessed. Use the actual floor reflectance for ρ_{FC} if the floor is the work plane.

4. Select the CU from fixture manufacturer's data. Adjust the CU if ρ_{FC} is other than 20%, using factor from table on page 161. The CU for this example will fall between the values given below for RCRs of 2 and 3. The data are obtained from the table on page 160.

| | **CU at** ρ_{CC} | |
RCR	70%	50%
2	0.57	0.47
3	0.50	0.42

By interpolation for RCR of 2.9 and wall reflectance of 50%

$$\text{CU at } \rho_{CC} \text{ of } 70\% = 0.57 - 0.07(0.9) = 0.51$$

$$\text{CU at } \rho_{CC} \text{ of } 50\% = 0.47 - 0.05(0.9) = 0.43$$

By interpolation for ρ_{CC} of 66%

$$\text{CU} = 0.51 - \frac{4}{20}(0.51 - 0.43) = 0.51 - 0.02 = \boxed{0.49}$$

Adjust CU for ρ_{FC} of 11% (see table on page 161).

$$\text{Adjusted CU} = \frac{0.49}{1.05} = \boxed{0.47}$$

5. Determine the required lamp lumens F and area per luminaire A_ℓ. Light loss factor LLF equals LLD times LDD.

$$F = \frac{E \times A}{CU \times LLF} = \frac{50 \times 20 \times 30}{0.47 \times 0.84 \times 0.85}$$

$$= \frac{30,000}{0.47 \times 0.714} = \boxed{89,397 \text{ lm}}$$

Each luminaire has two lamps with an initial output of 3150 lumens per lamp.

$$\text{Number of luminaires} = \frac{89,397}{2 \times 3150} = \boxed{14}$$

$$\text{Area per luminaire } A_\ell = \frac{20 \times 30}{14} = \boxed{43 \text{ ft}^2}$$

6. Check S:MH ratio. First, estimate spacing by taking the square root of the area per luminaire.

$$S \simeq \sqrt{A_\ell} \simeq \sqrt{43} = \boxed{6.6 \text{ ft}}$$

Next, try three continuous rows at 8-ft spacings (see reflected ceiling plan on page 157).

$$\frac{S}{MH} = \frac{8}{9.5} = \boxed{0.8}$$

This can be satisfactory for uniform illumination, as the S:MH ratio should be <1.3 for direct-indirect and diffuse luminaires and <1.5 for semi-indirect and indirect luminaires. Check with fixture manufacturers for recommended S:MH ratios.

The three rows are oriented parallel to the occupant's line of sight to front of classroom where over two-thirds of observations normally occur (e.g., viewing chalkboard, displays, and lecturer). In addition, this layout will reduce direct glare from luminaires by providing sidelighting for most viewing tasks in the classroom.

Room Identification: **Classroom**

Illuminance (in fc or lx): **50 fc**

Luminaire Data

Designation: **direct-indirect**

Lamps per Luminaire: **2**

LDD: **0.85 (24 mos., medium)**

Lamp Data

Designation: **F40 T12 CW**

Initial Output (in lm): **3150**

LLD: **0.84**

Lumens per Luminaire: **6300**

Step 1: Fill in dimensions and reflectances on sketch.

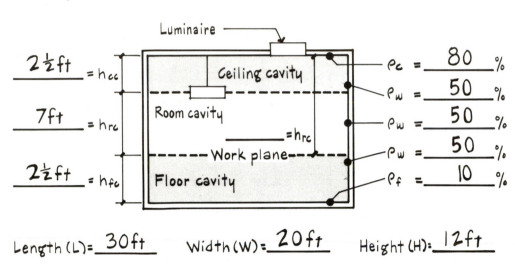

Length (L) = **30 ft**   Width (W) = **20 ft**   Height (H) = **12 ft**

Step 2: Using the formula

$$CR = 5h_c \left(\frac{L + W}{L \times W} \right)$$

or tables, determine the following cavity ratios:

Ceiling cavity ratio, CCR = **1.0**

Room cavity ratio, RCR = **2.9**

Floor cavity ratio, FCR = **1.0**

Step 3: Obtain effective ceiling cavity reflectance (ρ_{CC}) from table on page 251. ρ_{CC} = **66** %

Step 4: Obtain effective floor cavity reflectance (ρ_{FC}) from table on page 252. ρ_{FC} = **11** %

Step 5: Obtain CU from luminaire CU tables.

CU = 0.**49**

Note: If ρ_{FC} is other than 20%, adjust CU by factor from table on page 262.

Adjusted CU = 0.**47**

EXAMPLE PROBLEM (LUMEN METHOD)

Reflected Ceiling Plan

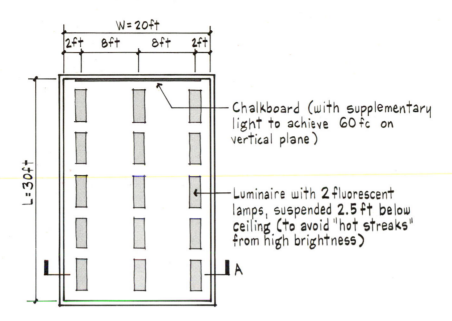

Chalkboard (with supplementary light to achieve 60 fc on vertical plane)

Luminaire with 2 fluorescent lamps, suspended 2.5 ft below ceiling (to avoid "hot streaks" from high brightness)

Note: Longitudinal rows can increase apparent length of room and reduce direct glare. Light directed toward ceiling prevents excessive contrast between luminaires and background. Luminaires with open top surfaces usually have less dirt accumulation if they allow smooth air circulation from convection due to lamp heat.

Section A

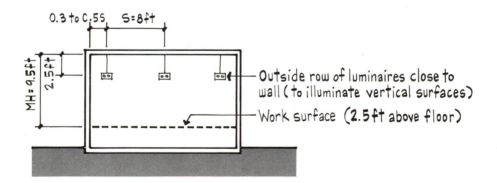

Outside row of luminaires close to wall (to illuminate vertical surfaces)

Work surface (2.5 ft above floor)

Note: For indirect luminaires, mounting height equals the ceiling height above work surface.

LUMINAIRE DIRT DEPRECIATION

Luminaire dirt depreciation is a factor used in lighting computations to account for reduced illumination due to dirt accumulation on luminaires. It depends on the frequency of cleaning and degree of dirtiness of rooms (i.e., very clean to very dirty). Use high LDD values when high-efficiency air-cleaning devices are incorporated into the air-distribution system or in spaces where smoking is not permitted. Example curves for two categories of luminaires are presented below.

Direct-Indirect Luminaire

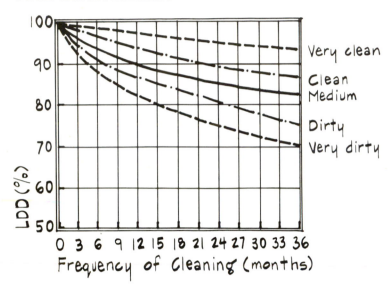

Indirect Luminaire (e.g., Cove)

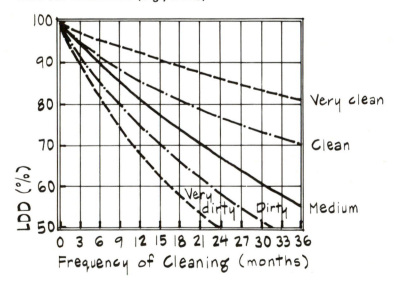

Note: For comprehensive procedures and data to evaluate LDD, see J. E. Kaufman (ed.), *IES Lighting Handbook* (1981 Reference Volume), pp. 9-2 to 9-5.

EFFECTIVE CEILING AND FLOOR CAVITY REFLECTANCES

The tables below present effective ceiling cavity reflectance ρ_{CC} and effective floor cavity reflectance ρ_{FC} values (in %). See page 251 for a comprehensive table.

Ceiling cavity reflectance

| CCR | $\rho_C = 90\%$ | | | | $\rho_C = 70\%$ | | | $\rho_C = 50\%$ | | |
| | ρ_W | | | | ρ_W | | | ρ_W | | |
	90%	70%	50%	30%	70%	50%	30%	70%	50%	30%
0	90	90	90	90	70	70	70	50	50	50
0.5	88	85	81	78	66	64	61	48	46	44
1	86	80	74	69	63	58	53	46	42	39
1.5	85	76	68	61	59	53	47	44	39	34
2	83	72	62	53	56	48	41	43	37	30
2.5	82	68	57	47	53	44	36	41	34	27
3	81	64	52	42	51	40	32	40	32	24
4	78	58	44	33	46	35	26	38	29	20
5	76	53	38	27	43	32	22	36	26	17

Floor cavity reflectance

| FCR | $\rho_F = 50\%$ | | | $\rho_F = 30\%$ | | | | $\rho_F = 10\%$ | | |
| | ρ_W | | | ρ_W | | | | ρ_W | | |
	70%	50%	30%	65%	50%	30%	10%	50%	30%	10%
0	50	50	50	30	30	30	30	10	10	10
0.5	48	46	44	29	28	27	25	11	10	9
1	46	42	39	29	27	24	22	11	9	8
1.5	44	39	34	28	25	22	18	12	9	7
2	43	37	30	28	24	20	16	12	9	6
2.5	41	34	27	27	23	18	14	13	9	6
3	40	32	24	27	22	17	12	13	8	5
4	38	29	20	26	21	15	9	13	8	4
5	36	26	17	25	19	13	7	14	8	4

COEFFICIENT OF UTILIZATION DATA (DIRECT-INDIRECT LUMINAIRE)

The table below presents CU data (in %) for typical direct-indirect luminaire with approximately equal light directed up and down. Data are given for ρ_{FC} of 20%.

RCR	$\rho_{CC} = 70\%$ ρ_W			$\rho_{CC} = 50\%$ ρ_W		
	50%	30%	10%	50%	30%	10%
1	0.64	0.61	0.60	0.52	0.51	0.50
2	0.57	0.53	0.50	0.47	0.45	0.42
3	0.50	0.46	0.43	0.42	0.39	0.37
4	0.45	0.40	0.37	0.38	0.35	0.32
5	0.40	0.36	0.32	0.34	0.30	0.28
10	0.25	0.20	0.17	0.21	0.18	0.15

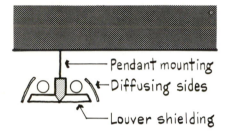

Pendant mounting

Diffusing sides

Louver shielding

Suspended Luminaire

Note: For comprehensive CU tables based on industry averages, see pages 253-261 in appendix or J.E. Kaufman (ed.), *IES Lighting Handbook* (1981 Reference Volume), pp. 9-13 to 9-32. CU data are also available from luminaire manufacturers.

FACTORS FOR EFFECTIVE FLOOR CAVITY REFLECTANCES OTHER THAN 20%

The table below presents factors to adjust CU values for effective floor cavity reflectances ρ_{FC} other than 15 to 25%. For $\rho_{FC} > 25\%$, multiply CU by factor from table to obtain adjusted CU. For $\rho_{FC} < 15\%$, divide CU by factor from table to obtain adjusted CU.

	$\rho_{CC} = 70\%$			$\rho_{CC} = 50\%$		
	ρ_W			ρ_W		
RCR	50%	30%	10%	50%	30%	10%
1	1.07	1.06	1.06	1.05	1.04	1.04
2	1.06	1.05	1.04	1.04	1.03	1.03
3	1.05	1.04	1.03	1.03	1.03	1.02
4	1.04	1.03	1.02	1.03	1.02	1.02
5	1.03	1.02	1.02	1.02	1.02	1.01
10	1.02	1.01	1.01	1.02	1.01	1.01

Note: For comprehensive tables of multiplying factors to adjust CU values for ρ_{FC} other than 20%, see J. E. Kaufman (ed.), *IES Lighting Handbook* (1981 Reference Volume), p. 9-33.

EXAMPLE PROBLEM (COVE LIGHTING)

The lumen method applied to a cove lighting system is outlined below.

1. Dimensions of example dining room lobby, surface reflectances, and luminaire and lamp data are given by worksheet on page 163.
2. Compute perimeter P of cove.

$$P = (2 \times 14) + (2 \times 20) = \boxed{68 \text{ ft}}$$

Reduce P by 5% to 65 ft to account for space taken up by bases, lampholders, and wiring channels.

3. Select CU from data on page 164. CU will fall between the values given below for RCRs of 4 and 5.

| | CU at ρ_{CC} | |
RCR	70%	50%
4	0.22	0.15
5	0.19	0.13

By interpolation for ρ_{CC} of 68% at RCR of 5

$$\text{CU} = 0.19 - \frac{2}{20}(0.19 - 0.13) = \boxed{0.18}$$

Adjust CU for ρ_{FC} of 10% (i.e., floor surface is work plane).

$$\text{Adjusted CU} = \frac{0.18}{1.02} = 0.176 = \boxed{0.18}$$

4. Find the required lumens to achieve desired 10 fc. LLF = LLD $\times$ LDD.

$$F = \frac{E \times A}{\text{CU} \times \text{LLF}} = \frac{10 \times 20 \times 14}{0.18 \times 0.76 \times 0.75}$$

$$= \frac{2800}{0.18 \times 0.57} = \boxed{27{,}290 \text{ lm}}$$

5. Determine the required lm/ft of cove.

$$\frac{27{,}290}{65} = \boxed{420 \text{ lm/ft}}$$

F42 T6 WW fluorescent lamps provide 536 lm/ft of cove, so maintained illumination level E will be:

$$E = \frac{536}{420} \times 10 \simeq \boxed{13 \text{ fc}}$$

This low level of illuminance on the horizontal work surface can be sufficient and appropriate if, for example, illuminated paintings and plants are used to reflect light, creating the desired relaxing atmosphere.

COEFFICIENT OF UTILIZATION WORKSHEET

Room Identification: **Lobby**

Illuminance (in fc or lx): **10fc**

Luminaire Data

Designation: **Cove Strip**

Lamps per Luminaire: **Strip**

LDD: **0.75** (18 mos., medium)

Lamp Data

Designation: **F42 T6 WW**

Initial Output (in lm): **1875**

LLD: **0.76**

Lumens per Luminaire: $\frac{1875}{3.5} = $ **536 lm/ft**

Step 1: Fill in dimensions and reflectances on sketch.

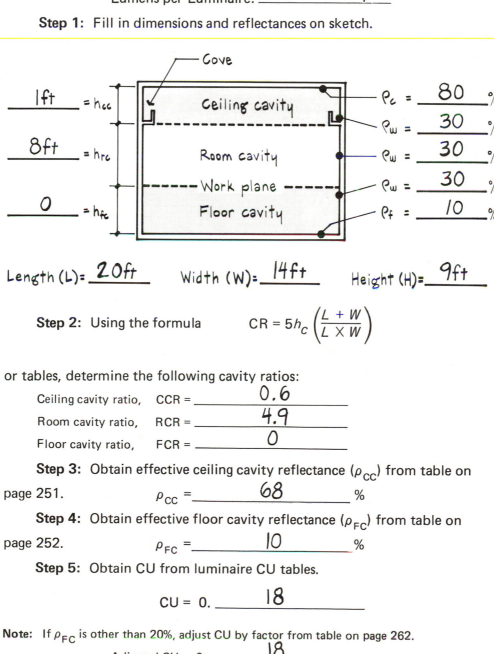

Length (L)= **20ft**   Width (W)= **14ft**   Height (H)= **9ft**

Step 2: Using the formula $CR = 5h_c \left(\dfrac{L + W}{L \times W} \right)$

or tables, determine the following cavity ratios:

Ceiling cavity ratio, CCR = **0.6**

Room cavity ratio, RCR = **4.9**

Floor cavity ratio, FCR = **0**

Step 3: Obtain effective ceiling cavity reflectance (ρ_{CC}) from table on page 251. $\rho_{CC} = $ **68** %

Step 4: Obtain effective floor cavity reflectance (ρ_{FC}) from table on page 252. $\rho_{FC} = $ **10** %

Step 5: Obtain CU from luminaire CU tables.

CU = 0.**18**

Note: If ρ_{FC} is other than 20%, adjust CU by factor from table on page 262.

Adjusted CU = 0.**18**

COEFFICIENT OF UTILIZATION DATA (COVE)

The table below presents CU data (in %) for typical indirect coves with a single row of fluorescent lamps. If two rows are used, multiply CU values from table by 0.93. Data are given for ρ_{FC} of 20%.

	ρ_{CC} = 70%			ρ_{CC} = 50%		
	ρ_W			ρ_W		
RCR	50%	30%	10%	50%	30%	10%
1	0.36	0.35	0.33	0.25	0.24	0.23
2	0.32	0.29	0.27	0.22	0.20	0.19
3	0.28	0.25	0.23	0.19	0.17	0.16
4	0.25	0.22	0.19	0.17	0.15	0.13
5	0.22	0.19	0.16	0.15	0.13	0.11
10	0.13	0.10	0.08	0.09	0.07	0.06

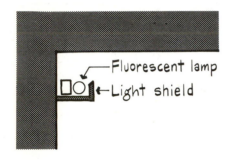

Cove

Note: For comprehensive CU tables based on industry averages, see pages 253-261 in appendix or J. E. Kaufman (ed.), *IES Lighting Handbook* (1981 Reference Volume), pp. 9-13 to 9-32. CU data are also available from luminaire manufacturers.

CHECKLISTS FOR ENERGY-CONSCIOUS DESIGN OF LIGHTING SYSTEMS

General Strategies

1. Avoid excessively high uniform illumination levels. After overall levels of 20 to 30 fc are achieved, provide selective lighting on tasks using portable fixtures, table lamps or floor-mounted lamps, furniture-integrated fixtures, and so on. To minimize veiling reflections, position local lighting so that light on visual tasks will come from the side, rather than from the front, of the task. Use other supplementary lighting to accent plants, paintings, entrances, etc.

2. Group together visual tasks which require similar lighting.

3. Where illumination level requirements are not constant, use state-of-the-art dimmers or multilevel ballasts for fluorescent lamps. Avoid block or group switching of fixtures, which may provide unused light.

4. Open-plan areas with partial-height barriers can reduce the amount of light that otherwise would be absorbed by walls in small, enclosed rooms. In open plans, provide separate circulation lighting to avoid the use of unnecessary ceiling fixtures.

5. Use a transparent material for the upper part of partitions in order to transmit interior light to corridors, where low illumination levels will be sufficient (e.g., about 10 fc).

Light Sources (See also Chap. 2)

1. For constant illumination level requirements, use single-wattage lamps at the wattage required to produce the necessary illumination rather than multilevel lamps which have lower light per watt output.

2. Because light output per watt increases with lamp wattage, use one incandescent lamp at the wattage required to produce the necessary illumination level rather than two or more lower-wattage lamps that equal or exceed the wattage of the single lamp.

3. Avoid using extremely long-life lamps which produce less light per watt than short-life lamps, unless short-life lamps present maintenance problems (e.g., where access for cleaning and relamping is complicated by hard-to-reach locations).

4. Use efficient lamps with high lm/W output and efficient, low-wattage-loss ballasts with discharge lamps. For outdoor lighting (e.g., parking, security), use HID lamps with timers or photocell devices to turn off lamps when they are not needed.

5. When fluorescent lamps are used outdoors in cold weather, use high-output or 1500-mA lamps in tightly enclosed, gasketed luminaires, or use a jacketed lamp when lamps are exposed.

Note: Be sure lamps are compatible with color rendition needs.

Luminaires

1. Use lower mounting heights for semi-direct luminaires and downlights to provide more light on tasks with less light absorbed by wall surfaces.

2. Specify luminaires with high CUs and high light loss factors (LLFs). LLF is decimal percent of actual to rated output.

3. Use heat-of-light systems, which use water or return air to transfer lamp and ballast heat away from luminaires (e.g., to building locations requiring heat), since they increase lamp efficacy by keeping surrounding air temperature below about 80°F. As low-wattage fluorescent lamps in troffer fixtures may operate at or near optimum temperatures, further cooling by return air could reduce light output and cause lamps to flicker.

4. Use pendant-supported or chain-suspended open fluorescent fixtures rather than enclosed luminaires, which reduce lm/W output due to buildup of heat from ballast and lamps.

5. For luminaire glare control, use prismatic plastic (or glass) and fresnel-type lenses, which transmit more light than parabolic wedge louvers, opal diffusers, or eggcrate louvers (e.g., louvers collect dirt and absorb light when slat elements are closely spaced).

6. To improve lm/W output of fluorescent lamps, use low-wattage-loss ballasts. Ballasts which operate at lower power after lamps have started are available.

Coordination with Daylighting (See also Chap. 6)

1. Use lighting systems that are zoned away from daylight sources (e.g., sidelighting at building perimeter, interior light wells) to allow easy independent switching. Locate tasks requiring highest illumination levels at locations where daylighting is best.

2. Use photocells, timers, or manual switches to reduce illumination at night or when daylight levels are sufficient. For fluorescent fixtures, consider using dimming and multilevel ballasts. For incandescent fixtures, use solid-state dimming devices, as rheostats consume energy continuously.

3. Use high-reflectance matte wall and ceiling surfaces (e.g., sloped white ceilings can provide useful reflected daylight). To increase efficiency of reflected light, use sloped surfaces, light shelves, and light-colored ground cover at base of buildings.

4. To control glare, use shading devices at window openings (e.g., drapes, fine-mesh screens, narrow-slat blinds) and at skylights (e.g., prismatic lenses). Window luminance normally should not exceed 300 fL in offices and classrooms.

Note: Be sure that energy consumption due to heat loss and heat gain through openings for daylighting does not exceed savings in reduced electric lighting energy consumption.

Chapter 6
Daylight and Design

ILLUMINANCE AND CREATIVITY

The more critical the visual task, the less freedom the designer has to create or manipulate space. As shown by the table below, there is an inverse relationship between the designer's opportunities for subjective or "intuitive" design expression and the user's critical seeing task needs. Spaces such as corridors, lobbies, and the like, where critical seeing task needs intermittently or rarely occur, offer the greatest freedom to manipulate space for daylighting. Other spaces, such as classrooms, banks, offices, and hospitals, must have carefully controlled daylighting which is often integrated with electrical task lighting.

Illuminance category*	Type of space (and activity)
A	Corridors (at night)
	Waiting rooms (such as medical diagnostic)
B	Dance halls, discotheques
	Dining halls
	Residences (for conversation, relaxation, and entertainment)
	Airport concourses
C	Corridors, lobbies, reception areas
	Churches (for main worship)
D	Hotels (bedrooms, lobby reading areas)
	Residences (kitchens, laundries, and sewing rooms)
E	Banks (teller areas)
	Churches (altar, reredos)
	Classrooms (science laboratories)
	Offices (for clerical tasks)
F	Drafting (low-contrast Mylar or vellum, sepia prints)
	Lecture rooms (for demonstrations)
G	Hospitals (autopsy tables)
H	Hospitals (operating tables)
I	Industrial (cloth inspection)

Increasingly Critical Visual Tasks (downward arrow on left)

Increasing Freedom for "Intuitive" Design Decisions (upward arrow on right)

*Illuminance category refers to a range of footcandle or lux values. Specific illuminance needs are established by considering the age of the building's occupants or workers, the speed and/or accuracy requirements of the visual tasks, and the reflectance of the task background. For comprehensive listings of recommended illuminance categories and illuminance values (or illumination levels) for a wide variety of indoor activities, refer to J. E. Kaufman (ed.), *IES Lighting Handbook* (1981 Application Volume), pp. 2-3 to 2-24.

Note: Achieved illuminance can be from daylighting, electrical lighting, or a combination of the two.

NATURAL LIGHT IN BUILDINGS

Daylight has predictable daily and seasonal variations and unpredictable patterns from cloud cover, atmospheric pollution, and other climatic variations. On the following pages are maps showing yearly weather conditions affecting available daylight in the United States.

Sunny Day

Clear skies (<30% cloud cover) can provide focus, and shadow and texture patterns as parts of the horizon will be brighter than overhead sky by as much as 12 to 1. Use sidelighting such as high window openings to achieve deep penetration of light.

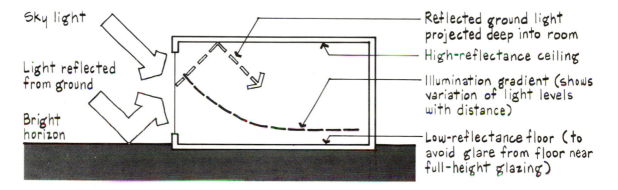

Overcast Day

Overcast skies (100% cloud cover, with sun not visible) are about 3 times brighter at the zenith than at the horizon. Therefore, openings which provide toplighting (e.g., skylights, clerestories) should be used to achieve an effective distribution of daylight at sites where overcast skies are frequent.

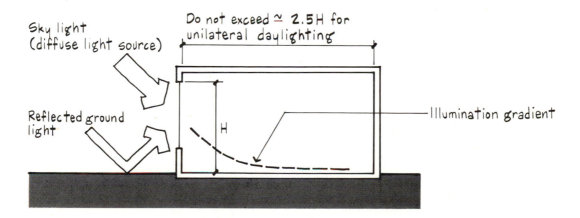

Note: For an overview of daylight design examples and principles, see "Natural Light," *AIA Journal,* September 1979, pp. 49-93.

CLEAR SKY CONDITIONS

The map below shows locations throughout the United States where yearly occurrences of clear sky conditions (<30% cloud cover) are high, medium, or low. High yearly occurrences mean that clear skies are present more than 180 days per year; medium, 100 to 180 days; and low, less than 100 days. The zones on the map indicate only the potential for available daylight, as weather conditions are highly variable and difficult to predict. When skies are bright and clear, glare must be controlled at building openings.

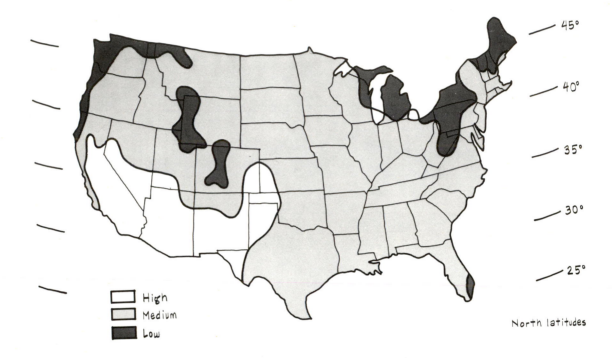

High
Medium
Low

North latitudes

Note: The north latitudes indicated on the map can be used to help determine sun angles for the lumen daylight design method developed by J. W. Griffith at Southern Methodist University. The method predicts illuminance from vertical glazing at three locations along the work plane in rooms. A booklet, "How to Predict Interior Daylight Illumination," describes the method and is available from Libbey-Owens-Ford Co., 811 Madison Avenue, Toledo, OH 43695.

CLOUDY SKY CONDITIONS

The map below shows locations throughout the United States where yearly occurrences of cloudy sky conditions (>70% cloud cover) are high, medium, or low. High yearly occurrences mean that cloudy skies are present more than 160 days per year; medium, 80 to 160 days; and low, less than 80 days. The zones on the map indicate only the potential for restricted daylight, as weather conditions are highly variable and difficult to predict. Daylight available from an overcast sky (100% cloud cover, with sun not visible) is relatively uniform and diffuse. However, its luminance can be one-eighth that of a clear sky.

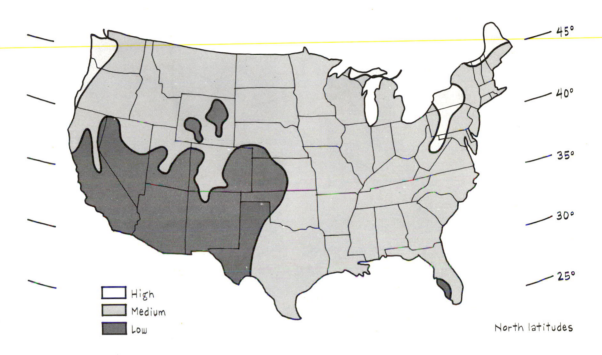

High

Medium

Low

North latitudes

SOLAR ANGLES

The position of the sun varies according to latitude (see map on preceding page), season, and time of day. As shown by the orbit sketch below, solar altitude angle ($\angle \alpha$) is measured between the horizon and the position of the sun above the horizon. Solar bearing angle ($\angle \beta$) is measured from the north-south axis to the vertical plane through the sun.

Sun's Orbit

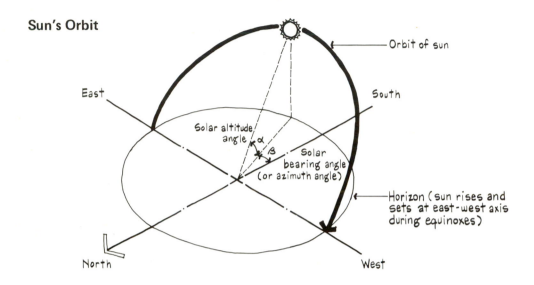

The table below presents solar altitude angle and bearing angle at various latitudes. Noon is the instant when the sun is at the highest point in its daily orbit.

North latitude	Solar angle (degrees)	Winter solstice (21 Dec.) 6 a.m. 6 p.m.	8 a.m. 4 p.m.	10 a.m. 2 p.m.	Noon	Spring equinox (21 Mar.) Fall equinox (21 Sep.) 6 a.m. 6 p.m.	8 a.m. 4 p.m.	10 a.m. 2 p.m.	Noon	Summer solstice (21 June) 6 a.m. 6 p.m.	8 a.m. 4 p.m.	10 a.m. 2 p.m.	Noon
46°	altitude (α)	—	2	15	21	—	20	37	44	17	37	57	67
	bearing (β)	—	52	28	0	90	67	39	0	107	88	58	0
42°	altitude (α)	—	4	19	25	—	22	40	48	16	38	60	71
	bearing (β)	—	53	29	0	90	69	41	0	108	89	63	0
38°	altitude (α)	—	7	23	28	—	23	43	52	14	37	61	75
	bearing (β)	—	54	30	0	90	71	43	0	109	90	70	0
34°	altitude (α)	—	9	26	33	—	25	46	56	13	37	62	79
	bearing (β)	—	54	30	0	90	72	46	0	110	95	78	0
30°	altitude (α)	—	12	29	37	—	26	49	60	12	37	63	83
	bearing (β)	—	54	32	0	90	74	49	0	111	99	84	0

Note: For comprehensive tables of solar angles at various latitudes, seasons, and times of day, refer to *ASHRAE Handbook* (1981 Fundamentals Volume), Atlanta, Ga., pp. 27.3 to 27.8, or J. E. Kaufman (ed.), *IES Lighting Handbook* (1981 Reference Volume), p. 7-4. For a graphic presentation of solar angles, sun angle calculators are available from Libbey-Owens-Ford Co., 811 Madison Avenue, Toledo, OH 43695.

DAYLIGHT ILLUMINANCE

The graph below presents average illuminance (in fc) for clear and overcast sky conditions. Actual levels may vary considerably due to changes in weather conditions.

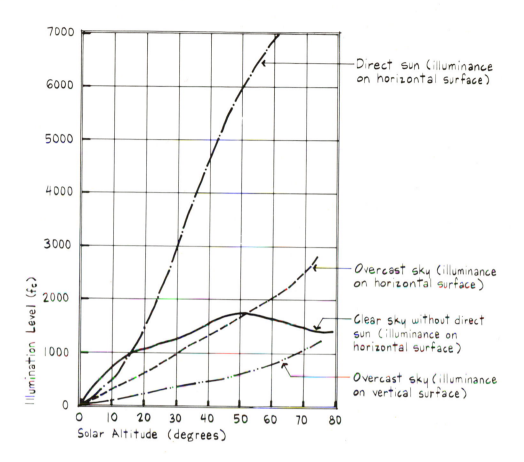

Note: For additional illuminance data, refer to J. E. Kaufman (ed.), *IES Lighting Handbook* (1981 Reference Volume), p. 7-8. Maps of the United States showing available daylight in numbers of days and hours per year are also presented in Chapter 7 of the handbook.

The brightness of the sky that can be seen through openings will determine the illuminance from daylight. For uniform illumination, the area of window openings should equal about one-fourth of the floor area. To minimize reflected glare, desks and tables should be oriented so that daylight comes to visual tasks from the direction normal to the side of occupants.

High

High, narrow openings (e.g., ribbon windows) can project light deep into rooms and achieve uniform distribution of daylight, but view of outdoors will be restricted. Ceiling and upper walls should be high-reflectance, matte surfaces.

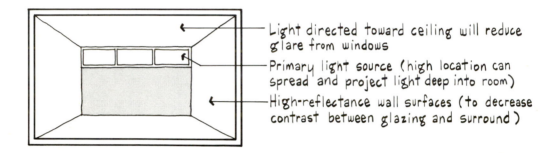

Light directed toward ceiling will reduce glare from windows

Primary light source (high location can spread and project light deep into room)

High-reflectance wall surfaces (to decrease contrast between glazing and surround)

Central

Openings with low sills project more light onto floor and permit better distribution of reflected ground light.

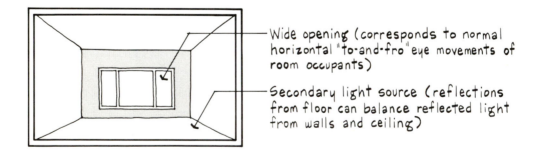

Wide opening (corresponds to normal horizontal "to-and-fro" eye movements of room occupants)

Secondary light source (reflections from floor can balance reflected light from walls and ceiling)

End

Openings at end of walls can help users understand size and shape of rooms by defining intersections of major surfaces. End openings also can reduce brightness ratios by illuminating adjacent surfaces. However, views of outdoors for time orientation and weather information will be restricted.

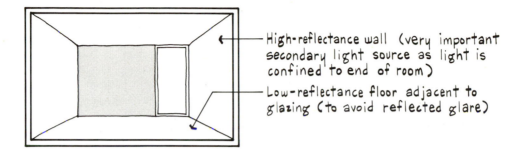

High-reflectance wall (very important secondary light source as light is confined to end of room)

Low-reflectance floor adjacent to glazing (to avoid reflected glare)

Reference

J. K. Holton, "Daylighting of Buildings," U.S. National Bureau of Standards, NBSIR 76-1098, October 1976.

High window placement can be used to project light deep into rooms. As shown below, reduced window height restricts the depth of daylight penetration. For example, under identical overcast sky conditions, reducing window height *H* from 14 to 8 ft will lower the illumination at the rear of a room by over 60%. Similar reductions will occur in rooms with bilateral openings (i.e., windows on both sides of a room), although illumination levels will be higher throughout room.

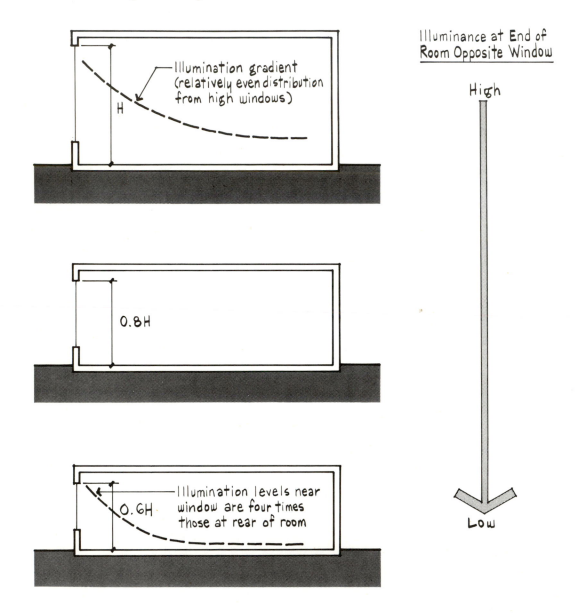

Illuminance at End of Room Opposite Window

Illumination gradient (relatively even distribution from high windows)

High

Illumination levels near window are four times those at rear of room

Low

Reference

B. H. Evans, *Daylight in Architecture,* McGraw-Hill, New York, 1981, pp. 56-57.

Wide window openings can provide greater depth of daylight penetration than narrow openings. The shape of wide openings also may correspond to the normal lateral scan of the eyes when room occupants are seeking information on weather, neighbors, and so on. Long, wide openings generally will be perceived as less glaring than tall, narrow openings of equal area and luminance. In addition, occupants generally prefer wider openings when the primary views of interest are of nearby objects or activities.

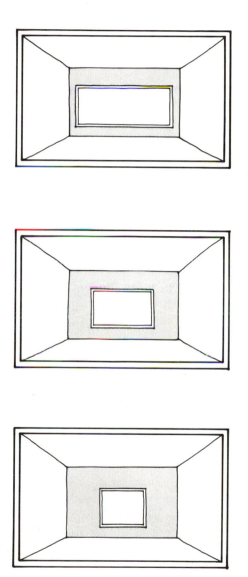

Illuminance at End of
Room Opposite Window

High

Low

In rooms with unilateral openings (i.e., windows on only one side), illumination levels at the end of the room opposite the windows are reduced as room depth D is increased. This is due to the fact that the transmitted light is spread over a greater area. To achieve effective distribution of light from unilateral daylighting, room depth should not exceed about 2.5H, where H is window height.

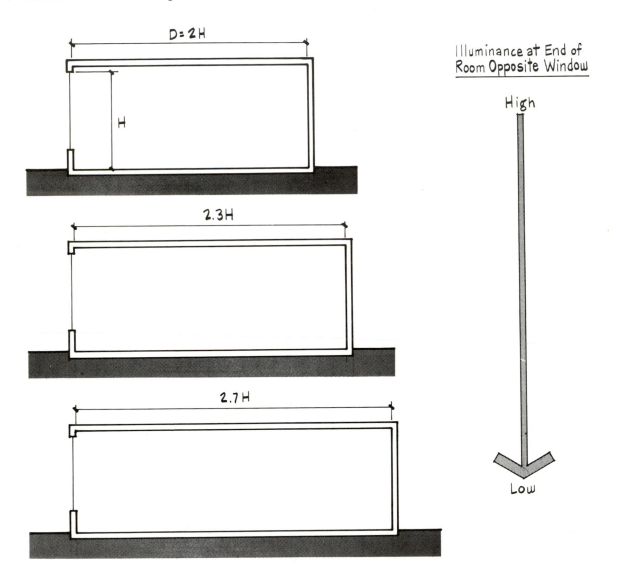

Illuminance at End of Room Opposite Window

High

Low

Reference

B. H. Evans, *Daylight in Architecture,* McGraw-Hill, New York, 1981, p. 59.

ROOF OVERHANGS

Illumination levels are reduced as the width of the overhang for sun control is increased. Although levels throughout the room are reduced, the greatest reduction occurs near the windows. Therefore, the distribution of light throughout the room is more uniform. Cantilevers can be used to project reflected ground light into rooms. Beyond about 40 ft from the building, however, ground conditions are not significant for single-story windows.

No Overhang

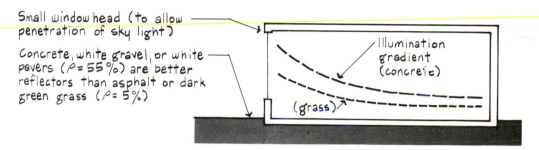

Small window head (to allow penetration of sky light)

Concrete, white gravel, or white pavers ($\rho = 55\%$) are better reflectors than asphalt or dark green grass ($\rho = 5\%$)

Illumination gradient (concrete)

(grass)

Short Cantilever

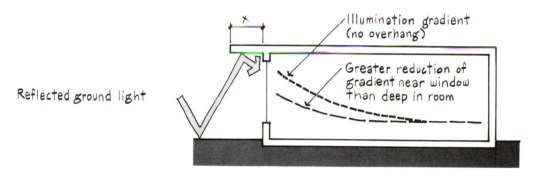

x

Illumination gradient (no overhang)

Reflected ground light

Greater reduction of gradient near window than deep in room

Wide Cantilever

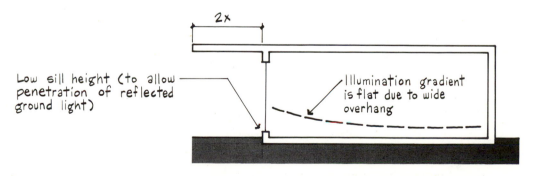

2x

Low sill height (to allow penetration of reflected ground light)

Illumination gradient is flat due to wide overhang

Note: Window added to rear wall can raise and flatten illumination gradient and reduce harsh shadows.

Contours of equal illumination levels in footcandle, lux, or DF (called *isoilluminance diagrams*) can be used to show the pattern of daylighting produced by openings and the illumination levels throughout a room. As shown in the bilaterally illuminated room below, the daylight factor (and illuminance) is extremely high adjacent to window openings, and penetration is deep because of the multiple sources of daylight. The *daylight factor* (DF) is the percentage of light from outdoors at a point indoors. For example, 600 fc from an overcast sky and a DF of 1% will result in an illumination level of 6 fc (i.e., 0.01×600) on a horizontal surface indoors.

Plan

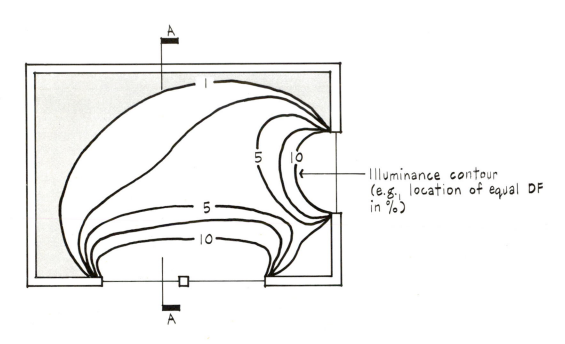

Illuminance contour (e.g., location of equal DF in %)

Section A-A

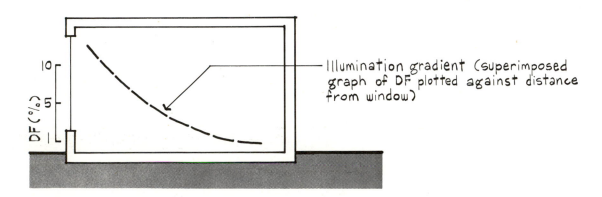

Illumination gradient (superimposed graph of DF plotted against distance from window)

ISOILLUMINANCE CONTOURS FOR SIDELIGHTING

Isoilluminance contours can be used to show the pattern of light distribution. In the examples of window openings of equal area shown below, the distribution of daylight is deepest through the tall window and widest through the multiple window openings. Obstructions such as horizontal and bay window overhangs will reduce the penetration of light.

Single Opening

When wide openings are placed high in walls, surfaces beneath can appear dark. Electric light sources providing low illumination levels on these surfaces can prevent gloomy conditions.

Wide   **Tall**

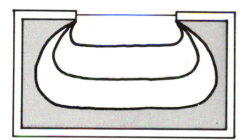   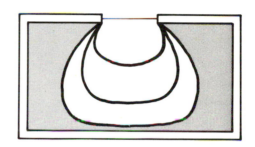

Multiple Openings

Wall surfaces between widely spaced windows also can appear too dark. Splayed jambs and chamfered ceilings can lower brightness ratios and reduce apparent darkness.

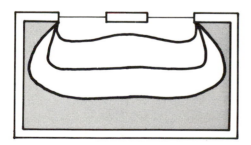

Note: For a description of a graphic method to predict daylighting levels using standard light distribution plots, see M. S. Millet and J. R. Bedrick, "Predicting Daylight Distribution in Proposed Interior Designs," *Lighting Design & Application,* March 1980.

Toplighting distributes light over a greater horizontal area than side-lighting. At locations where overcast skies are more frequent than clear skies, toplighting can be more effective than sidelighting. Be careful, however, as skylights located in the offending zone can produce veiling reflections at work stations.

Central Skylight

For even illumination, spacing between skylights should not exceed room height *H* for small skylights and *2H* for large skylights (e.g., open area > 30 ft²). Be sure skylights do not allow direct glare from the sun on critical seeing tasks.

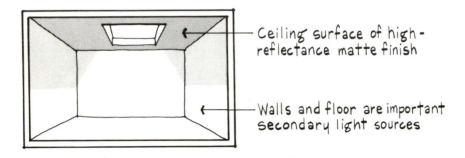

Ceiling surface of high-reflectance matte finish

Walls and floor are important secondary light sources

Unilateral Clerestory

For clerestories facing north, light will be diffuse, cool, and uniform; whereas for those facing south, light will be bright and variable and will provide strong modeling effects. Be careful when clerestories face east or west as solar radiation can complicate thermal comfort system designs.

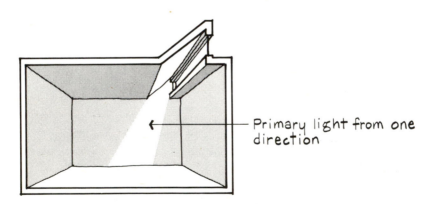

Primary light from one direction

Bilateral Clerestories

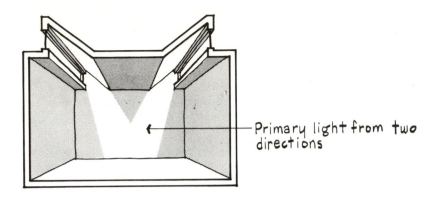

Primary light from two directions

Reflective Clerestory

Reflective clerestories can project daylight into lower-level spaces by reflection and provide dramatic effects on vertical surfaces by a wash of indirect light.

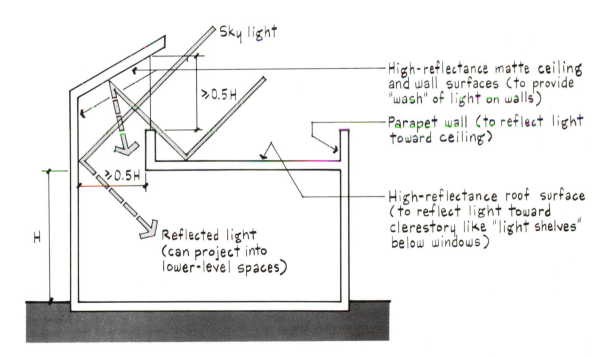

Sky light

≥0.5H

≥0.5H

H

Reflected light (can project into lower-level spaces)

High-reflectance matte ceiling and wall surfaces (to provide "wash" of light on walls)

Parapet wall (to reflect light toward ceiling)

High-reflectance roof surface (to reflect light toward clerestory like "light shelves" below windows)

Sawtooth Skylight

Sawtooth skylights can provide more uniform lighting than a unilateral clerestory of equal glazing area.

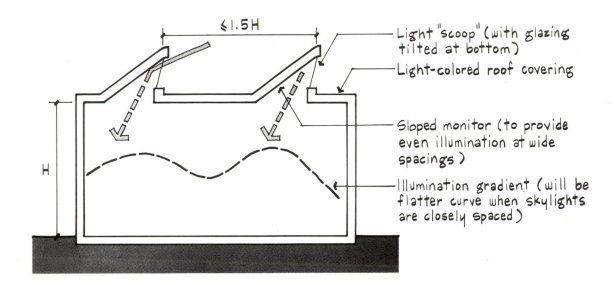

Note: For a method to determine horizontal illuminance on work surfaces and potential energy savings from skylights, refer to J. B. Murdoch, "A Procedure for Calculating the Potential Savings in Lighting Energy from the Use of Skylights," *Journal of the Illuminating Engineering Society,* July 1977.

LIGHT WELLS

Light wells with sloped surfaces are toplighting devices which can soften the brightness ratios at the boundary of the view of sky and ceiling. The sides of the well should have a high-reflectance, matte finish. Avoid glossy finishes which can create hot spots. For efficient distribution of transmitted daylight, the well index should be less than 0.9. Efficient shapes for well openings are wide and long, but narrow in depth. The well index I_W can be found by the following formula.

$$I_W = 0.5H\left(\frac{W + L}{W \times L}\right)$$

where I_W = well index (no units)

   W = width of well opening (ft)

   L = length of well opening (ft)

   H = depth of well opening (ft)

Pyramidal Well

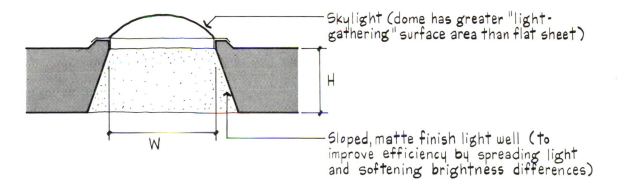

Skylight (dome has greater "light-gathering" surface area than flat sheet)

H

Sloped, matte finish light well (to improve efficiency by spreading light and softening brightness differences)

Note: Double-dome acrylic skylights can have translucent glass-fiber insulation in air-space to provide diffuse light and increase resistance to heat flow. However, these luminous ceiling elements could be perceived as being dull and gloomy.

Clerestory openings, or a series of openings such as sawtooth skylights or monitors, can be used to project light deep into large spaces. With glazing tilted inward at bottom or roof overhang elements, as shown below, clerestories on southern exposures can be designed to admit the winter sun but exclude the summer sun. The height of a clerestory opening H_c should be at least one-half the height of the window opening H_W. For uniform illumination, the distance from clerestory opening to rear wall should not exceed $2H_T$, where H_T is the height of the clerestory above the floor.

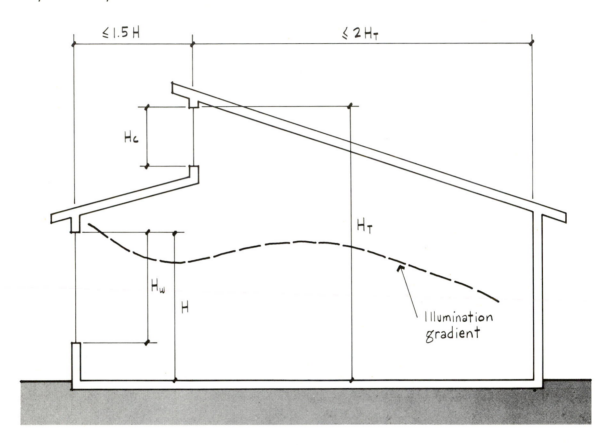

Reference

J. E. Flynn and A. W. Segil, *Architectural Interior Systems,* Van Nostrand Reinhold, New York, 1970, p. 115.

REFLECTED AND BEAM DAYLIGHTING

Reflected Daylighting

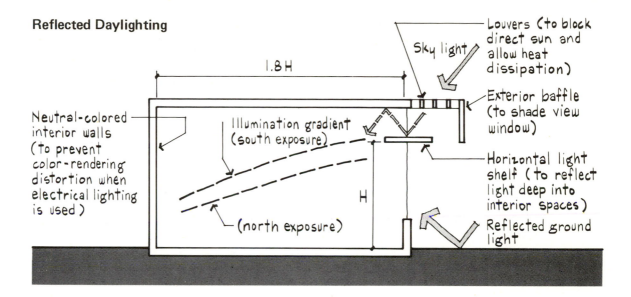

Note: Daylighting can be complemented by ceiling fixtures and task lighting at work stations.

Reference

"Engineered Daylighting for an Energy Company in Houston," *Architectural Record,* Mid-August 1979, p. 105.

Beam Daylighting (Reflected Direct Light from Sun)

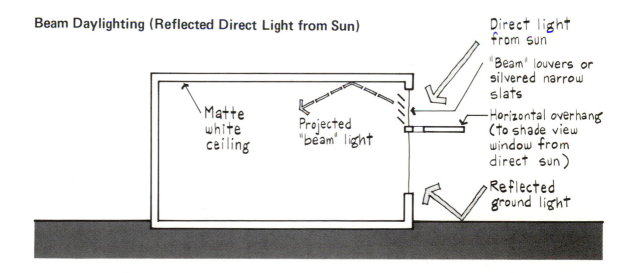

Note: Glass block, with a prismatic inner surface, can be used above the overhang to direct light toward a reflective ceiling. Control of beam lighting is difficult, as louver or slat devices must adapt to changes in the sun's angle.

Reference

A. H. Rosenfeld and S. E. Selkowitz, "Beam Daylighting: An Alternative Illumination Technique," *Energy and Buildings,* May 1977, pp. 43-50.

REFLECTED DAYLIGHTING EXAMPLES

As shown by the examples below, reflectors can project light deep into rooms. When windows are located at seated eye height, the view of the horizon (needed for physical orientation) and the ground (needed for information on nature and people) can be sufficient, and glare from the sky and sun is shielded at most viewing positions.

Curved Collector/Reflector

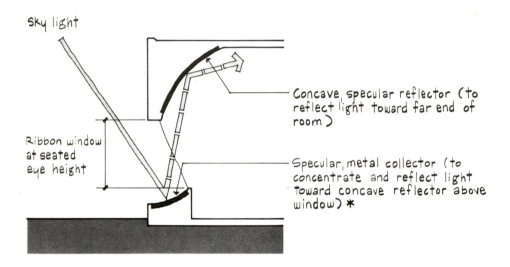

Sky light

Ribbon window at seated eye height

Concave, specular reflector (to reflect light toward far end of room)

Specular, metal collector (to concentrate and reflect light toward concave reflector above window) *

*For maximum efficiency, collector should be adjustable to accommodate seasonal changes.

Sloped Reflector

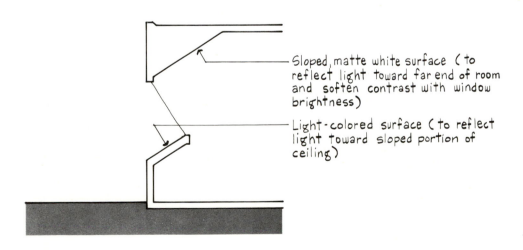

Sloped, matte white surface (to reflect light toward far end of room and soften contrast with window brightness)

Light-colored surface (to reflect light toward sloped portion of ceiling)

GLARE CONTROL FOR WINDOWS

As daylight constantly changes, the most effective controls are those which can be adjusted by the user or are automated by photocell devices.

Blinds

Blinds and narrow-slat louvers can be oriented to reflect light toward ceiling and control direct glare from the sky.

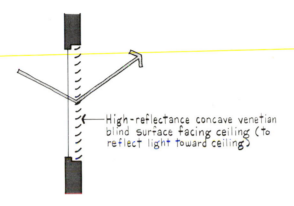

High-reflectance concave venetian blind surface facing ceiling (to reflect light toward ceiling)

Screen (or Fine-Mesh Drapes)   Film

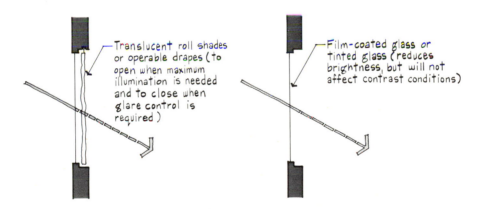

Translucent roll shades or operable drapes (to open when maximum illumination is needed and to close when glare control is required)

Film-coated glass or tinted glass (reduces brightness, but will not affect contrast conditions)

Reflective and low-transmittance films can be applied to glass surfaces to diffuse light and lower brightness. However, brightness ratios in the room will be unaffected. Low-transmittance films or coatings reduce daylight penetration but do not prevent glare from direct sun. They also can cause glare and visual noise at night by reflecting images of bright lighting fixtures.

Note: Do not use tinted glass adjacent to clear glass as artificial gloom can be created.

LOW-TRANSMITTANCE GLASS

Avoid using low-transmittance glass (i.e., tinted glass, glass block) adjacent to clear glass in doors or windows. Low-transmittance glass can restrict useful contact with the outdoors for time orientation and can generate gloom when a comparison is made to actual outdoor conditions through adjacent clear glass. For similar reasons, large, translucent skylights (e.g., double-dome with glass-fiber core) can simulate overcast sky conditions at all times during the day, regardless of the actual weather conditions.

Low-Transmittance Glass Block

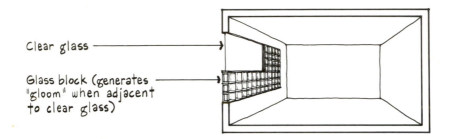

Clear glass

Glass block (generates "gloom" when adjacent to clear glass)

Low-Transmittance Tinted Glass

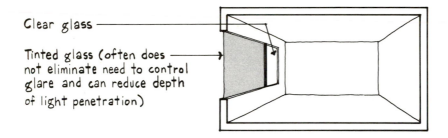

Clear glass

Tinted glass (often does not eliminate need to control glare and can reduce depth of light penetration)

Reference

M. S. Millet, "Energy in Design," *Proceedings of CCAIA Energy Conference,* Pacific Grove, Calif., August 1981.

GLARE CONTROL FOR SKYLIGHTS

External Louvers

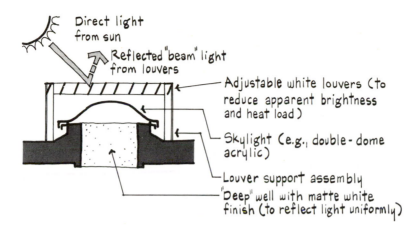

Direct light from sun

Reflected "beam" light from louvers

Adjustable white louvers (to reduce apparent brightness and heat load)

Skylight (e.g., double-dome acrylic)

Louver support assembly

"Deep" well with matte white finish (to reflect light uniformly)

Prismatic Lens

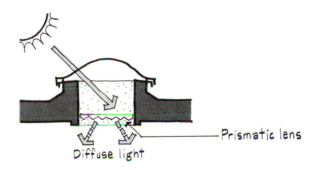

Prismatic lens

Diffuse light

Pyramidal Well

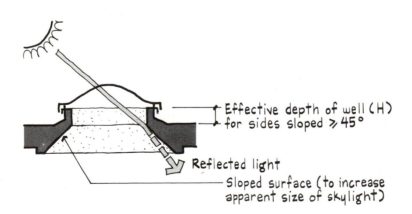

Effective depth of well (H) for sides sloped ≥ 45°

Reflected light

Sloped surface (to increase apparent size of skylight)

Reference

F. S. Dubin and C. G. Long, Jr., *Energy Conservation Standards,* McGraw-Hill, New York, 1978, pp. 220-221.

BUILDING SHAPES AND LAYOUTS

Shapes

Building shapes have a significant effect on the distribution of daylight. For example, narrow buildings (<30 ft wide) can allow complete penetration of daylight; stepped sections with setback floor levels and reflective roof surfaces can project daylight into upper stories; and stepped plans, atria, or light wells can open buildings to allow deep penetration of daylight.

Hollow Rectangular   **Stepped**   **U-shaped**

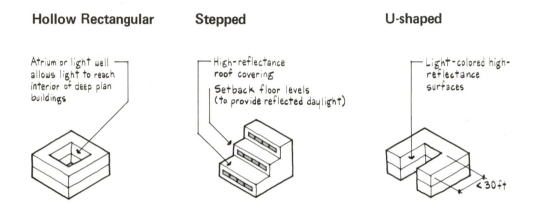

Atrium or light well allows light to reach interior of deep plan buildings

High-reflectance roof covering

Setback floor levels (to provide reflected daylight)

Light-colored high-reflectance surfaces

<30 ft

Note: Windows can be protected from environmental noise by building elements such as balconies, setback floors, and light wells. For example, these elements can act as noise-reduction barriers by shielding windows from direct exposure to noise from automobiles and trucks at ground level. (For a method to estimate noise reduction by outdoor barriers, see M. D. Egan, *Concepts in Architectural Acoustics,* McGraw-Hill, New York, 1972, pp. 92-93.)

Layouts

Offset building layouts allow significantly more daylight penetration than parallel building layouts.

Parallel Rows   **Offset 90°**

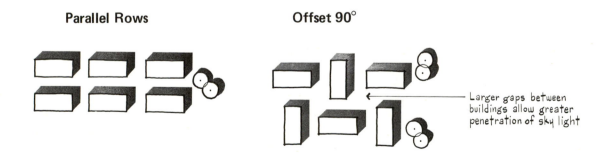

Larger gaps between buildings allow greater penetration of sky light

DAYLIGHTING TERMS FOR DAYLIGHT FACTOR METHOD

The daylight factor method was developed during the 1920s in England, where overcast sky conditions are frequent. The daylight factor (DF) is the percentage of external illumination from an unobstructed sky at a point on a horizontal plane in a room. In this method, DF is the sum of the following terms or components:

sky component (SC) — the amount of sky light directly incident on window opening

externally reflected component (ERC) — the light reflected from outdoor objects (e.g., fences, buildings, etc.)

internally reflected component (IRC) — the light reflected from interior surfaces

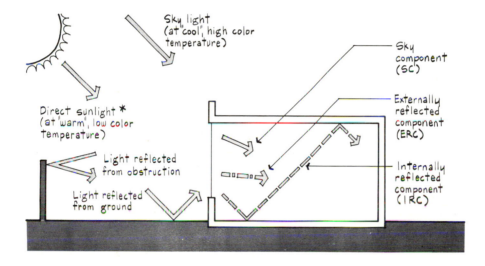

*Direct sunlight should usually be excluded from buildings by shading devices, as it can result in excessive glare, overheating, and thermal discomfort. However, in spaces where critical visual tasks are infrequent, the modeling and contrast effects of sunlight can provide interest and drama. In addition, objects seen partially in silhouette can be pleasant.

Note: A plot of daylight factors (i.e., gradients or contours) represents the variation in ratio of actual light indoors on a horizontal surface to available light outdoors.

EXAMPLE PROBLEM (DAYLIGHT FACTOR METHOD)

Artist's studio in Washington, D.C. residence at a built-up, clean location is described below.

Plan

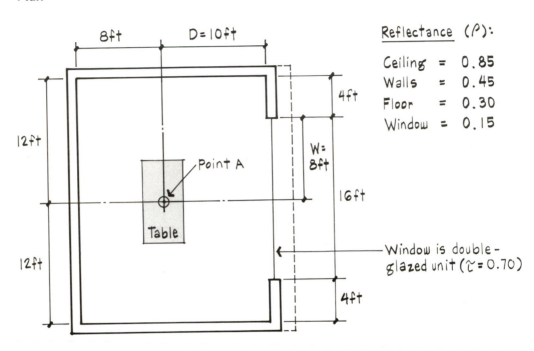

Reflectance (ρ):

Ceiling = 0.85
Walls = 0.45
Floor = 0.30
Window = 0.15

Window is double-glazed unit ($\tau = 0.70$)

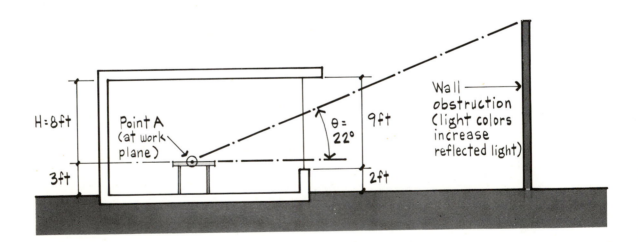

DAYLIGHT FACTOR METHOD

The daylight factor (%) is the sum of the sky component, externally reflected component, and internally reflected component, as defined on page 193. The step-by-step procedure to find interior illumination by the daylight factor method is outlined below using a solution for an artist's studio in a residence as an example (see page 194).

1. Find the sky component (SC). See SC graph for overcast sky conditions on page 198. Shape ratios will be $W/D = 8/10 = 0.8$ and $H/D = 8/10 = 0.8$. The angle of obstruction ($\angle\theta$) = 22°.

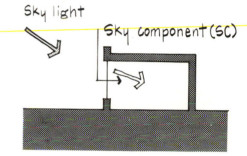

$$SC = (SC_w - SC_o)\,\tau$$
$$SC = (2.6 - 0.75)\,0.7 = 1.3\%$$

where SC_w = sky component of window opening (%)

   SC_o = obstructed sky component (%)

   τ = transmittance (%)

Total SC (i.e., reference point is opposite center of window) will be

$$\text{Total SC} = 2 \times 1.3 = \boxed{2.6\%}$$

(Without wall obstruction, total SC would be 2 × 1.82 = 3.6%.)

2. Find the externally reflected component (ERC). To account for brightness of obstructions, use a coefficient (C_b) of 0.2 when obstruction is below 20°, 0.1 when obstruction is above 20°, and 0 for open sites without obstructions.

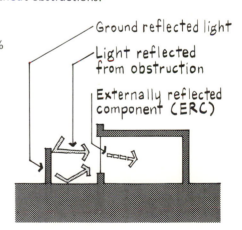

$$ERC = C_b\,(SC_o)\tau$$
$$ERC = 0.1 \times 0.75 \times 0.7 = 0.05\%$$
$$\text{Total ERC} = 2 \times 0.05 = \boxed{0.1\%}$$

3. Find the internally reflected component (IRC). First, find the total interior surface area A_{tot}.

$$A_{tot} = 2[(18 \times 11) + (24 \times 11) + (18 \times 24)] = 1788 \text{ ft}^2$$

The weighted average reflectance of all surfaces (ρ_{avg}) is found by dividing the sum of $A \times \rho$ values by the total area.

	A (ft^2)	ρ	$A \times \rho$
Ceiling	432	0.85	367
Floor	432	0.30	130
Walls	780	0.45	351
Glass	144	0.15	22
Total	1788		870

$$\rho_{avg} = \frac{870}{1788} = 0.49$$

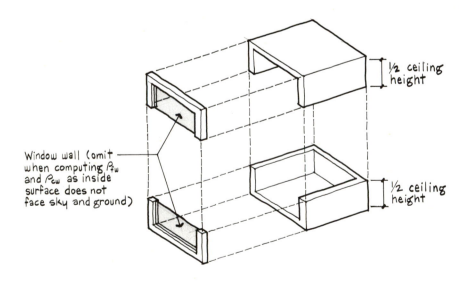

Window wall (omit when computing ρ_{fw} and ρ_{cw} as inside surface does not face sky and ground)

½ ceiling height

½ ceiling height

Next, find average reflectance below midheight of room ρ_{fw} and above midheight of room ρ_{cw}. Floor area (432 ft^2) plus one-half wall area (330 ft^2) is 762 ft^2. Exclude window wall area from this computation, as it does not face the sky. (See sketch above dividing room in half.)

$$\rho_{fw} = \frac{(330 \times 0.45) + (432 \times 0.3)}{762} = \frac{278}{762} = 0.36$$

Ceiling area (432 ft^2) plus one-half wall area (330 ft^2) is 762 ft^2. Again, exclude window wall area from this computation, as it does not face the ground.

$$\rho_{cw} = \frac{(330 \times 0.45) + (432 \times 0.85)}{762} = \frac{516}{762} = 0.68$$

Next, find the average internally reflected component IRC.

$$IRC = \frac{0.85 A_w}{A_{tot}(1 - \rho_{avg})}(C\rho_{fw} + 5\rho_{cw})$$

$$IRC = \frac{0.85 \times 144}{1788 (1 - 0.49)} [(30 \times 0.36) + (5 \times 0.68)]$$

$$= \frac{122}{912}(10.8 + 3.4) = \boxed{1.9\%}$$

where A_w = area of window less frame, bars, etc. (ft^2)

C = obstruction coefficient (from table on page 200)

4. Finally, find the daylight factor (DF).

$$DF = SC + ERC + IRC$$
$$= 2.6 + 0.1 + 1.9 = \boxed{4.6\%}$$

This value would be appropriate for sidelighting (see table on page 200).

Note: To find illuminance E_I on horizontal plane indoors for overcast sky conditions, refer to table on page 201 which presents average external illumination levels E_o.

$$E_I = E_o \times DF \times DDF$$
$$E_I = 800 \times 0.046 \times 0.8 = \boxed{29 \text{ fc}} \text{ (on table, 10 ft from}$$
window on overcast day)

where DDF = dirt depreciation factor (for built-up residential locations, use 0.8 for "clean" occupancy, 0.6 for "dirty" occupancy; for rural locations, use 0.9 for "clean" occupancy, 0.7 for "dirty" occupancy)

Without the wall obstruction, the DF would be 3.6 + 0 + 1.9 = 5.5% increasing the illuminance by 20% to 35 fc. Under clear sky conditions the increase would be even greater.

Sky component values can be found for overcast sky conditions by the graph below. The sky component is the percentage of light from the sky which is directly incident on window openings. To use the graph, first find the window shape ratios of W/D and H/D

where H = height of window above work plane (ft)

            W = width of window to one side of center of work plane, i.e., $2W$ is full width of window (ft)

            D = distance from window to point of interest (ft)

If outdoor obstructions occlude view of sky from window opening, use W/D ratio and angle of obstruction (i.e., angle measured from work plane to boundary of obstruction) to find obstructed SC, then subtract from unobstructed SC. For example, a window with W/D = 0.8, H/D = 0.8 and angle of obstruction $\angle\theta$ = 22° would have unobstructed SC = 2.6% and obstructed SC = 0.75%. (See dashed lines on graph.) Consequently, SC for opening will be 2.6 − 0.75 = 1.85%. This SC value will be reduced by the glazing. Transmittance values are given in the table on the following page.

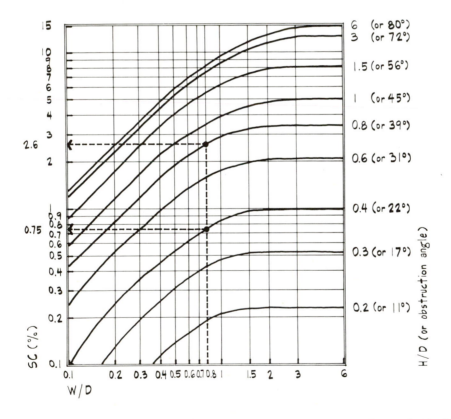

Note: For comprehensive tables of SC values for overcast skies, see R. G. Hopkinson, *Architectural Physics: Lighting,* Her Majesty's Stationery Office, London, 1963, pp. 56-57. For clear sky conditions, see H. J. Bryan, "A Simplified Procedure for Calculating the Effects of Daylight from Clear Skies," *Journal of the Illuminating Engineering Society,* April 1980.

TRANSMITTANCE

Transmittance (τ) values for glass and plastic, in percent of incident light that is transmitted, are given below. For other materials, see the table on page 30.

Type	Transmittance (%)
Clear plate glass, tempered glass, wired glass, clear plastic*	80-90
Patterned glass, frosted glass	70-75
Heat-absorbing glass	65-85
Clear double-pane glass	65-80
Glass block	40-75
Tinted glass, bronze	50
Tinted glass, gray	40

*Transmittance of plastic can be greatly reduced by weathering.

Note: Transmittance values can vary widely. Values in table are average for varieties of glass and plastic at different thicknesses. Consult the manufacturer's literature for specific data from certified laboratory tests.

References

J. H. Callender (ed.), *Time-Saver Standards,* McGraw-Hill, New York, 1974, p. 925.

J. E. Kaufman (ed.), *IES Lighting Handbook* (1981 Reference Volume), p. 7-10.

OBSTRUCTIONS

The obstruction coefficient for overcast sky conditions, given in the table below, is used to compute the internally reflected component. The coefficient varies with the angle between the horizontal at the work plane and the end or boundary of the obstruction.

Angle of obstruction ($\angle \theta$)	Obstruction coefficient (C)
80	5
70	7
60	10
50	14
40	20
30	25
20	31
10	35
0 (no obstruction)	39

Reference

R. G. Hopkinson, *Architectural Physics: Lighting,* Her Majesty's Stationery Office, London, 1963, p. 184.

DAYLIGHT FACTOR FOR ILLUMINATION BY WINDOWS

The table below can be used as a guide to evaluate the effectiveness of openings for sidelighting during the schematic stages of a project's design development. Suggested minimum daylight factor and ratio of open area of window A_w to floor area A_f are given below. Complement daylighting with electrical lighting for use when sky luminance is low.

Type of space	DF (%)	A_w/A_f (%)
Art studios, altars (if strong emphasis is desired)	4-6	20-30
Laboratories (e.g., work benches)	3	15
General offices, banks (e.g., typing, accounting), classrooms, gymnasiums, swimming pools	2	10
Lobbies, lounges, living rooms	1	5
Corridors, bedrooms	0.5	2.5

AVERAGE OVERCAST SKY ILLUMINANCE

The table below presents average external illumination levels E_o (in fc) from overcast sky conditions, available about 85% of the day from 8 a.m. to 4 p.m. Data are given for example north latitude locations.

North latitude (degrees)	Illumination level (fc)	Example locations
46	700	Montréal; Minneapolis; Portland, Oreg.
42	750	New York; Chicago; Eureka, Calif.
38	800	Washington, D.C.; Denver; San Francisco
34	850	Clemson, S.C.; Albuquerque; Los Angeles
30	900	New Orleans; San Antonio; Ensenada, Mex.

Note: For comprehensive tables of external illumination levels (in fc) and sky brightness (in fL) at various latitudes, seasons, and times of day, see J. E. Kaufman (ed.), *IES Lighting Handbook* (1981 Reference Volume), pp. 7-5 to 7-7 or J. H. Callender (ed.), *Time-Saver Standards,* McGraw-Hill, New York, 1966, pp. 922-923.

1. Complement daylighting with electrical lighting (e.g., use electric light sources near wall which is opposite windows, where desired illumination levels cannot be achieved by daylighting). Window openings which allow daylight penetration can enhance modeling effects, reduce veiling reflections, and provide time orientation from visual contact with outdoor conditions. Window openings also provide visual rest when used in work environments. However, avoid direct sunlight and sky light on critical seeing tasks.

Daylight Complemented by Electric Light Sources

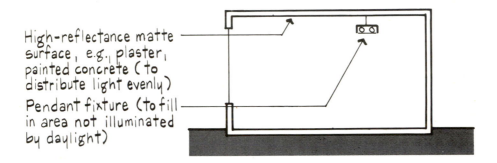

High-reflectance matte surface, e.g., plaster, painted concrete (to distribute light evenly)

Pendant fixture (to fill in area not illuminated by daylight)

Illumination Gradients

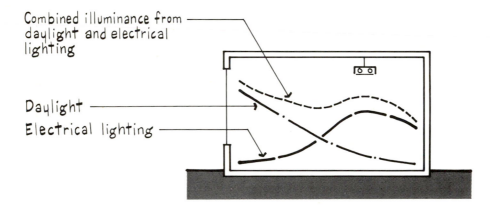

Combined illuminance from daylight and electrical lighting

Daylight

Electrical lighting

2. When daylighting is sufficient, switch or dim lighting fixtures to lower illumination levels or turn them off (e.g., by digital on-off, multilevel, continuous dimming). Avoid using switches which control large areas or entire rooms.

3. Use neutral-colored interior surfaces to avoid color-rendering distortion when electrical lighting is used with daylighting. Avoid using dark-colored surfaces adjacent to windows, as uncomfortably high contrast conditions can be created.

4. Admit daylight from two or more sides of a room to avoid sharp contrast between daylight and adjacent wall surfaces. In addition, the side of the room opposite unilateral openings (i.e., windows on only one side) can be perceived as gloomy because of the occupant's adaptation to daylight.

Gloom from Unilateral Daylight

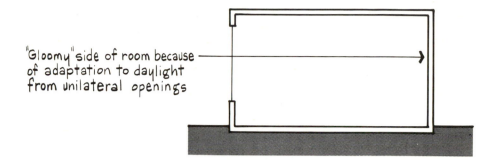

"Gloomy" side of room because of adaptation to daylight from unilateral openings

5. Admit daylight from high locations (e.g., window height at least one-half of room depth) that are away from the occupant's line of sight. Use transparent interior partitions (or upper parts of partitions, transoms) to transmit daylight into interior spaces (e.g., to corridors which require low illumination levels).

High Openings

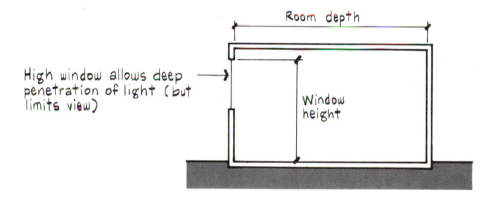

Room depth

High window allows deep penetration of light (but limits view)

Window height

Low Openings

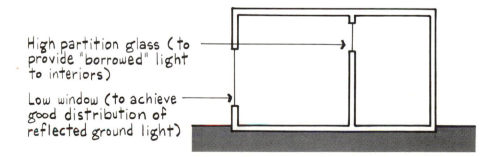

High partition glass (to provide "borrowed" light to interiors)

Low window (to achieve good distribution of reflected ground light)

6. Avoid sharp-cornered openings which can create high brightness ratios and glare. Use splayed jambs, sloped light wells, and the like to lower brightness ratios. Electrical lighting at low illumination levels also reduces window glare and brightness ratios by illuminating mullions, frames, and adjacent surfaces.

Splayed Wall

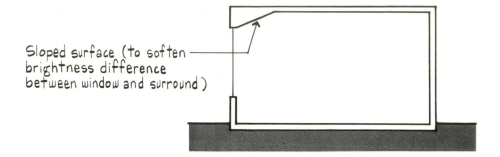

Sloped surface (to soften brightness difference between window and surround)

Straight Wall (with Electrical Lighting)

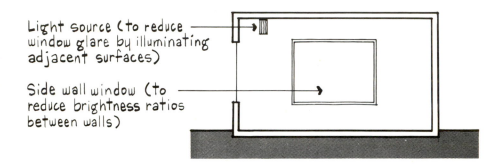

Light source (to reduce window glare by illuminating adjacent surfaces)

Side wall window (to reduce brightness ratios between walls)

7. Baffle daylighting openings so that view of the sky is shielded from occupants in most viewing positions. Use large-scale elements (e.g., horizontal overhangs, deep reveals, light shelves) or use fine-mesh screens, drapes, or narrow-slat blinds which can be adjusted or raised when not needed. Exterior shading devices (e.g., louvers, overhangs) can mitigate unwanted "greenhouse" effects.

Deep Window Reveal

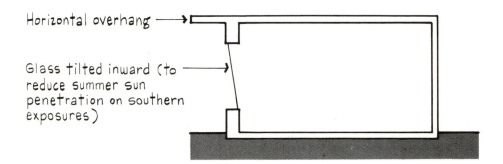

Horizontal overhang

Glass tilted inward (to reduce summer sun penetration on southern exposures)

Interior Shading

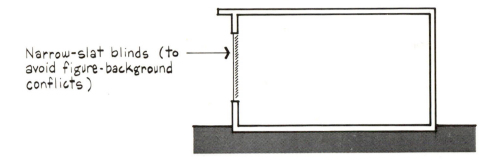

Narrow-slat blinds (to avoid figure-background conflicts)

8. Use horizontal overhangs to project reflected ground light into rooms. Concrete, white gravel, white pavers, water, etc., are better ground reflectors of light than asphalt or grass. Beyond about 40 ft from a building, however, ground reflectance is not significant for single-story windows.

Exterior Shading (Wide Cantilever)

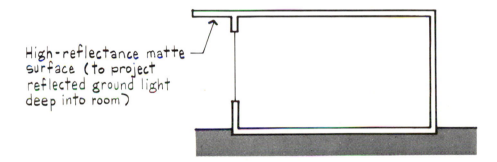

High-reflectance matte surface (to project reflected ground light deep into room)

9. Increase the level of daylight in rooms by using reflectors or toplighting in areas without a view (e.g., clerestories, monitors, light shelves with mirrored top surfaces) to project daylight deep into interior spaces. Use high-reflectance roof coverings to increase quantity of light admitted by clerestories, monitors, and other toplighting devices. In multi-story buildings, use light wells to project daylight into lower-level spaces.

Clerestory

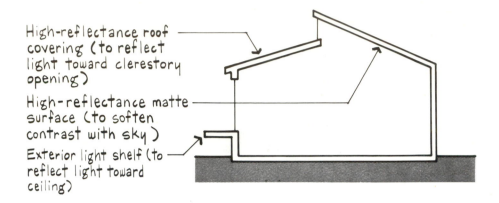

High-reflectance roof covering (to reflect light toward clerestory opening)

High-reflectance matte surface (to soften contrast with sky)

Exterior light shelf (to reflect light toward ceiling)

Skylight (or Monitor)

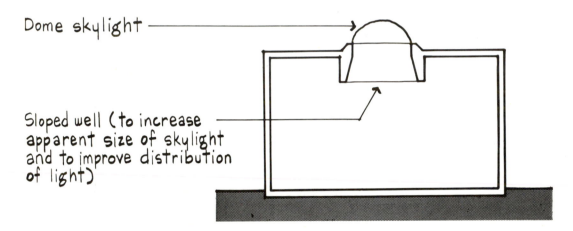

Dome skylight

Sloped well (to increase apparent size of skylight and to improve distribution of light)

10. Use high-reflectance matte finishes on interior surfaces to maximize effectiveness of both daylighting and electrical lighting and to soften contrast with the sky. The reflectance of sound-absorbing ceiling board is determined in testing laboratories according to provisions of ASTM C 523.

Chapter 7
Illuminated Models

ILLUMINATED MODEL STUDIES

Photographs and projected slide images of illuminated models can be used to help designers experience, evaluate, and predict the appearance of lighted interiors prior to actual construction. With illuminated models, designers can

1. Create, evaluate, and vary design concepts that respond to the client's visual needs. For example, the effects of alternative lighting systems can be compared using slides and photographs of the same model.
2. Make changes in scale, finishes, openings, etc., that would not be feasible at full-scale or even with mock-ups.
3. Show the interaction of light with complex surfaces and forms that cannot be readily computed (e.g., delineation of shadow patterns on curved surfaces).
4. Convey an impression of illuminated designs to clients by projected slide images. This allows evaluation based on the illusion of full-scale space and eliminates visual noise from surroundings which occurs when the actual model is viewed (cf., R. Corth, "Can Models Predict the Real World?," *Lighting Design & Application*, January 1980).
5. Complement computational procedures such as the lumen method, the point method, and the daylight factor method. (See Chaps. 5 and 6.)
6. Study the performance of unusual daylighted designs (e.g., roof monitors for sky light and light shelves for reflected-sun beam lighting).

SCALE OF MODELS

Models which are convenient to build generally have scale ratios in the range of 1:8 to 1:32 (i.e., 1-inch in model equals 32-inch in prototype being studied). Usually, the larger the scale ratio, the easier it will be to fabricate complex shapes for the model. Listed below are typical scale ratios along with corresponding conventional drawing scales.

Drawing scale of models (in = ft)	Scale ratio	Drawing scale of models (in = ft)	Scale ratio
Illuminated (or interior):		Massing and exterior:	
3 = 1	1 : 4	1/4 = 1	1 : 48
1 1/2 = 1	1 : 8	3/16 = 1	1 : 64
1 = 1	1 : 12	1/8 = 1	1 : 96
3/4 = 1	1 : 16	3/32 = 1	1 : 128
1/2 = 1	1 : 24*	1/16 = 1	1 : 192
3/8 = 1	1 : 32†	1 = 20	1 : 240
		1/32 = 1	1 : 384
		1 = 40	1 : 480
		1 = 50	1 : 600

*Scale ratios should not be smaller than 1 : 24 for daylighting models.

†For example:

$$\frac{1}{x} = \frac{3/8 \text{ in}}{12 \text{ in}} \qquad \frac{3}{8}x = 12 \qquad x = \frac{8}{3} \times 12 = 32 \text{ or a scale ratio of } \boxed{1 : 32}$$

ROOM FINISH MATERIALS AND FURNISHINGS FOR ILLUMINATED MODELS

Listed below are a wide variety of materials which can be used in illuminated models to simulate full-scale finishes and furnishings. Be sure to establish scale within the model with furnishings or with cardboard-mounted color photos of people. This technique can contribute a sense of full-scale space to the projected color slides. As it is often time-consuming to construct furnishings, try to use a limited number of tables and chairs. For example, do not construct six chairs when one can represent the furnished conditions.

Brick:
Chipboard (handpainted and scored with ink or knife to represent joints)
Sandpaper (painted red or brown and scored with knife)

Carpet:
Burlap
Crushed corduroy
Felt
Velour paper
Velvet

Ceramic Tile:
Painted and scored chipboard or acetate

Concrete:
Flock
Painted sandpaper
Plain or pebbled illustration board or chipboard, depending on texture desired

Concrete Block:
Scored pebbled illustration board

Draperies:
Cloth (Check size of weave to ensure that it will be small scale.)

Furniture:[a]
Charms
Cove base molding (to model church pews)
Dollhouse furniture
Handmade (e.g., Styrofoam or polyurethane foam for cushions with scrap cloth for upholstery, steel wire for metal chair frames, stained balsa for desks, etc.)
Perfume bottles (to model vases)

Glass Block:
Scored Plexiglas or sheet plastic

Glazing:[b]
Acetate
Glass (1/8 in thick or less)
Opaque acrylic
Plexiglas or sheet plastic (sanded with fine sandpaper to simulate translucent glass)

[a] Commercial sources for scale model furnishings include local hobby shops, model train shops, and the like. For a comprehensive listing of suppliers of model materials, see S. Hohauser, *Architectural and Interior Models*, Van Nostrand Reinhold, New York, 1970, pp. 203-206.

[b] For daylighting models, be sure transmittance is identical to prototype or apply correction factor to model illuminance measurements.

Plexiglas with black paper on back surface (to represent reflective glass)
Polymer-based plastic sheet diffuser (available from theatrical supply houses
or from Rosco, 36 Bush Avenue, Port Chester, NY 10573)

Gypsum Board:
Nonskid floor covering
Painted chipboard
Painted sandpaper
Pebbled illustration board (smooth board can also represent acoustical board)
Velour paper (large scale)

Marble:
Handpainted board
Marbleized paper
White opaque acrylic

Metals:[c]
Aluminum
Brass
Copper
Steel

Mirrors:
Mirror
Silvered acetate (or Mylar)
Silvered Plexiglas

People:[d]
Magazine pictures mounted on thin illustration board or cardboard

Plaster:[e]
Painted chipboard
Painted sandpaper
Pebbled illustration board
Velour paper (large scale)

Skylights (Plastic Dome):
Acetate
Glass
Tracing paper

Stone:
Contact paper
Cork (e.g., automotive gaskets)
Pieces of paper cut out and glued on illustration board
Plaster of paris

Terrazzo:
Handpainted board
Speckled wrapping paper

Vinyl Wall Covering:
Contact paper
Linen
Plastic placemats

[c] In most situations, the actual material may be used since the grain will not show. For example, aluminum foil can be used to represent etched aluminum.

[d] Department and clothing store catalogs (e.g., Sears, Saks Fifth Avenue) and magazines are sources for pictures of people. Select carefully, as lighting in pictures of people should match lighting in model.

[e] Texture for stucco can be achieved using bird gravel and sawdust.

Water:
Cellophane
Mirror
Plexiglas with black film on back surface

Window Frames and Mullions:^{f}
Balsa wood
Cardboard glued to acetate or glass
Opaque paper

Wood
Scaled color photos of natural materials
Stained (or natural) balsa or basswood

^{f}Size and reflectance of sill must be carefully controlled for daylighting studies.

Note: Small-scale materials (e.g., floor coverings, wallpaper, rugs) are commercially available for use in dollhouses. For a catalog and ordering information, contact: Dover Publications, Inc., 180 Varick St., New York, NY 10014.

LUMINAIRE MODELING TECHNIQUES

Listed below are materials that can be used in illuminated models to simulate the overall lighting pattern of a variety of luminaires. The modeling of the candlepower distribution characteristics of a luminaire is extremely complicated and requires the fabrication of small-scale components such as reflectors, lenses, and baffles. Therefore, the techniques below can only be used for qualitative analyses. Nevertheless, care should be taken to ensure that the modeled luminaires perform as nearly like the actual luminaires as possible.

Luminaire (lamp or lens)	Model materials
Recessed downlight	Metal (or plastic) grommet Metal (or plastic) washer Gummed reinforcement (for holes in three-ringed notebook paper)

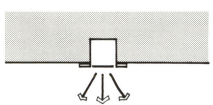

Surface-mounted downlight	Copper or aluminum tubing Drinking straw (with contact paper cover) Hollow arrow shaft

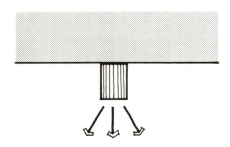

Suspended downlight	Copper tubing Metal container lids (e.g., caps for felt tip markers, refills for lead pencils) Small arms cartridge

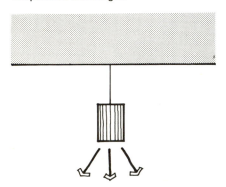

Luminaire (lamp or lens)	Model materials
Suspended globe* 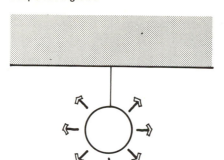	Ping-pong or bingo ball (with "grain of wheat" or miniature tungsten-halogen lamp inside) Miniature lamps (e.g., for switchboards, instruments, or annunciator panels)
Plastic lens	Acetate Polymer-based plastic sheet diffuser Scored Plexiglas Vellum tracing paper Lenses from luminaires
Parabolic louvers 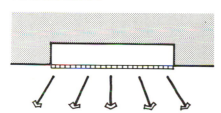	Dark acetate Metal insect screen Parawedge
Eggcrate louvers	Fine-mesh solar screen Plastic needlepoint canvas
Fluorescent lamp, bare	Neon tubes
Chandelier	Jewelry beads

*Miniature lamps are available from hardware stores and hobby shops (e.g., miniature tungsten-halogen lamps by Sylvania or General Electric). For catalogs of miniature lamps, see "Sylvania Miniature Lighting Products," Sylvania Catalog #304, 1979, which is available from GTE Products Corp., West Main Street, Hillsboro, NH 03244 and "Miniature & Sub-Miniature Lamps," General Electric Catalog 208-9165, Cleveland, December 1979.

Parabolic Louver (to avoid direct glare from fixture)

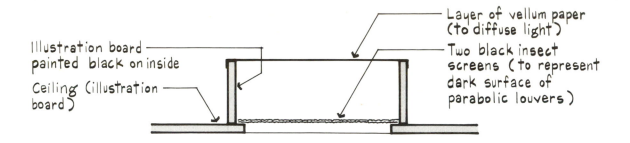

Layer of vellum paper (to diffuse light)

Two black insect screens (to represent dark surface of parabolic louvers)

Illustration board painted black on inside

Ceiling (illustration board)

Indirect Fixture (to illuminate ceiling and convey cheerful sense of spaciousness)

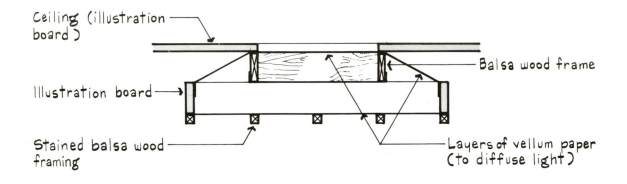

Ceiling (illustration board)

Balsa wood frame

Illustration board

Layers of vellum paper (to diffuse light)

Stained balsa wood framing

Recessed Downlight (to achieve focal glow)

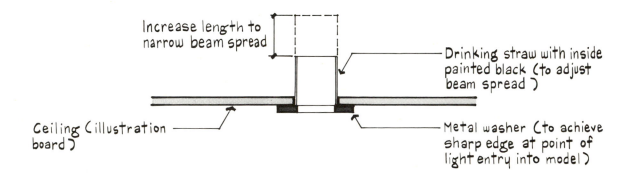

Increase length to narrow beam spread

Drinking straw with inside painted black (to adjust beam spread)

Ceiling (illustration board)

Metal washer (to achieve sharp edge at point of light entry into model)

HOW TO PHOTOGRAPH ILLUMINATED MODELS

1. To take photographs, set model on table or desk of sufficient size to permit adjustment of the model's position. Position the lamps above the model and prevent glare from entering the lens by using chipboard shields. (See model setup on page 216.) Avoid placing lamps too close to model, as excessive heat buildup can damage the model or even cause ignition. Be sure an all-purpose portable fire extinguisher is nearby during photography sessions.

2. Use 250- or 500-W photoflood lamps (3200 K color temperature) in ceramic fixtures or aluminum reflectors. The average model may need three lamps to get satisfactory results. Obtain diffuse light by placing tissue paper or glass wool between the lamps and the model.

3. Check for light leaks in the model prior to taking photographs. If necessary, use opaque masking tape or aluminum foil on the outside of the model to seal joints and other openings.

4. Use a tripod and cable shutter release to keep the camera stable and level.

5. Use wide-angle lenses (e.g., 35 mm, 28 mm, etc.) to achieve greater depth of field and more realistic projected slide images.

6. Aim the exposure meter at the predominant features when taking exposure readings of light in the model. Avoid taking readings of excessively bright areas or dark shadows. Take additional shots one-half to one f stop above and below exposure meter reading so that a range of different exposures will be available to select from. When exposure time exceeds 1/10 s, check film instruction sheet for information on correction for "reciprocity failure" (e.g., color shifts with light lost).

7. Typical exposure times range from 1 to 1/30 s at $f/11$ to $f/16$. Use smaller f stops to get an acceptable depth of field (i.e., zone of acceptable sharp focus). Assure proper focus and depth of field by using depth-of-field scale or preview device on camera. Try to achieve sense of room enclosure by having floor, ceiling, and three walls in frame.

8. Decide what you want to show in the slide, then move camera in or out to frame the desired view. Try to frame the shot within the limits of the model. If this is not possible, the finished slide can be masked with opaque photographic masking tape. Use screw-in type close-up lenses if camera lens does not allow close enough focus.

9. Shoot at "standing eye level" in the model to achieve realism. Use model scale figures or furnishings to define eye level.

10. Use both horizontal and vertical formats for a variety of views. More than one removable wall will increase the number of potential views available to photograph.

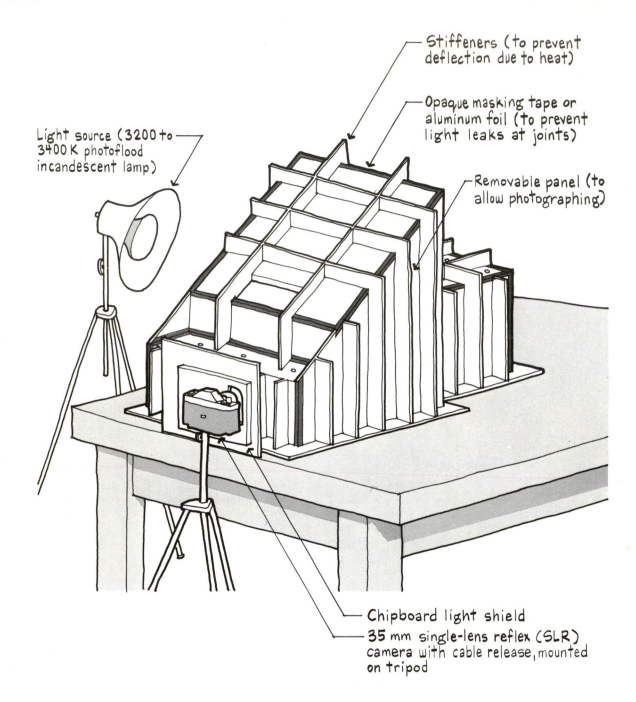

Stiffeners (to prevent deflection due to heat)

Opaque masking tape or aluminum foil (to prevent light leaks at joints)

Light source (3200 to 3400 K photoflood incandescent lamp)

Removable panel (to allow photographing)

Chipboard light shield

35 mm single-lens reflex (SLR) camera with cable release, mounted on tripod

SUGGESTED FILMS

For Slides

1. Ektachrome 160 (Type B) is generally preferred because of its favorable light sensitivity. Its rated speed (ASA 160)* can be doubled by the use of special processing. Color is balanced for 3200 K tungsten lamps.

2. Kodachrome 64 is a sharp, fine-grain film. It is less prone to fading and generally less expensive than Ektachrome 160. Kodachrome 64 color is balanced for daylight and electronic flash. However, it can be used with 3200 K lamps by adding a #80A filter to the camera lens and increasing exposure time by two f stops.

3. Other possible choices (usually by special order) include Ektachrome 50 (Type B) balanced for 3200 K photoflood lamps and Kodachrome 40 (Type A) balanced for 3400 K photoflood lamps.

4. Ektachrome 400 (ASA 400) and Ektachrome 200 (ASA 200) are daylight-balanced films that can be used with daylighting models when films more sensitive to light are required.

5. Fujichrome 100 (ASA 100) and Fujichrome 400 (ASA 400). Fujichrome 400, when used with some fluorescent lamps, has minimal greenish distortion.

For Color Prints (Custom-Made Slides, Black-and-White Prints)

1. Kodacolor 400 (ASA 400) balanced for daylight
2. Kodacolor II (ASA 100) balanced for daylight
3. Vericolor L (ASA 100) balanced for 3200 K lamps

For Black-and-White Prints

1. Kodak Plus-X pan (ASA 125)
2. Ilford FP4 (ASA 125)
3. Agfapan 100 (ASA 100)

Note: To avoid color exaggeration and distortion, do *not* use different types of exterior light sources to simulate illumination in the same model (e.g., cool white fluorescent lamps and 3200 K incandescent lamps) at same time.

*ASA designation refers to the film's sensitivity to light—the higher ASAs are more sensitive and require less light on the subject.

Scale model studies of daylighting can be conducted under actual or artificial sky conditions. When testing models outdoors, be sure that sky and ground conditions are comparable to those at the actual building site. Avoid performing measurements under partly cloudy conditions where sky brightness will vary rapidly. To compare design modifications under identical sky conditions, two models could be tested simultaneously. For reference purposes, always measure sky illuminance outside the model prior to, during, and after recording illuminance in the model. Techniques for modeling window openings and skylights are listed on pages 209 and 210.

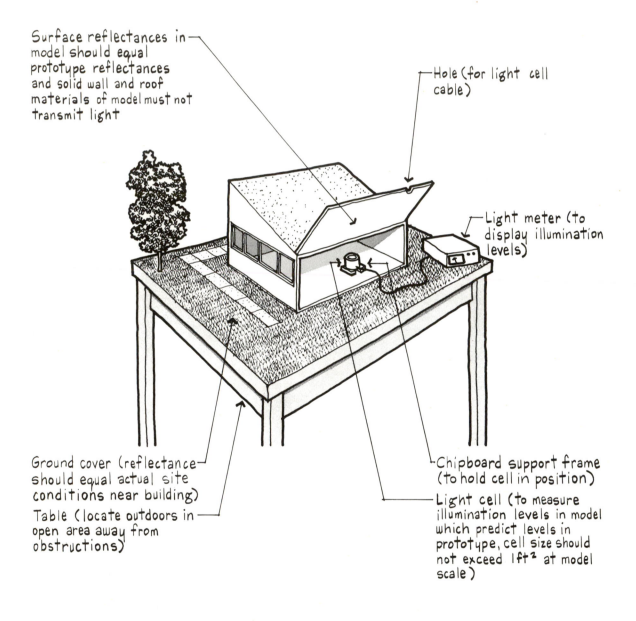

Surface reflectances in model should equal prototype reflectances and solid wall and roof materials of model must not transmit light

Hole (for light cell cable)

Light meter (to display illumination levels)

Ground cover (reflectance should equal actual site conditions near building)

Table (locate outdoors in open area away from obstructions)

Chipboard support frame (to hold cell in position)

Light cell (to measure illumination levels in model which predict levels in prototype, cell size should not exceed 1 ft² at model scale)

Note: Interior surface details are not critical when only illumination levels are desired and color slides are not to be used for evaluation of appearance of daylighted models. For example, smooth surfaces can be used to represent carpet, dark paint can duplicate the reflectance of various colored finishes, and so on.

ARTIFICIAL SKIES

Artificial skies (e.g., hemispherical or mirrored rectilinear shapes) allow studies of daylighting under constant sky conditions to be conducted on scale models. Artificial skies in the United States are located at Virginia Polytechnic Institute and State University (Blacksburg), University of California (Berkeley), and University of Washington (Seattle). Typical dimensions for hemispherical skies are a 24-ft diameter with a 15-ft floor-to-dome-apex height.

Hemispherical

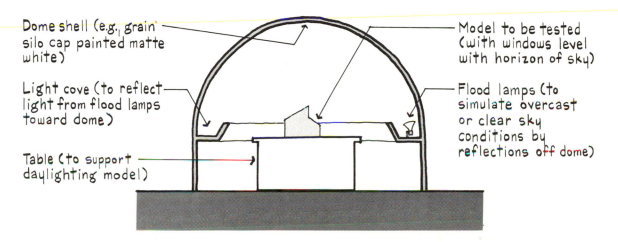

Dome shell (e.g., grain silo cap painted matte white)

Light cove (to reflect light from flood lamps toward dome)

Table (to support daylighting model)

Model to be tested (with windows level with horizon of sky)

Flood lamps (to simulate overcast or clear sky conditions by reflections off dome)

Rectilinear

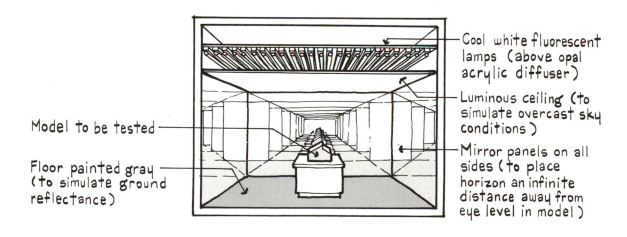

Model to be tested

Floor painted gray (to simulate ground reflectance)

Cool white fluorescent lamps (above opal acrylic diffuser)

Luminous ceiling (to simulate overcast sky conditions)

Mirror panels on all sides (to place horizon an infinite distance away from eye level in model)

An illuminated model was used to study design concepts for a branch bank. Two example concepts are shown at the right (rectangular pattern of direct light from recessed troffers) and at the left of the page (indirect light from suspended architectural elements). Details for modeling light sources are shown on page 214.

Recessed Troffer

This type of fixture provides direct light on work activities and ambient light by reflection from room surfaces. (See photo at right.)

Indirect Light Source

This type of lighting provides uplight on ceiling, creating a feeling of spaciousness, and light on activity tasks at teller/counter areas. In addition, surface-mounted downlights provide focus on elements in the lounge area.

Note: Scale ratio for model was 1:12. It was constructed and photographed by Clemson University College of Architecture students Michael Barr, Stephen Bridges, Peter Porretta, and Denise Thompson.

In the open-plan office area of the bank interior shown below, ambient light is provided by fluorescent tubes mounted on the edge of cantilevered baffle elements and by ceiling fixtures. For additional photos and drawings of this project, see *Architectural Record*, January 1976, pp. 94-95.

Luminous Sloped Edges

The photo of the illuminated model shows the undulating pattern created by the fluorescent strips on the edges of the white baffles.

View of Lighting in Existing Building

Lighting conditions in the actual office are shown in the photo below. The mirrored rear wall is used to visually enlarge the space.

Note: Model was constructed and photographed by Clemson University College of Architecture students Richard Beale, Carl Berry, and John Butch. This building, the County Federal Savings and Loan Association in Greens Farms, Conn., was designed by Moore Grover Harper, P. C., Architects.

A daylighting illuminated model was used to study redesign concepts for an existing conference room. The photos below show the existing room (left photo) and the illuminated model (right photo). The model was modified to study the effects of removing glazing from one wall and to evaluate the brightness patterns from central skylights.

Existing Conference Room   **Daylighted Model**

The photo of the existing conference room shows sidelighting by extensive clear glazing on the east and south building exposures. The model was photographed at the building site to depict conditions of bright openings and dark coffered ceiling. (See above photos.)

Daylighted Model

A redesign alternate eliminated sidelighting on one wall and introduced toplighting. The central skylights create a dramatic, striped pattern of sunlight on the east wall.

Note: Scale ratio for model was 1:12. It was constructed and photographed by Georgia Institute of Technology students James Hudgins and Dean Daley for the College of Architecture Daylight Design Studio conducted by Professor Charles C. Benton.

SELECTED REFERENCES ON INTERIOR MODELS

1. H. J. Cowan et al., *Models in Architecture*, American Elsevier, New York, 1968. See pp. 159-163 and 198-205.

2. B. H. Evans, *Daylight in Architecture*, McGraw-Hill, New York, 1981. For techniques to evaluate design alternatives with daylighting models, see pp. 107-138.

3. S. Hohauser, *Architectural and Interior Models*, Van Nostrand Reinhold, New York, 1970. For interior design modeling techniques, see pp. 154-162 and 184-189.

4. W. M. C. Lam, *Perception and Lighting as Formgivers for Architecture*, McGraw-Hill, New York, 1977. For examples of models used in lighting consulting practice, see pp. 90-95 and 274.

5. T. M. Lemons and R. B. MacLeod, Jr., "Scale Models Used in Lighting System Design and Evaluation," *Lighting Design & Application*, February 1972.

6. H. E. Rodman, "Models in Architectural Education and Practice," *Lighting Design & Application*, June 1973.

7. J. Taylor, *Model Building for Architects and Engineers*, McGraw-Hill, New York, 1971. See pp. 133-140.

Chapter 8
Illustrated Glossary

A

absorption   process by which incident light is dissipated, usually by conversion to heat

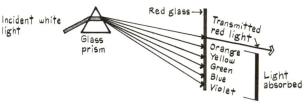

color produced by absorption

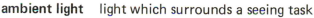

accent light   directional light which emphasizes objects or draws attention to a part of the visual field

accommodation   ability of the eye to change the shape of the lens to focus on near or distant objects

acuity   see *visual acuity*

adaptation   ability of the eye to adjust to different levels of light by change in size of pupil and by chemical changes in the photosensitive pigments of the retina

afterimage   visual effect which occurs after light stimulus has been removed

aiming angle   angle (in degrees) between center line of beam from point source of light and line perpendicular to surface containing source (usually at nadir)

ambient light   light which surrounds a seeing task

ampere   unit of intensity (or rate of flow) of electric current. Amperage is equal to wattage divided by voltage

angle of incidence $\angle \alpha$ angle at which light ray strikes surface, measured between ray and line perpendicular to surface

angstrom   unit of wavelength for light equal to 10^{-10} m

aperture fluorescent lamp   fluorescent lamp with reflective coating underneath phosphor coating and small, clear aperture to provide directional control of light output

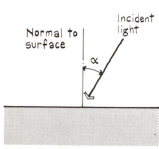

aiming angle

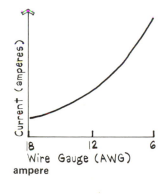

ampere

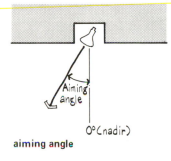

angle of incidence

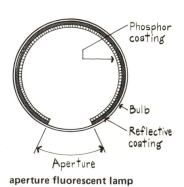

aperture fluorescent lamp

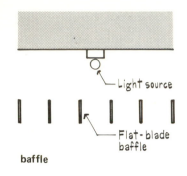

baffle

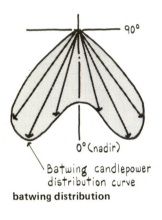

batwing distribution

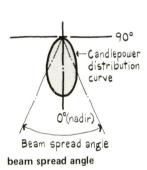

beam spread angle

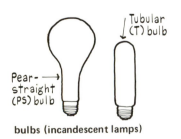

bulbs (incandescent lamps)

apparent color   perceived visual sensation determined by wavelength, intensity, mixture of wavelengths, and eye adaptation of observer

arc tube   enclosure which contains arc discharge (e.g., glass for fluorescent lamps, quartz for mercury and metal halide lamps, translucent alumina ceramic for high-pressure sodium lamps)

B

baffle   opaque or translucent element used to shield light source from direct view at certain angles

ballast   electrical device which supplies proper voltage, current, and wave form conditions to start and operate discharge lamps (e.g., fluorescent, mercury, high-pressure sodium)

batwing distribution   light from fixtures that is directed out to sides rather than down, where reflected glare can occur. The candlepower distribution curve looks like a bat's wing

beam cutoff angle   angle measured from vertical axis (i.e., nadir) and first line of sight at which bare light source is not visible

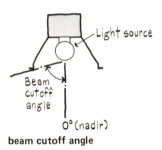

beam cutoff angle

beam daylighting   daylighting technique in which sunlight is reflected (e.g., by blinds located behind clerestory openings, light shelves at window openings) onto high-reflectance ceilings which project light deep into buildings

beam spread angle   angle between two end directions of beam of light in which candlepower usually equals 10% or more of maximum candlepower in beam

binocular vision   vision by both eyes

blackbody curve   spectrum describing a radiator that absorbs all radiant energy falling onto it. The continuous spectrum for an incandescent lamp approximates the blackbody curve

black hole effect   perceived light-draining characteristic of windows at night when viewed from the inside looking out

blind spot   point of exit of optic nerve from retina. There are no rods or cones at this point, and consequently there is no response to light

brightness   subjective impression of light reaching the eye. Subjective brightness does not vary directly with measured brightness

brightness constancy   perception of familiar objects as having the same brightness under different levels of illumination

brightness ratio   ratio between measured brightnesses of two elements in a visual field. Also referred to as *luminance ratio*

bulb   outer envelope of light source, usually quartz or glass

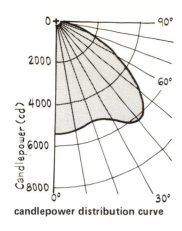
candlepower distribution curve

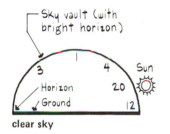
clear sky

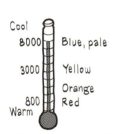
color temperatures for blackbody (in K)

candela (cd)   unit of luminous intensity equal to one candlepower. To convert lumens to candelas, divide by 12.57

candlepower (cp)   intensity of light produced by light source, measured in candelas

candlepower distribution curve   curve, generally plotted on polar coordinates, which represents variation in intensity of light (in cd) from bare lamp or luminaire

cavity ratio (CR)   number which indicates the size or proportions of a cavity calculated from its length, width, and height

chroma   purity or saturation of color

chromaticity   relative evaluation of color temperature (warmth or "coolth") of a light source

ciliary muscle   muscle which changes the shape of the lens for near and distant vision

clear sky   sky with < 30% cloud cover. Relative brightnesses for clear sky conditions are represented by numbers on sky vault sketch in the margin

clerestory   upper part of a wall which projects above roof plane, containing openings for daylighting of interiors

cloudy sky   sky with > 70% cloud cover

coefficient of utilization (CU)   ratio of lumens on the work surface to lumens emitted by the lamps of a luminaire. CU value is influenced by room surface reflectances, size and shape of room, location of luminaires, and design of luminaires

color constancy   perception of familiar objects as having the same color under different light sources

color contrast   relationship between the color of an object or area of interest and that of its immediate surround. Color contrast occurs even when two colors have the same measured brightness

color rendering index (CRI)   number obtained by comparing light sources to standard reference sources by measuring color shifts on eight color test samples. A CRI of 100 means the tested source exactly matches the reference source. The chromaticity of lamps must be nearly the same if the color rendering indexes are to be compared

color rendition   effect of a light source on the color appearance of objects

color temperature   temperature (in K) to which a blackbody radiator must be raised to match the color of a light source

cones   cone-shaped cells of the retina which function in bright light, perceiving color and detail

conspicuity   how well details stand out from their background

constancy   characteristics of objects (e.g., brightness, color, size, and shape) which are perceived as remaining unchanged even when they are seen under different conditions. Constancy is the ability to see as we feel objects should be rather than as they are

CONTRAST

contrast

$$E_2 = E_1 \cos \propto$$

cosine law

dazzle (from disappearing spots)

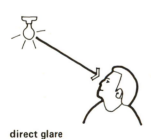

direct glare

contrast　relationship between brightness (or color) of an object and that of its immediate surrounding

contrast rendition factor (CRF)　ratio of visual task contrast measured under a given lighting environment to contrast measured under sphere illumination. The CRF will exceed 1 when lighting conditions have fewer veiling reflections than the reference sphere illumination

contrast sensitivity　ability to detect luminous, or brightness, differences

cornea　transparent coating of eyeball covering iris and pupil. Focuses light on retina by refraction

cornice lighting　lighting from sources behind panel, parallel to wall, and attached to ceiling. Light is distributed over walls

cosine law　law stating that illumination level (E) on any surface varies with the cosine of angle of incidence ($\angle \alpha$)

cove lighting　lighting from sources shielded by molding, ledge, or horizontal recess. Light is distributed over upper walls and ceiling

D

dark adaptation　process by which retina adapts to luminance less than about 0.01 footlambert. Complete dark adaptation can take up to one hour

daylight factor method　computational procedure for daylighting to determine percentage of external illumination on a point in a room. The daylight factor (DF) is the sum of the sky component, the externally reflected component, and the internally reflected component

dazzle　intense light or high-contrast pattern of identical figure and background shapes which overpowers or reduces visual acuity. (The pattern of squares shown in the margin creates dazzle from gray spots which disappear when focused upon.)

dichroic coating　film layers on incandescent bulb which remove heat from light beam by transmitting one color and reflecting its complement

diffuse　having the property of scattering incident light over a wide range of angles (e.g., materials like plaster, wood, brick have diffuse surfaces). See also *matte*

diffuser　device, object, or surface that scatters light from a source

dimmer　control device used to provide variable light output from lamps

direct glare　glare caused by bright source directly in field of vision

dirt depreciation factor (DDF)　factor used in daylighting computations to account for reduced illumination due to dirt accumulation on glazing

disability glare　glare which reduces ability to perceive visual information needed for task performance; too much light becomes scattered inside the eye

discomfort glare　glare which is distracting, annoying, or uncomfortable but does not significantly reduce the ability to perform visual tasks

downlight　small lighting fixture which directs light downward. Can be recessed, surface-mounted, or suspended

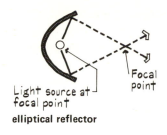

elliptical reflector

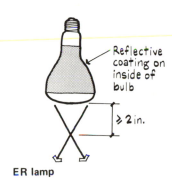

Reflective coating on inside of bulb

≥ 2 in.

ER lamp

effective ceiling cavity reflectance (ρ_{CC})   represents combined reflectance effect of all surface areas above plane of luminaire

effective floor cavity reflectance (ρ_{FC})   represents combined reflectance effect of all surface areas below plane of work surface

efficacy of light sources   luminous efficiency (in lm/W) expressed by lumen output of lamps per power input in watts

efficiency of luminaires   luminous efficiency expressed as ratio of lumen output of fixture to lumen output of lamps alone

elliptical (or ellipsoidal) reflector   light reflector shaped as ellipse so that light source placed at one focal point will cause light rays to converge at other focal point

ER lamp   elliptical reflector lamp which focuses light about two inches in front of lamp

equivalent sphere illumination (ESI)   level of sphere illumination (in fc or lx) which would produce task visibility equivalent to that produced by a specific lighting environment

externally reflected component (ERC)   light reflected from outdoor objects (e.g., fences, buildings) onto indoor plane of interest

figure-background   two aspects of visual perception which influence each other: a figure which has good contour and is separate from the background, and a background which is relatively homogeneous and not clearly patterned

flood lamp   incandescent lamp which produces a relatively wide beam of light

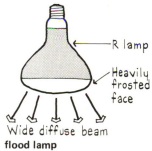

R lamp

Heavily frosted face

Wide diffuse beam
flood lamp

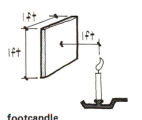

1 ft
1 ft
1 ft

footcandle

fluorescence   ability of materials to convert ultraviolet energy into visible light

fluorescent lamp   discharge lamp which emits electron arc stream from cathodes at ends. Fluorescent phosphor coating on inside of bulb transforms ultraviolet energy into visible light

footcandle (fc)   quantity of light on one square foot of surface area one foot away from light source of one candela. (Metric measure is *lux*; to convert footcandles to lux, multiply by 10.76.)

footlambert (fL)   quantity of light reflected from or transmitted through an object. (Metric measure is cd/m² or *nit.*)

fovea   small depression at center of retina which contains only cones. Site of the most distinct vision and best color response

fresnel lens   thin glass or plastic plano-convex lens used in downlights or spotlights to concentrate light into beam pattern

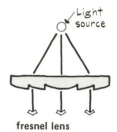

fresnel lens

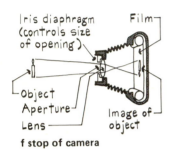

f stop of camera

f stop   indicates relative size of aperture in front of camera lens through which light passes. The higher the number, the smaller the size of the aperture opening

G

gestalt   figure or pattern whose integrated whole is perceived as being different from the sum of its parts

glare   harsh, uncomfortably bright light source or reflection which interferes with visual perception. Light from the wrong place at greater brightness than that to which eyes are adapted. See also *disability glare* and *discomfort glare*

glass block   hollow block of clear or translucent glass used in non-load-bearing walls

glitter   see *sparkle*

glossy   having the reflective properties of a mirror. Example finishes are marble, polished aluminum, and enamel paint

grazing light   directional light which emphasizes texture on plane surfaces by placing source (e.g., incandescent lamp with spread lens) near to and parallel with surfaces

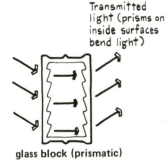

glass block (prismatic)

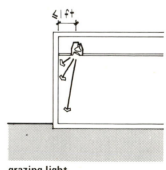

grazing light

HID lamps

ground light light from sun and sky reflected by ground cover (e.g., concrete, grass, pavers)

H

hard wiring permanent electrical connections, without plugs or user-operable connectors

high-intensity discharge (HID) lamp discharge lamp which passes a high-pressure electron arc stream through a gas vapor. Examples are mercury, metal halide, and high-pressure sodium lamps

high-pressure sodium lamp HID light source in which radiation from sodium vapor produces visible light. Pressure is about 0.1 atm during operation

hue classification of color. Red, yellow, green, blue, and purple are the primary hues in the Munsell color system

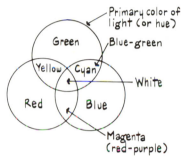

additive primary colors of light (produce white light when projected on same surface)

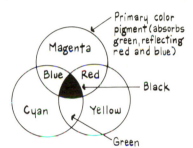

subtractive primary pigments (complementary colors are opposite in diagram, e.g., blue is complement of yellow)

I

illuminance (E) see *illumination level*

illuminated ceiling ceiling directly illuminated by sources which are suspended, on wall surfaces, or in room furniture

illumination gradient graphic representation of variation in illumination levels along an axis of measurement

illumination level (E) quantity of light (in fc or lx) which reaches a surface. To convert lux to footcandles, multiply by 0.09

incandescent lamp lamp in which light is produced by heating filament to incandescence (i.e., point of emitting light) by means of an electric current

incident light light which falls onto a surface or object

indirect lighting lighting achieved by reflection, usually from wall and ceiling surfaces. An example would be a space with a high-reflectance ceiling illuminated by uplight from lamps integrated into furniture

$$E = \frac{CP}{r^2}$$

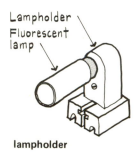

inverse-square law

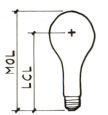

lampholder

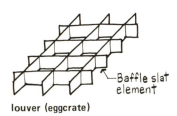

light center length (and maximum overall length)

internally reflected component (IRC)   light reflected from interior room surfaces onto indoor plane of interest

inverse-square law   law stating that illumination level (E) on a surface varies directly with candlepower (cp) of point source and inversely with square of distance (r) between point source and surface (distance should be at least 5 times the maximum dimension of the bare lamp source or luminaire)

iris   diaphragm which controls the size of the pupil opening, depending on amount of light available to eye

isofootcandle contours   lines plotted to show all points on a surface where illumination level (in fc) is the same

isoilluminance contours   see *isofootcandle* and *isolux contours*

isolux contours   lines plotted to show all points on a surface where illumination level (in lx) is the same

L

lamp   complete light source unit, usually consisting of light-generating element (arc tube or filament), support hardware, enclosing envelope (bulb), and base

lampholder   device to provide mechanical support and electrical connections (base pins and contacts) for fluorescent lamps

lamp lumen depreciation (LLD)   factor used in lumen method computations to account for reduced lumen output due to aging of lamp sources

lens   shielding or diffusing portion of fixture which controls luminance and directs light. Also, transparent oval body behind iris which adjusts eye's focus on retina for near and distant vision

light adaptation   process by which retina adapts to luminance greater than about one footlambert. Complete light adaptation takes about one minute

light center length (LCL)   for incandescent and HID lamps, the distance from center of light source to reference point on base

light loss factor (LLF)   see *maintenance factor.* LLF also takes into account temperature and voltage variations, aging of luminaire finish, dirt accumulation on room surfaces (RSDD), lamp burnouts (LBO), and other factors

light well   shaft, open to outside at top, used for daylighting of buildings

lighting fixture   see *luminaire*

linear perspective   depth cue of parallel straight lines which appear to converge at distant vanishing point

louver   series of baffles (e.g., eggcrate, parabolic) used to shield light sources from view at certain angles

lumen (lm)   unit of light energy used to specify light output of sources. It is the rate at which light falls on one square foot of surface area one foot from a source of one candela

lumen method   computational procedure for lighting to determine average room illumination level by taking into account both direct and interreflected light

louver (eggcrate)

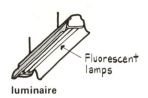

luminaire

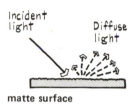

matte surface

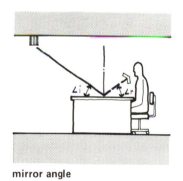

mirror angle

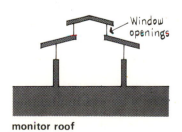

monitor roof

luminaire   complete lighting unit consisting of lamp (or lamps) together with parts to position and protect lamp, direct light, and connect lamp to a power supply. Also referred to as a *fixture*

luminaire dirt depreciation (LDD)   factor used in lumen method computations to account for reduced illumination due to dirt accumulation on luminaires

luminance (*L*)   see *measured brightness*

luminous ceiling   ceiling of backlighted translucent material which provides light by diffusion

luminous efficacy   see *efficacy of light sources*

luminous intensity (*I*)   see *candlepower*

lux (lx)   metric unit of quantity of light on 1 square meter of surface area 1 meter away from light source of 1 candela. (1 lux is equal to 0.09 footcandle.)

M

maintained illumination level   initial illumination level from luminaires adjusted for depreciation of lamp lumens by aging, effects of dirt accumulation on luminaire surfaces, and other factors

maintenance factor (MF)   ratio of illumination on a given area after a period of time to initial illumination on same area. MF is equal to LDD times LLD

matte   having the property of scattering incident light. Example matte finishes are flat paint, plaster, and limestone

maximum overall length (MOL)   longest length of lamp

measured brightness (*L*)   luminous intensity of a surface or object, often referred to as *luminance*. Objectively measured light (in fL or nt) reflected from or transmitted through an object. To convert footlamberts to nits, multiply by 3.43

mercury lamp   HID light source in which radiation from mercury vapor produces visible light. Mercury lamps that are self-ballasted are available

metal halide lamp   HID light source in which radiation from mixture of metallic vapor and products of dissociation of halides (e.g., sodium, thallium, indium) produces visible light

mirror angle   angle equal to and opposite the viewing angle between line of sight and plane of surface under observation. See also *specular*

modeling   having the property of revealing three-dimensional form by emphasizing highlights and shadows

moiré   clouded, wavy, or frosted appearance (e.g., on textiles, postage stamps, metals)

monitor roof   raised section of roof, usually straddling ridge, with window openings for daylighting

monocular vision   vision by one eye

Munsell color system   system for ordering surface colors by specifying *hue* (color), *value* (lightness or darkness), and *chroma* (saturation)

N

nadir   angle equal to zero degrees and oriented vertically downward

nanometer (nm)   unit of wavelength for light equal to 10^{-9} m

near point   point at which observer's lenses have reached maximum curvature and cannot focus clearly if object is moved closer to eyes

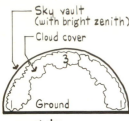

overcast sky

nit (nt)   metric unit of quantity of light reflected from or transmitted through an object. To convert nits to footlamberts, multiply by 0.29
noise   see *visual noise*

O

offending zone   location of light source which produces maximum veiling reflections or reflected glare
optic nerve   bundle of nerve fibers which carries light-generated impulses from eye to brain
overcast sky   sky with 100% cloud cover, completely occluding view of sun. Relative brightnesses for overcast sky conditions are represented by numbers on sky vault sketch in the margin

P

PAR lamp   parabolic aluminized reflector lamp with accurate beam control. Hard glass incandescent lamp with inside reflecting surface, precisely placed filament, and lens to control beam spread
parabolic reflector   light reflector shaped as paraboloid to concentrate light beam parallel to axis of reflector

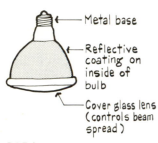

PAR lamp

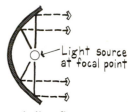

parabolic reflector

partly cloudy sky   constantly changing sky with 30 to 70% cloud cover
peripheral vision   ability to see objects outside central visual field, beyond near visual surround
phosphorescence   ability of material to retain and release light energy after the stimuli are removed
photometry   measurement of quantities associated with light
photoperiodism   light-rhythm characteristic of plants (i.e., light versus dark hours in a 24-hour cycle). Incandescent, fluorescent, and HID lamps can be used to promote or retard flowering
photopic vision   vision by cones with eye adaptation to luminance of at least one footlambert. See also *light adaptation*
phototropism   attraction toward light
point method   computational procedure for lighting to determine direct illumination level by use of photometric data. Interreflected light from room surfaces is accounted for separately
point source   light source with dimensions less than about one-fifth the distance between source and surface to be illuminated

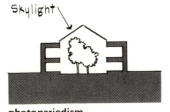

photoperiodism

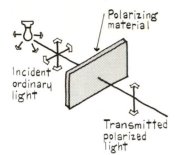

polarized light

polarized light   light waves vibrating in a single plane

presbyopia   loss of lens flexibility of eyes due to aging

prismatic lens   glass or plastic consisting of prisms which refract transmitted light

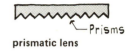

prismatic lens

pupil   opening in center of iris that controls amount of light admitted into eye

Purkinje effect   shift from perception by cones to perception by rods. For example, blue flowers seem brighter than red flowers when viewed in low levels of light

Q

quartz lamp   see *tungsten-halogen lamp*

R

reflectance (ρ)   percentage of incident light on surface which is re-radiated. It depends on angle of incidence and other factors

reflected glare   glare from specular reflections of high brightness off polished or glossy surfaces. Position of human eye provides poor shielding for reflected glare off desk tops or floors. See also *veiling reflections*

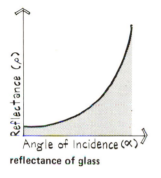

reflectance of glass

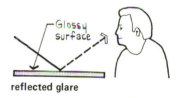

reflected glare

reflector   device used to redirect light from a source

refractor   device used to redirect light. Light rays change direction when passing obliquely from one medium (air) to another (glass or plastic)

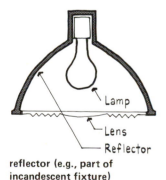

reflector (e.g., part of incandescent fixture)

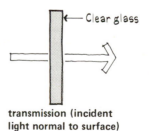

transmission (incident light normal to surface)

refraction (due to configurated surface)

RLM dome fixture

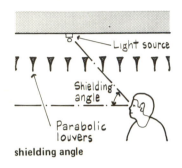
shielding angle

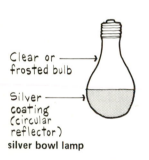
silver bowl lamp

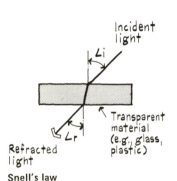
Snell's law

regular reflection   see *specular*

retina   lining at back of inside of eye which consists of cones and rods that are sensitive to color and light and nerve cells which transmit signals to optic nerve

R lamp   reflector incandescent lamp with frosting on the face of the lamp to control beam spread

RLM fixture   porcelain-on-steel incandescent lamp reflector fixture. RLM refers to Registered Luminaire Manufacturers Institute

rods   rod-shaped cells of the retina which are sensitive at low levels of light. Rod vision is achromatic (i.e., shades of gray)

S

saturation   purity or richness of color (i.e., measure of how much white or gray is in mixture). See also *chroma*

scale ratio   ratio of physical dimension in model to physical dimension in full-scale structure or prototype

sclera   white, thick outer coating that maintains the shape of the eye

scotopic vision   vision by rods with eye adaptation to luminance less that about 0.01 footlambert. See also *dark adaptation*

self-ballasted lamp   discharge lamp with integral ballast

shielding angle   maximum angle between the horizontal and an observer's line of sight to the shielding materials when the lamps first can be seen

shielding material   see *diffuser, lens, baffle,* and *louver*

signal-to-noise ratio   ratio of desired or needed visual information to undesired or competing visual signals

silver bowl lamp   incandescent lamp with silver reflective coating on lower half of bulb to provide indirect light by reflection

simultaneous contrast   heightening of difference in color or brightness when objects are placed next to each other

size constancy   perception of familiar objects as being unchanged in size regardless of distance from which they are viewed

sky component (SC)   light from sky directly incident onto indoor plane of interest

sky light   light from sun redirected by atmosphere

skylight   opening in roof, glazed with transparent or translucent material, for daylighting

sky vault   hemispherical shape of sky as viewed from earth

Snell's law   law which states that ratio of indices of refraction of two media are inversely proportional to the sine of angle of refraction and angle of incidence. It predicts amount of bending when light in air enters and leaves glass or plastic because the speed of light changes from one medium to another

soffit lighting   lighting from sources in undersurface of beam, balcony, vault, and so on

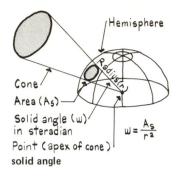

solid angle

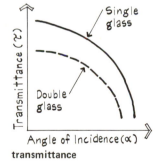

transmittance

solid angle   three-dimensional angle formed by three or more planes meeting at a point (e.g., apex of cone, pyramid, or the like). Unit of measure for solid angle is steradian

sparkle   attractive, extreme brightness which results from a pleasant composition of luminous brilliance (e.g., chandeliers in lobbies or dining rooms, lights on theater marquees, glass-enclosed elevators decorated with small incandescent light sources)

specular   having the reflective properties of a mirror where angle of incidence is equal to angle of reflection. Example finishes are polished aluminum, stainless steel, and tin. Angles are usually measured between light ray and line perpendicular to surface as shown below

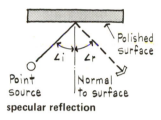

specular reflection

sphere illumination   illumination from light source which provides equal candlepower from all directions onto the task

spot lamp   incandescent lamp which provides relatively narrow beam of light. For example, R lamp with lightly-frosted face or PAR lamp with stipled lens

spot relamping   replacement of lamps on a one-by-one basis

T

task light   light on a seeing task which has visual information an observer is attempting to see and comprehend

textural perspective   crowding and blending of details (e.g., pebbles in a field) as they are seen from increasingly greater distances away

texture   pattern of highlight and shadow

toplighting   lighting from skylights, clerestories, and light wells

torchère   indirect floor-mounted lamp which directs most of its light upward

transmittance (τ)   ratio (in %) of transmitted light to incident light. It depends on angle of incidence, measurement method, and other factors

troffer   recessed, long lighting fixture, usually installed with its housing flush with the ceiling

tungsten-halogen lamp   incandescent light source containing halogen gas which reacts with tungsten evaporated from filament to redeposit it on the filament

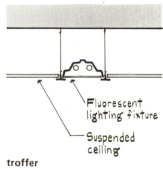

troffer

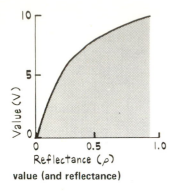

value (and reflectance)

valance longitudinal shielding member mounted across the top of a window or along a wall to conceal light sources which provide up and down light

value (V) lightness or darkness of color, measured by scale from perfect white (10) to perfect black (0). The graph in the margin shows the relationship between value and reflectance

veiling reflections reflections of incident light superimposed on diffuse reflections. They partially or totally obscure details by reducing contrast. The effect is most severe when the light source is above and in front of the work surface

viewing angle angle formed between an observer's line of sight and the normal to plane of surface under observation

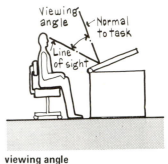

viewing angle

visibility how well a scene or object can be seen

visible spectrum small band of the electromagnetic spectrum, about 380 to 780 nanometers, which contains all wavelengths observers with normal color vision can perceive as visible colors

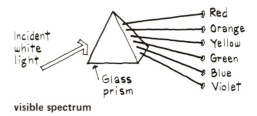

visible spectrum

visual acuity capacity to discriminate fine details of objects

visual comfort probability index (VCP) rating scheme for arrangements of fixtures in terms of percentage of viewers who would find direct glare conditions tolerable at a specified location and direction of view

visual efficiency quantitative assessment of task performance based on speed and accuracy of test subjects

visual field extent of space where objects can be seen when the head and eyes are stationary

visual noise undesirable or distracting visual stimuli which interfere or compete with desired signals

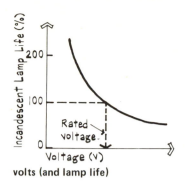

volts (and lamp life)

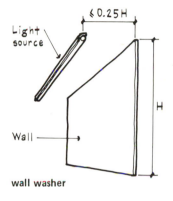

wall washer

visual surround   all portions of visual field except the visual task and its immediate background

visual task   details and objects that must be seen for performance of a given activity, including immediate background of details or objects

volt   unit of electromotive force (or pressure of electricity). One volt in a circuit of one ohm resistance will cause one ampere of current to flow. Amperage is equal to voltage divided by resistance (called *Ohm's law*)

W

wall washer   light source, located close to wall plane, which distributes light on wall

watt (W)   unit of electrical power. Wattage is equal to voltage times amperage

wavelength   distance between two similar points of a given wave. Unit of measure for wavelengths of light is the nanometer

white-dog effect   increase in apparent contrast between white and gray colors due to large reduction of illumination

wiring channel   metal enclosure containing ballast, starter, lamp-holders, and wiring for fluorescent lamp. Called *fluorescent strip* when used with bare fluorescent lamp

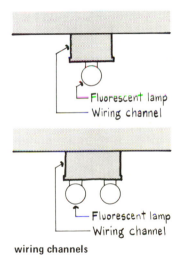

wiring channels

work surface   plane at which work is performed, usually on horizontal surface 30 in above floor. Also referred to as *work plane*

wraparound fixture   surface-mounted or suspended fixture with one-piece plastic lens to enclose (or "wrap") lamp compartment on both sides and bottom

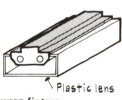

wrap fixture

Z

zonal cavity method   see *lumen method*

References for Glossary

1. C. M. Harris (ed.), *Dictionary of Architecture and Construction*, McGraw-Hill, New York, 1975.

2. J. E. Kaufman (ed.), *IES Lighting Handbook* (Reference Volume), Illuminating Engineering Society, New York, 1981, pp. 1-1 to 1-31.

3. W. M. C. Lam, *Perception and Lighting as Formgivers for Architecture*, McGraw-Hill, New York, 1977, pp. 7-9.

4. R. L. Mackey, *Lighting Discipline*, Westinghouse Electric Corporation, Vicksburg, Miss., 1977, pp. 6-13.

5. T. K. McGowan, "All About Sources," *Progressive Architecture*, September 1973.

6. C. G. Mueller and M. Rudolph, *Light and Vision*, Time-Life Books, New York, 1966, pp. 194-195.

7. J. L. Nuckolls, "Furniture Integrated Lighting," The Shaw-Walker Company, Muskegon, Mich., 1979, pp. 24-27.

8. A.I. Rubin and J. Elder, *Building for People*, U.S. National Bureau of Standards, Washington, D.C., June 1980, pp. 275-288.

Selected References on Lighting

LIGHTING FUNDAMENTALS AND VISION

C. A. Bennett, *Spaces for People*, Prentice-Hall, Englewood Cliffs, N.J., 1977, pp. 87-112.

P. R. Boyce, *Human Factors in Lighting*, Macmillan Publishing, New York, 1981.

L. Erhardt, *Radiation, Light, and Illumination*, Camarillo Reproduction Center, Camarillo, Calif., 1977.

W. Faulkner, *Architecture and Color*, John Wiley and Sons, New York, 1972.

R. E. Fischer (ed.), *Architectural Engineering-Environmental Control*, McGraw-Hill, New York, 1965, pp. 118-180.

J. E. Flynn and S. M. Mills, *Architectural Lighting Graphics*, Van Nostrand Reinhold, New York, 1962.

J. E. Flynn and A. W. Segil, *Architectural Interior Systems*, Van Nostrand Reinhold, New York, 1970, pp. 3-46 and 101-148.

J. P. Frier and M. E. G. Frier, *Industrial Lighting Systems*, McGraw-Hill, New York, 1980.

General Electric Company (General Electric Lighting Institute, Nela Park, Cleveland, OH 44112) technical publications:

"Industrial Lighting," TP-108R, March 1977.

"Light and Color," TP-119, February 1978.

"Light Measurement and Control," TP-118, March 1965.

A. O. Halse, *The Use of Color in Interiors*, McGraw-Hill, New York, 1978.

R. G. Hopkinson, *Architectural Physics: Lighting*, Her Majesty's Stationery Office, London, England, 1963.

R. G. Hopkinson and J. D. Kay, *The Lighting of Buildings*, Praeger Publishers, New York, 1969.

L. C. Kalff, *Creative Light*, Van Nostrand Reinhold, New York, 1971.

J. E. Kaufman (ed.), *IES Lighting Handbook* (Application Volume), Illuminating Engineering Society, New York, 1981.

J. E. Kaufman (ed.), *IES Lighting Handbook* (Reference Volume), Illuminating Engineering Society, New York, 1981.

W. M. C. Lam, *Perception and Lighting as Formgivers for Architecture*, McGraw-Hill, New York, 1977.

L. L. Langley et al., *Dynamic Anatomy & Physiology*, McGraw-Hill, New York, 1974, pp. 304-329.

J. L. Nuckolls, *Interior Lighting for Environmental Designers*, John Wiley and Sons, New York, 1976.

D. Phillips, *Lighting in Architectural Design*, McGraw-Hill, New York, 1964.

R. N. Helms, *Illumination Engineering for Energy Efficient Luminous Environments*, Prentice-Hall, Englewood Cliffs, N.J., 1980.

How to Predict Interior Daylight Illumination, Libbey-Owens-Ford Company, Toledo, Ohio, 1976.

J. E. Kaufman (ed.), *IES Lighting Handbook* (Reference Volume), Illuminating Engineering Society, New York, 1981, pp. 9-1 to 9-95.

Lighting Handbook, Westinghouse Electric Corporation, Bloomfield, N.J., 1978.

R.L. Mackey, *Lighting Discipline*, Westinghouse Electric Corporation, Vicksburg, Miss., 1977.

W. J. McGuinness et al., *Mechanical and Electrical Equipment for Buildings*, John Wiley and Sons, New York, 1980, pp. 707-994.

J. Pohl, *The Layman's Lumen*, California Polytechnic State University, San Luis Obispo, Calif., 1974.

DAYLIGHTING

J. H. Callender (ed.), *Time-Saver Standards*, McGraw-Hill, New York, 1974, pp. 921-934.

B. H. Evans, *Daylight in Architecture*, McGraw-Hill, New York, 1981.

R. G. Hopkinson et al., *Daylighting*, William Heineman Ltd., London, England, 1966.

J. E. Kaufman (ed.), *IES Lighting Handbook* (Reference Volume), Illuminating Engineering Society, New York, 1981, pp. 9-81 to 9-94.

J. A. Lynes, *Principles of Natural Lighting*, Elsevier, Amsterdam, 1968.

Appendix A:
Summary of Useful Formulas

Visual Angle

$$\alpha \simeq \frac{57h}{D}$$

where α = visual angle (degrees)
h = object height (ft)
D = distance from eye to object (ft)

Note: $\simeq$ means approximately equal to.

Contrast

$$C = \frac{L_t - L_s}{L_s}$$

where C = contrast (no units)
L_t = luminance (or measured brightness) of task or detail (fL)
L_s = luminance (or measured brightness) of surround or background (fL)

$$C = \frac{\rho_t - \rho_s}{\rho_s}$$

where C = contrast, independent of illumination level (no units)
ρ_t = reflectance of task (%)
ρ_s = reflectance of surround (%)

Reflectance

$$\rho \simeq V(V - 1)$$

where ρ = reflectance (%)
V = Munsell value (no units)

Brightness

$$L = E \times \rho$$

where L = luminance or measured brightness (fL)

E = illumination level or illuminance (fc)

ρ = reflectance (%)

$$L = E \times \tau$$

where L = luminance or measured brightness (fL)

E = illumination level or illuminance (fc)

τ = transmittance (%)

Light Flow

$$F = 4\pi \text{ cp}$$

where F = rate of flow of visible radiation (lm)

cp = mean spherical candlepower (or luminous intensity) of light source (cd)

Note: cp is the abbreviation for candlepower used throughout the book. The symbol I for luminous intensity also is candlepower in cd units.

Inverse-Square Law

$$E = \frac{\text{cp}}{r^2}$$

where E = illumination level directly below light source (fc)

cp = candlepower of source of light (cd)

r = distance from source of light to point of interest (ft)

Note: Candlepower varies with angle, usually expressed in degrees from nadir. Find candlepower for a given angle or direction from photometric data.

Point Method

$$E = \frac{\text{cp}}{r^2} \cos\theta$$

where E = illumination level on horizontal plane (fc)

cp = candlepower of source of light (cd)

r = distance from source of light to point of interest (ft)

θ = angle between vertical line from light source and line from light source to point of interest (degrees)

Note: Angle α can be used in formula when θ equals α (i.e., the angle between ray of light and the normal to surface at point of interest).

$$E = \frac{cp}{r^2} \sin \theta$$

where E = illumination level on vertical plane (fc)
    cp = candlepower of source of light (cd)
    r = distance from source of light to point of interest (ft)
    θ = angle between vertical line from light source and line
       from light source to point of interest (degrees)

$$E = \frac{cp}{H^2} \cos^3 \theta$$

where E = illumination level on horizontal plane (fc)
    cp = candlepower of source of light (cd)
    H = height or perpendicular distance from plane containing
       source of light to plane at point of interest (ft)
    θ = angle between vertical line from light source and line
       from light source to point of interest (degrees)

$$E = \frac{cp}{H^2} \cos^2 \theta \sin \theta$$

where E = illumination level on vertical plane (fc)
    cp = candlepower of source of light (cd)
    H = height or perpendicular distance from plane containing
       source of light to plane at point of interest (ft)
    θ = angle between vertical line from light source and line
       from light source to point of interest (degrees)

Accent Light

$$x = 0.6H - 3$$

where x = distance from wall (ft)
    H = floor-to-ceiling height (ft)

Lumen Method

$$CR = 5h_C \left(\frac{L + W}{L \times W} \right)$$

where CR = cavity ratio (no units)
    h_C = height of cavity (ft)
    L = length of cavity (ft)
    W = width of cavity (ft)

$$CR = \frac{5h_C}{r}$$

where CR = cavity ratio (no units)
    h_C = height of cavity (ft)
    r = radius of cavity (ft)

$$F = \frac{E \times A}{CU \times LLF}$$

where F = initial generated light from lamps of luminaire (lm)
E = illumination level or illuminance (fc)
A = area of work plane (ft²)
CU = coefficient of utilization (decimal %)
LLF = $LLD \times LDD$ (decimal %)

Note: CU data can be obtained from luminaire manufacturers. For composite data of generic luminaire types, refer to the *IES Lighting Handbook* or Appendix C. Lamp lumen depreciation (LLD) and luminaire dirt depreciation (LDD) data are available from tables.

$$S \simeq \sqrt{A_\ell}$$

where S = spacing between adjacent luminaires (ft)
A_ℓ = area per luminaire, i.e., the area of work plane divided by the number of luminaires (ft²)

Line Sources

$$E = \frac{L \times w}{2H}$$

where E = illumination level directly below line of light sources (fc)
L = luminance of light source (fL)
w = width of light source (ft)
H = height or perpendicular distance from row of fixtures to point of interest (ft)

Area Sources

$$E = \frac{L \times A \cos \beta \cos \alpha}{\pi D^2}$$

where E = illumination level (fc)
L = luminance of area light source (fL)
A = area of large (or area) light source (ft²)
D = distance from area source to point of interest (ft)
β = angle between normal to the area source and line drawn to the point of interest (degrees)
α = angle between normal to the plane of interest and line drawn from the area source (degrees)

Light Wells

$$I_w = 0.5H \left(\frac{W + L}{W \times L} \right)$$

where I_w = well index (no units)
H = depth of well opening (ft)
W = width of well opening (ft)
L = length of well opening (ft)

Daylight Factor Method

$$SC = (SC_w - SC_o)\,\tau$$

where SC = sky component (%)
            SC_w = sky component of window opening (%)
            SC_o = obstructed sky component (%)
            τ = transmittance (%)

Note: Sky components are found in tables or graphs.

$$SC \simeq \frac{10}{D}\left(\frac{W \times H^2}{D^2 + H^2}\right)\tau$$

where SC = sky component (%)
            W = width of window to one side of center of work plane (ft)
            H = height of window above work plane (ft)
            D = distance from window to point of interest (ft)
            τ = transmittance (%)

$$ERC = C_b(SC_o)\,\tau$$

where ERC = externally reflected component (%)
            C_b = obstruction brightness coefficient (use 0.2 when obstruction is below 20°, 0.1 when above 20°, and 0 for open sites)
           SC_o = obstructed sky component (%)
            τ = transmittance (%)

$$IRC = \frac{0.85A_w}{A_{tot}(1 - \rho_{avg})}\,(C\rho_{FW} + 5\rho_{CW})$$

where IRC = internally reflected component (%)
           A_w = open area of windows (ft²)
           A_{tot} = total interior surface area of room (ft²)
           ρ_{avg} = average reflectance of room surfaces (%)
           C = obstruction coefficient (no units)
           ρ_{FW} = average reflectance of room surfaces below midheight of room (%)
           ρ_{CW} = average reflectance of room surfaces above midheight of room (%)

Note: When computing ρ_{FW} and ρ_{CW}, exclude area of window wall.

$$C \simeq 40 - \frac{\theta}{2}$$

where C = obstruction coefficient (no units)
            θ = angle of obstruction above horizontal plane (degrees)

$$DF = SC + ERC + IRC$$

where DF = daylight factor (%)
           SC = sky component (%)

ERC = externally reflected component (%)
IRC = internally reflected component (%)

$$E_I = E_o \times DF \times DDF$$

where E_I = average interior illumination level on horizontal plane (fc or lx)
   E_o = average external illumination level (fc or lx)
   DF = daylight factor (%)
   DDF = dirt depreciation factor (decimal %)

Note: Find E_o values from tables of illuminance for overcast sky conditions. DDF also is available from tables.

Screen Luminance

$$L = \frac{F \times \rho}{A}$$

where L = luminance of screen (fL)
   F = light output of projection lamp (lm)
   ρ = reflectance of screen (%)
   A = area of screen (ft^2)

Electricity

$$I = \frac{V}{R}$$

where I = current (amperes)
   V = voltage (volts)
   R = resistance (ohms)

Note: This formula is referred to as Ohm's law.

$$W = VI$$

where W = power (watts)
   V = voltage (volts)
   I = current (amperes)

Note: To compute power in alternating current systems, multiply equation by appropriate power factor.

Heat from Light Sources

$$H = 3.4W$$

where H = heat (Btuh)
   W = power supplied to lamps and ballasts (watts)

Appendix B:
Conversion Factors

The table below presents conversion factors for common lighting units to corresponding metric system units, often referred to as le Système Internationale d'Unités (SI units). The basic SI units are expressed as follows: length by meter (abbreviated m), mass by kilogram (kg), time by second (s), and temperature by degree kelvin (K). For a comprehensive presentation of metric system units, refer to "Standard for Metric Practice," ASTM E 380. This publication is available from the American Society for Testing and Materials (ASTM), 1916 Race Street, Philadelphia, PA 19103.

To convert	Into	Multiply by*	Conversely, Multiply by*
atmosphere (atm)	psi	14.7	6.8×10^{-2}
Btu	joule	1055	9.479×10^{-4}
Btuh	watt	0.293	3.413
cd/in^2	cd/m^2	1550	6.452×10^{-4}
cd/m^2	cd/in^2	6.452×10^{-4}	1550
	fL	0.2919	3.426
	lambert	3.142×10^{-4}	3183
$^\circ$C	$^\circ$F	$(^\circ C \times 9/5) + 32$	$(^\circ F - 32) \times 5/9$
	K	$^\circ C + 273$	$K - 273$
cm	in	0.3937	2.54
	ft	3.281×10^{-2}	30.48
	mm	10	10^{-1}
	m	10^{-2}	10^2
deg (angle)	radian	1.745×10^{-2}	57.3
$^\circ$F	$^\circ$C	$(^\circ F - 32) \times 5/9$	$(^\circ C \times 9/5) + 32$
	K	$(^\circ F + 460) \times 5/9$	$1.8 K - 460$
ft	in	12	0.0833
	mm	304.8	3.281×10^{-3}
	cm	30.48	3.281×10^{-2}
	m	0.3048	3.281
ft^2	in^2	144	6.944×10^{-3}
	cm^2	9.29×10^2	0.01076
	m^2	9.29×10^{-2}	10.76
ft^3	in^3	1728	5.787×10^{-4}
	cm^3	2.832×10^4	3.531×10^{-5}
	m^3	2.832×10^{-2}	35.31

*Round converted quantity to proper number of significant digits commensurate with the intended precision.

To convert	Into	Multiply by*	Conversely, Multiply by*
footcandle (fc)	lux (lx)	10.76	0.0929
footlambert (fL)	cd/m^2	3.426	0.2919
	cd/in^2	0.00221	452
	cd/ft^2	0.3183	3.142
	stilb (cd/cm^2)	0.00034	2.919×10^3
in	ft	0.0833	12
	mm	25.4	0.03937
	cm	2.54	0.3937
in	m	0.0254	39.37
in^2	ft^2	0.006944	144
	cm^2	6.452	0.155
	m^2	6.452×10^{-4}	1550
in^3	ft^3	5.787×10^{-4}	1.728×10^3
	cm^3	16.388	6.102×10^{-2}
	m^3	1.639×10^{-5}	6.102×10^4
K	°C	K − 273	°C + 273
	°F	1.8 K − 460	(°F + 460) × 5/9
	°R (Rankine)	1.8 K	°R × 5/9
kilowatt (kW)	horsepower (hp)	1.341	0.7457
lux (lx)	fc	0.0929	10.76
m	in	39.37	0.0254
	ft	3.281	0.3048
	yd	1.0936	0.9144
	mm	10^3	10^{-3}
	cm	10^2	10^{-2}
mil	in	10^{-3}	10^3
miles	ft	5280	1.894×10^{-4}
	km	1.6093	0.6214
nit	fL	0.2919	3.426
watt (W)	Btuh	3.413	0.293
	hp	1.341×10^{-3}	745.7
W/ft^2	W/m^2	10.76	9.29×10^{-2}

*Round converted quantity to proper number of significant digits commensurate with the intended precision.

Appendix C:
IES Tables for Lumen Method*

Percent Effective Ceiling or Floor Cavity Reflectances for Various Reflectance Combinations

Per Cent Base* Reflectance →	90										80										70										60										50									
Per Cent Wall Reflectance → / Cavity Ratio ↓	90	80	70	60	50	40	30	20	10	0	90	80	70	60	50	40	30	20	10	0	90	80	70	60	50	40	30	20	10	0	90	80	70	60	50	40	30	20	10	0	90	80	70	60	50	40	30	20	10	0
0.2	89	88	88	87	86	85	84	84	84	82	79	78	78	77	77	76	76	75	74	72	70	69	68	68	67	67	66	66	65	64	60	59	59	59	58	57	56	56	55	53	50	50	49	49	48	48	47	46	46	44
0.4	88	87	86	85	84	83	81	80	79	76	79	77	76	75	74	73	71	70	68	68	69	68	67	66	65	64	63	62	61	58	60	59	59	58	57	55	54	53	52	50	50	49	48	48	47	46	45	45	44	42
0.6	87	86	84	82	80	79	77	76	74	73	78	76	75	73	71	70	68	66	65	63	69	67	65	64	63	61	59	58	57	54	60	58	57	56	55	53	51	50	50	46	50	48	48	47	46	46	43	42	41	38
0.8	87	85	82	80	77	75	73	71	69	67	78	75	73	71	69	67	65	63	61	57	68	66	64	62	60	58	56	55	53	50	59	57	56	55	54	51	48	47	46	43	50	48	47	46	45	44	42	41	38	36
1.0	86	83	80	77	75	72	69	66	64	62	77	74	72	69	67	65	62	60	57	55	68	65	62	60	58	55	53	52	50	47	59	57	55	53	51	48	46	44	43	41	50	48	46	45	44	43	41	38	36	34
1.2	85	82	78	75	72	69	66	63	60	57	76	73	70	67	64	61	58	55	53	51	67	64	61	59	57	54	51	49	47	44	59	56	54	51	49	46	44	42	40	38	50	47	45	43	41	39	36	35	34	29
1.4	85	80	77	73	69	65	62	59	57	52	76	72	68	65	62	59	55	53	50	48	67	63	60	58	55	51	49	47	45	41	59	56	53	49	47	44	41	39	38	36	50	47	45	42	40	38	35	34	32	27
1.6	84	79	75	71	67	63	59	56	53	50	75	71	67	63	60	57	53	50	47	44	67	62	59	56	53	49	47	45	43	38	59	55	52	48	45	42	39	37	35	33	50	47	44	41	39	36	33	32	30	26
1.8	83	78	73	69	64	60	56	53	50	48	75	70	66	62	58	54	50	47	44	41	66	61	58	54	51	46	45	42	40	35	58	55	51	47	44	40	37	35	33	31	50	46	43	40	38	35	31	30	28	25
2.0	83	77	72	67	62	58	53	50	47	43	74	69	64	60	56	52	48	45	41	38	66	60	56	52	49	45	42	40	38	33	58	54	50	46	43	39	35	33	31	29	50	46	43	40	37	34	30	28	26	24
2.2	82	76	70	65	59	54	50	47	44	40	74	68	63	58	54	49	45	42	38	35	66	60	55	51	48	43	40	38	36	32	58	53	48	44	42	38	34	31	29	28	50	46	42	38	36	33	29	27	25	22
2.4	82	75	69	64	58	53	48	45	41	37	73	67	61	56	52	47	43	40	36	33	65	60	54	50	46	41	37	35	33	30	58	53	47	44	41	37	32	30	27	26	50	46	42	37	35	31	27	25	23	21
2.6	81	74	67	62	56	51	46	42	38	35	73	66	60	55	50	45	41	38	34	31	65	59	53	49	45	40	36	33	31	28	58	53	48	43	39	35	31	28	26	24	50	46	41	37	34	30	26	23	21	20
2.8	81	73	66	60	54	49	44	40	36	34	73	65	59	53	48	43	39	36	32	29	65	59	53	48	43	38	35	32	30	26	57	52	47	42	38	34	30	27	24	22	50	45	41	36	33	29	25	22	20	18
3.0	80	72	64	58	52	47	42	38	34	30	72	65	58	52	47	42	37	34	30	27	64	58	52	47	42	37	34	31	27	24	57	52	46	41	37	32	29	25	23	20	49	44	40	33	32	28	24	21	19	17
3.2	79	71	63	56	50	45	40	36	32	28	72	64	57	51	45	40	35	33	28	25	64	58	51	46	41	36	31	28	25	23	57	51	45	40	36	31	28	23	22	18	49	44	39	32	31	27	23	20	18	16
3.4	79	70	62	54	48	43	38	34	30	27	72	64	56	49	44	39	34	32	27	24	64	57	50	45	39	35	29	27	24	22	57	51	45	40	35	31	27	23	20	17	48	43	38	31	30	26	22	19	17	15
3.6	78	69	61	53	47	42	36	32	28	25	71	63	54	48	43	38	33	29	27	23	63	56	49	44	38	33	28	25	22	20	57	50	44	39	34	30	26	22	19	16	48	42	37	30	29	25	21	18	16	14
3.8	78	69	60	51	45	40	35	31	27	23	70	62	53	47	41	36	32	27	23	20	63	56	49	43	37	32	27	24	21	19	57	50	43	38	33	29	25	21	17	15	48	41	36	29	28	24	20	17	15	13
4.0	77	68	58	51	44	39	33	29	25	22	70	61	53	46	40	35	30	26	22	19	63	55	48	42	36	31	26	23	20	17	57	49	42	37	32	28	23	20	18	14	47	40	35	28	27	23	20	17	15	12
4.2	77	67	57	50	43	37	32	28	24	21	69	60	52	45	39	34	29	25	21	18	62	55	47	41	35	30	25	22	19	16	56	49	41	36	31	27	22	19	17	14	47	40	34	27	26	22	19	16	14	12
4.4	76	66	56	49	42	36	31	27	23	20	69	60	51	44	38	33	28	24	20	17	62	54	46	40	34	29	24	21	18	15	56	49	40	36	31	26	22	19	16	13	46	39	33	26	26	22	18	15	13	11
4.6	76	65	54	47	41	35	30	26	22	19	69	60	50	43	37	32	27	23	19	16	62	53	45	39	33	28	24	19	16	14	56	48	39	34	30	26	21	18	16	13	46	38	32	26	25	21	18	15	13	10
4.8	75	64	52	46	40	34	28	25	21	18	68	59	49	42	36	31	26	22	18	14	62	53	45	38	32	27	23	18	15	13	56	48	39	34	29	25	21	18	15	12	45	37	31	25	24	20	17	14	12	09
5.0	75	63	51	45	38	33	28	24	20	16	68	59	48	41	35	30	25	21	18	14	61	52	44	36	31	26	22	19	16	12	56	48	41	34	28	24	20	17	14	11	45	36	30	24	23	19	17	14	12	09
6.0	73	61	49	41	34	29	24	20	16	11	66	55	44	38	31	27	22	18	14	11	60	51	41	35	28	24	19	16	13	09	55	45	37	31	25	21	17	14	11	07	42	34	27	22	20	17	14	12	09	06
7.0	70	58	45	38	31	25	21	17	13	08	64	53	41	35	28	24	19	16	12	07	58	48	38	32	26	22	17	14	11	06	54	43	35	30	24	20	15	12	09	05	41	32	25	21	19	16	13	10	08	05
8.0	68	55	42	35	29	23	19	15	12	06	62	50	38	32	26	22	17	14	11	06	57	46	35	29	23	19	15	13	10	05	53	42	33	28	22	18	14	11	08	03	40	30	24	20	18	15	13	10	07	03
9.0	66	52	40	31	25	21	16	14	11	05	61	49	36	30	23	19	15	13	10	05	56	45	33	27	21	18	14	12	09	04	52	40	31	26	20	16	12	10	07	03	39	29	22	18	16	14	11	09	07	03
10.0	65	51	36	28	22	19	15	11	09	04	59	46	33	27	21	18	14	11	08	03	55	43	31	25	19	16	12	10	08	03	51	39	29	24	18	15	11	09	07	02	37	27	21	17	14	12	09	07	06	02

* Ceiling, floor or floor of cavity.

*The tables in this appendix section have been reproduced with the permission of the Illuminating Engineering Society of North America (IES).

Continued

Per Cent Base* Reflectance	40										30										20										10										0									
Per Cent Wall Reflectance \ Cavity Ratio	90	80	70	60	50	40	30	20	10	0	90	80	70	60	50	40	30	20	10	0	90	80	70	60	50	40	30	20	10	0	90	80	70	60	50	40	30	20	10	0	90	80	70	60	50	40	30	20	10	0
0.2	40	40	39	39	39	39	38	38	37	36	31	31	30	30	29	29	29	28	28	27	21	20	20	20	20	19	19	19	19	17	11	11	11	10	10	10	10	09	09	09	02	02	01	01	01	01	01	00	00	0
0.4	41	40	39	39	38	37	36	35	34	34	31	31	30	30	29	28	28	27	26	25	22	21	20	19	19	19	18	18	18	16	12	11	11	11	10	10	10	09	09	08	04	03	03	02	02	02	01	01	00	0
0.6	41	40	39	38	37	36	34	33	32	31	32	31	31	29	28	27	26	26	25	23	23	22	21	20	19	18	18	17	16	15	13	13	12	11	11	10	10	09	08	08	05	05	04	03	03	02	02	01	01	0
0.8	41	40	38	37	36	35	33	32	31	29	32	31	30	29	28	27	26	25	23	22	24	22	21	20	19	18	17	16	16	14	14	13	12	12	11	11	10	09	08	07	07	06	05	04	04	03	02	02	01	0
1.0	42	40	38	37	35	33	32	31	29	27	33	32	30	29	27	25	24	23	22	20	25	23	22	20	19	18	17	16	15	13	16	14	13	12	12	11	10	09	08	07	08	07	06	05	04	03	03	02	01	0
1.2	42	40	38	36	34	32	30	29	27	25	33	32	30	28	27	25	23	22	21	19	25	23	22	20	19	17	16	14	12	12	17	15	14	13	12	11	10	09	07	06	10	08	07	06	05	04	03	02	01	0
1.4	42	39	37	35	33	31	29	27	25	23	34	32	30	28	26	24	22	21	19	18	26	24	22	20	18	17	15	13	12	12	18	16	14	13	12	11	10	09	07	06	11	09	08	07	06	04	03	02	01	0
1.6	42	39	37	35	32	30	27	25	23	22	34	33	29	27	25	23	22	20	18	17	26	24	22	20	18	16	15	13	11	11	19	17	15	14	12	11	10	08	07	06	12	10	09	07	06	05	03	02	01	0
1.8	42	39	36	34	31	29	26	24	22	21	35	33	29	27	25	23	21	19	17	16	27	25	23	20	18	16	14	13	11	10	19	17	15	14	13	11	09	08	06	06	13	11	09	08	07	05	04	03	02	0
2.0	42	39	36	34	31	28	25	23	21	19	35	33	29	26	24	22	20	18	16	14	28	25	23	20	18	16	14	13	11	09	20	18	16	14	13	11	09	08	06	05	14	12	10	09	07	05	04	03	02	0
2.2	42	39	36	33	30	27	24	22	19	18	36	32	29	26	24	22	19	17	15	13	28	25	23	20	18	16	14	12	10	09	21	19	16	14	13	11	09	07	06	05	15	13	11	09	07	06	04	03	02	0
2.4	43	39	35	33	29	26	24	21	18	17	36	32	29	26	24	22	19	16	14	12	29	26	23	20	18	16	14	12	10	08	22	19	17	15	13	11	09	07	06	05	16	14	11	10	08	06	04	03	02	0
2.6	43	39	35	32	29	25	23	20	17	15	36	32	29	25	23	21	18	16	14	12	29	26	23	20	18	16	14	11	09	08	23	20	17	15	13	11	09	07	06	04	17	14	12	10	08	06	05	03	02	0
2.8	43	39	35	32	28	25	22	18	16	14	37	33	29	25	23	20	18	15	13	11	30	27	23	20	17	15	13	11	09	07	23	20	18	16	13	11	09	07	05	03	17	15	13	10	08	07	05	04	02	0
3.0	43	39	35	31	27	24	21	18	16	13	37	33	29	25	22	20	17	15	12	10	30	27	23	20	17	15	13	11	09	07	24	21	18	16	13	11	09	07	05	03	18	16	13	11	09	07	05	04	03	0
3.2	43	39	35	31	27	23	20	71	15	13	37	33	29	25	22	19	16	14	12	10	31	27	23	20	17	15	12	11	09	06	25	21	18	16	13	11	09	07	05	03	19	16	14	11	09	07	05	04	03	0
3.4	43	39	34	30	26	23	20	17	14	12	37	33	29	25	22	19	16	14	11	09	31	27	23	20	17	15	12	11	08	06	26	22	18	16	15	11	09	07	05	03	20	17	14	12	09	07	06	04	03	0
3.6	44	39	34	30	26	22	19	16	14	11	38	33	29	24	21	18	15	13	10	09	32	27	23	20	17	15	12	10	08	05	26	22	19	16	13	11	09	06	04	03	20	17	15	12	10	08	06	04	03	0
3.8	44	38	33	29	25	22	18	16	13	10	38	33	28	24	21	18	15	13	10	08	32	28	23	20	17	15	12	10	07	05	27	23	19	17	14	11	09	06	04	02	21	18	15	12	10	08	06	05	04	0
4.0	44	38	33	29	25	21	18	15	12	10	38	33	28	24	21	18	14	12	09	07	33	28	23	20	17	14	11	09	07	05	27	23	20	17	14	11	09	06	04	02	22	18	15	13	10	08	06	05	04	0
4.2	44	38	33	29	24	21	17	15	12	10	38	33	28	24	20	17	14	12	09	07	33	28	23	20	17	14	11	09	07	04	28	24	20	17	14	11	09	06	04	02	22	19	16	13	10	08	06	05	04	0
4.4	44	38	33	28	24	20	17	14	11	09	39	33	28	24	20	17	14	11	09	06	34	28	24	20	17	14	11	09	07	04	28	24	20	17	14	11	08	06	04	02	23	19	16	13	10	08	06	05	04	0
4.6	44	38	32	28	23	19	16	14	11	08	39	33	28	24	20	17	13	11	08	06	34	29	24	20	17	14	11	09	07	04	29	25	20	17	14	11	08	06	04	02	23	20	17	13	11	08	06	05	04	0
4.8	44	38	32	27	22	19	16	13	10	08	39	33	28	24	20	17	13	11	08	05	35	29	24	20	16	13	10	08	06	04	29	25	20	17	14	11	08	06	04	02	24	20	17	14	11	08	06	05	04	0
5.0	45	38	31	27	22	19	15	13	10	07	39	33	28	24	19	16	13	10	08	05	35	29	24	20	16	13	10	08	06	04	30	25	20	17	14	11	08	06	04	02	25	21	17	14	11	09	06	05	04	0
6.0	44	37	30	25	20	17	13	11	08	05	39	33	27	23	18	15	11	09	06	04	36	30	24	20	16	13	10	08	05	02	31	26	21	18	14	11	08	06	03	01	27	23	18	15	12	09	06	05	04	0
7.0	44	36	29	24	19	16	12	10	07	04	40	33	26	22	17	14	10	08	05	03	36	30	24	20	15	12	09	07	04	02	32	27	21	17	14	11	08	06	03	01	28	24	19	15	12	09	06	05	04	0
8.0	44	35	28	23	18	15	11	09	06	03	40	33	26	21	16	13	09	07	04	02	37	30	23	19	15	12	08	06	03	01	33	27	21	17	13	10	07	05	03	01	30	25	20	15	13	09	07	06	04	0
9.0	44	35	26	21	16	13	10	08	05	02	40	33	25	20	15	12	09	07	04	02	37	29	23	19	14	11	08	06	03	01	34	28	21	17	13	10	07	05	02	01	31	25	20	15	13	09	07	06	04	0
10.0	43	34	25	20	15	12	08	07	05	02	40	32	24	19	14	11	08	06	03	01	37	29	22	18	13	10	07	05	03	01	34	28	21	17	12	10	07	05	02	01	31	25	20	15	12	09	07	06	04	0

* Ceiling, floor or floor of cavity.

Coefficients of Utilization

Typical Luminaire	Typical Intensity Distribution and Per Cent Lamp Lumens	Maint. Cat.	SC	RCR ↓	ρcc → 80			70			50			30			10			0
				ρw →	50	30	10	50	30	10	50	30	10	50	30	10	50	30	10	0
					Coefficients of Utilization for 20 Per Cent Effective Floor Cavity Reflectance (ρFC = 20)															
1 — Pendant diffusing sphere with incandescent lamp (35½%↑ 45%↓)		V	1.5	0	.87	.87	.87	.81	.81	.81	.70	.70	.70	.59	.59	.59	.49	.49	.49	.45
				1	.71	.67	.63	.66	.62	.59	.56	.53	.50	.47	.45	.42	.38	.37	.35	.31
				2	.60	.54	.49	.56	.50	.45	.47	.43	.39	.39	.36	.33	.32	.29	.27	.23
				3	.52	.45	.39	.48	.42	.37	.41	.36	.31	.34	.30	.26	.27	.24	.22	.18
				4	.46	.38	.33	.42	.36	.30	.36	.30	.26	.30	.26	.22	.24	.21	.18	.15
				5	.40	.33	.27	.37	.30	.25	.31	.26	.22	.26	.22	.18	.21	.18	.15	.12
				6	.36	.28	.23	.33	.26	.21	.28	.23	.19	.23	.19	.16	.19	.15	.13	.10
				7	.32	.25	.20	.29	.23	.18	.25	.20	.16	.21	.16	.13	.17	.13	.11	.09
				8	.29	.22	.17	.26	.20	.16	.23	.17	.14	.19	.15	.12	.15	.12	.09	.07
				9	.26	.19	.15	.24	.18	.14	.20	.15	.12	.17	.13	.10	.14	.11	.08	.06
				10	.23	.17	.13	.22	.16	.12	.19	.14	.10	.16	.12	.09	.13	.09	.07	.05
2 — Concentric ring unit with incandescent silvered-bowl lamp (83%↑ 3½%↓)		II	N.A.	0	.83	.83	.83	.72	.72	.72	.50	.50	.50	.30	.30	.30	.12	.12	.12	.03
				1	.72	.69	.66	.62	.60	.57	.43	.42	.40	.26	.25	.25	.10	.10	.10	.03
				2	.63	.58	.54	.54	.50	.47	.38	.36	.33	.23	.22	.21	.09	.09	.08	.02
				3	.55	.49	.45	.48	.43	.39	.33	.30	.28	.20	.19	.17	.08	.08	.07	.02
				4	.48	.42	.37	.42	.37	.33	.29	.26	.24	.18	.16	.15	.07	.07	.06	.02
				5	.43	.36	.32	.37	.32	.28	.26	.23	.20	.16	.14	.13	.06	.06	.05	.01
				6	.38	.32	.27	.33	.28	.24	.23	.20	.17	.14	.12	.11	.06	.05	.04	.01
				7	.34	.28	.23	.30	.24	.21	.21	.17	.15	.13	.11	.09	.05	.04	.04	.01
				8	.31	.25	.20	.27	.21	.18	.19	.15	.13	.12	.10	.08	.05	.04	.03	.01
				9	.28	.22	.18	.24	.19	.16	.17	.14	.11	.10	.09	.07	.04	.03	.03	.01
				10	.25	.20	.16	.22	.17	.14	.16	.12	.10	.10	.08	.06	.04	.03	.03	.01
3 — Porcelain-enameled ventilated standard dome with incandescent lamp (0%↑ 83½%↓)		IV	1.3	0	.99	.99	.99	.97	.97	.97	.93	.93	.93	.89	.89	.89	.85	.85	.85	.83
				1	.88	.85	.82	.86	.83	.81	.83	.80	.78	.79	.78	.76	.77	.75	.73	.72
				2	.78	.73	.68	.76	.72	.67	.73	.69	.66	.71	.67	.64	.68	.65	.63	.61
				3	.69	.62	.57	.67	.61	.57	.65	.60	.56	.63	.58	.55	.61	.57	.54	.52
				4	.61	.54	.49	.60	.53	.48	.58	.52	.48	.56	.51	.47	.54	.50	.46	.45
				5	.54	.47	.41	.53	.46	.41	.51	.45	.41	.50	.44	.40	.48	.43	.40	.38
				6	.48	.41	.35	.47	.40	.35	.46	.39	.35	.44	.39	.34	.43	.38	.34	.32
				7	.43	.35	.30	.42	.35	.30	.41	.34	.30	.39	.34	.30	.39	.33	.29	.28
				8	.38	.31	.26	.38	.31	.26	.37	.30	.26	.36	.30	.26	.35	.30	.26	.24
				9	.35	.28	.23	.34	.27	.23	.33	.27	.23	.32	.27	.23	.31	.26	.22	.21
				10	.31	.25	.20	.31	.24	.20	.30	.24	.20	.29	.24	.20	.29	.23	.20	.18
4 — Prismatic square surface drum (18½%↑ 60½%↓)		V	1.3	0	.89	.89	.89	.85	.85	.85	.77	.77	.77	.70	.70	.70	.63	.63	.63	.60
				1	.78	.75	.72	.74	.72	.69	.68	.66	.64	.62	.60	.58	.56	.55	.54	.51
				2	.69	.65	.61	.66	.62	.58	.61	.57	.54	.56	.53	.50	.51	.49	.47	.44
				3	.62	.57	.52	.60	.55	.50	.55	.51	.47	.50	.47	.44	.46	.43	.41	.39
				4	.56	.50	.46	.54	.49	.44	.50	.45	.42	.46	.42	.39	.42	.39	.37	.35
				5	.51	.45	.40	.49	.43	.39	.45	.41	.37	.42	.38	.35	.39	.36	.33	.31
				6	.46	.40	.36	.45	.39	.35	.42	.37	.33	.39	.35	.31	.36	.32	.30	.28
				7	.42	.36	.32	.41	.35	.31	.38	.33	.29	.35	.31	.28	.33	.29	.27	.25
				8	.38	.32	.28	.37	.32	.28	.35	.30	.26	.32	.28	.25	.30	.27	.24	.22
				9	.35	.29	.25	.34	.29	.25	.32	.27	.24	.30	.26	.23	.28	.24	.22	.20
				10	.32	.27	.23	.31	.26	.22	.29	.25	.21	.27	.23	.20	.26	.22	.20	.18
5 — R-40 flood without shielding (0%↑ 100%↓)		IV	0.8	0	1.19	1.19	1.19	1.16	1.16	1.16	1.11	1.11	1.11	1.06	1.06	1.06	1.02	1.02	1.02	1.00
				1	1.09	1.07	1.04	1.07	1.05	1.02	1.03	1.01	.99	.99	.98	.96	.96	.95	.93	.92
				2	1.01	.97	.93	.99	.95	.92	.96	.93	.90	.93	.90	.88	.90	.88	.86	.84
				3	.93	.88	.84	.92	.87	.83	.89	.85	.81	.87	.83	.80	.84	.81	.79	.77
				4	.87	.81	.76	.85	.80	.75	.83	.78	.75	.81	.77	.74	.79	.76	.73	.71
				5	.80	.74	.69	.79	.73	.69	.77	.72	.68	.76	.71	.67	.74	.70	.67	.65
				6	.74	.68	.63	.73	.67	.63	.72	.66	.62	.70	.66	.62	.69	.65	.61	.60
				7	.69	.62	.57	.68	.62	.57	.67	.61	.57	.65	.60	.56	.64	.60	.56	.55
				8	.64	.57	.53	.63	.57	.52	.62	.56	.52	.61	.56	.52	.60	.55	.52	.50
				9	.59	.52	.48	.59	.52	.48	.58	.52	.48	.57	.51	.48	.56	.51	.47	.46
				10	.55	.49	.44	.55	.48	.44	.54	.48	.44	.53	.48	.44	.52	.47	.44	.42
6 — R-40 flood with specular anodized reflector skirt; 45° cutoff (0%↑ 85%↓)		IV	0.7	0	1.01	1.01	1.01	.99	.99	.99	.94	.94	.94	.90	.90	.90	.87	.87	.87	.85
				1	.96	.94	.92	.94	.92	.91	.90	.89	.88	.87	.86	.85	.84	.84	.83	.82
				2	.91	.88	.86	.90	.87	.85	.87	.85	.83	.84	.83	.82	.82	.81	.80	.79
				3	.87	.84	.81	.86	.83	.81	.84	.81	.79	.82	.80	.78	.80	.78	.77	.76
				4	.83	.80	.77	.82	.79	.77	.81	.78	.76	.79	.77	.75	.78	.76	.74	.73
				5	.79	.76	.73	.79	.75	.73	.77	.74	.72	.76	.73	.71	.75	.73	.71	.70
				6	.76	.73	.70	.76	.72	.70	.75	.72	.69	.74	.71	.69	.73	.70	.68	.67
				7	.73	.69	.66	.73	.69	.66	.72	.68	.66	.71	.68	.66	.70	.67	.65	.64
				8	.70	.66	.63	.70	.66	.63	.69	.65	.63	.68	.65	.63	.67	.65	.63	.62
				9	.67	.63	.60	.67	.63	.60	.66	.62	.60	.65	.62	.60	.65	.62	.60	.59
				10	.64	.60	.58	.64	.60	.58	.63	.60	.58	.63	.60	.57	.62	.59	.57	.56

Continued

Typical Luminaire	Maint. Cat.	SC	RCR ↓	ρcc → 80, ρw 50	30	10	70, 50	30	10	50, 50	30	10	30, 50	30	10	10, 50	30	10	0
7 — EAR-38 lamp above 51 mm (2″) diameter aperture (increase efficiency to 54 ½% for 76 mm (3″) diameter aperture)* (0% ↑, 43½% ↓)	IV	0.7	0	.52	.52	.52	.51	.51	.51	.48	.48	.48	.46	.46	.46	.45	.45	.45	.44
			1	.49	.48	.48	.48	.48	.47	.47	.46	.46	.45	.45	.44	.44	.43	.43	.42
			2	.47	.46	.45	.46	.45	.44	.45	.44	.43	.44	.43	.42	.43	.42	.42	.41
			3	.45	.44	.43	.45	.43	.42	.44	.42	.42	.43	.42	.41	.42	.41	.40	.40
			4	.43	.42	.41	.43	.41	.40	.42	.41	.40	.41	.40	.39	.41	.40	.39	.38
			5	.42	.40	.39	.41	.40	.38	.41	.39	.38	.40	.39	.38	.39	.38	.38	.37
			6	.40	.39	.37	.40	.38	.37	.39	.38	.37	.39	.38	.37	.38	.37	.36	.36
			7	.39	.37	.36	.39	.37	.36	.38	.37	.35	.38	.36	.35	.37	.36	.35	.35
			8	.37	.36	.34	.37	.35	.34	.37	.35	.34	.36	.35	.34	.36	.35	.34	.33
			9	.36	.34	.33	.36	.34	.33	.35	.34	.33	.35	.34	.33	.35	.33	.33	.32
			10	.35	.33	.32	.35	.33	.32	.34	.33	.32	.34	.33	.32	.34	.32	.31	.31
8 — Medium distribution unit with lens plate and inside frost lamp (0% ↑, 54½% ↓)	V	1.0	0	.65	.65	.65	.63	.63	.63	.60	.60	.60	.58	.58	.58	.55	.55	.55	.54
			1	.60	.58	.57	.58	.57	.56	.56	.55	.54	.54	.53	.52	.52	.52	.51	.50
			2	.55	.53	.51	.54	.52	.50	.52	.50	.49	.51	.49	.48	.49	.48	.47	.46
			3	.51	.48	.46	.50	.47	.45	.49	.46	.44	.47	.45	.44	.46	.44	.43	.42
			4	.47	.44	.41	.47	.44	.41	.45	.43	.41	.44	.42	.40	.43	.41	.40	.39
			5	.44	.40	.38	.43	.40	.38	.42	.39	.37	.41	.39	.37	.40	.38	.37	.36
			6	.41	.37	.35	.40	.37	.35	.39	.36	.34	.39	.36	.34	.38	.36	.34	.33
			7	.38	.34	.32	.37	.34	.32	.37	.34	.31	.36	.33	.31	.35	.33	.31	.30
			8	.35	.32	.29	.35	.31	.29	.34	.31	.29	.34	.31	.29	.33	.30	.29	.28
			9	.33	.29	.27	.32	.29	.27	.32	.29	.26	.31	.28	.26	.31	.28	.26	.25
			10	.30	.27	.25	.30	.27	.24	.30	.27	.24	.29	.26	.24	.29	.26	.24	.23
9 — Recessed baffled downlight, 140 mm (5 ½″) diameter aperture—150-PAR/FL lamp (0% ↑, 68½% ↓)	IV	0.5	0	.82	.82	.82	.80	.80	.80	.76	.76	.76	.73	.73	.73	.70	.70	.70	.69
			1	.78	.77	.76	.77	.76	.75	.74	.74	.73	.72	.71	.71	.69	.69	.69	.68
			2	.76	.74	.73	.75	.73	.72	.73	.71	.70	.71	.70	.69	.69	.68	.67	.67
			3	.74	.72	.70	.73	.71	.70	.71	.70	.69	.70	.69	.68	.68	.67	.67	.66
			4	.72	.70	.68	.71	.69	.68	.70	.68	.67	.69	.67	.66	.67	.66	.66	.65
			5	.70	.68	.66	.69	.67	.66	.68	.67	.65	.67	.66	.65	.67	.65	.64	.64
			6	.69	.66	.65	.68	.66	.65	.67	.66	.64	.67	.65	.64	.66	.65	.64	.63
			7	.67	.65	.63	.67	.65	.63	.66	.64	.63	.65	.64	.63	.65	.64	.62	.62
			8	.66	.64	.62	.65	.63	.62	.65	.63	.62	.64	.63	.62	.64	.62	.61	.61
			9	.65	.63	.61	.64	.62	.61	.64	.62	.61	.63	.62	.61	.63	.62	.61	.60
			10	.63	.61	.60	.63	.61	.60	.63	.61	.60	.62	.61	.60	.62	.61	.60	.59
10 — Recessed baffled downlight, 140 mm (5 ½″) diameter aperture—75ER30 lamp (0% ↑, 85% ↓)	IV	0.5	0	1.01	1.01	1.01	.99	.99	.99	.95	.95	.95	.91	.91	.91	.87	.87	.87	.85
			1	.97	.95	.94	.95	.94	.92	.92	.91	.90	.88	.88	.87	.86	.85	.84	.83
			2	.93	.91	.89	.91	.89	.88	.89	.87	.86	.86	.85	.84	.84	.83	.82	.81
			3	.90	.87	.85	.89	.86	.84	.87	.85	.83	.85	.83	.82	.83	.82	.81	.79
			4	.87	.84	.82	.86	.83	.81	.84	.82	.80	.83	.81	.79	.81	.80	.79	.78
			5	.84	.81	.79	.83	.80	.78	.82	.79	.78	.81	.79	.77	.80	.78	.76	.75
			6	.82	.79	.76	.81	.78	.76	.80	.78	.76	.79	.77	.75	.78	.76	.75	.74
			7	.79	.76	.74	.79	.76	.74	.78	.75	.73	.77	.75	.73	.76	.74	.73	.72
			8	.77	.74	.72	.77	.74	.72	.76	.73	.71	.75	.73	.71	.75	.72	.71	.70
			9	.75	.72	.70	.75	.72	.70	.74	.71	.69	.73	.71	.69	.73	.71	.69	.68
			10	.73	.70	.68	.73	.70	.68	.72	.69	.68	.72	.69	.67	.71	.69	.67	.67
11 — Wide distribution unit with lens plate and inside frost lamp (0% ↑, 53½% ↓)	V	1.4	0	.63	.63	.63	.62	.62	.62	.59	.59	.59	.57	.57	.57	.54	.54	.54	.53
			1	.58	.56	.54	.57	.55	.54	.54	.53	.52	.52	.51	.50	.50	.50	.49	.48
			2	.53	.50	.48	.52	.49	.47	.50	.48	.46	.48	.47	.45	.47	.45	.44	.43
			3	.48	.45	.42	.47	.44	.42	.46	.43	.41	.44	.42	.40	.43	.41	.40	.39
			4	.44	.40	.37	.43	.40	.37	.42	.39	.37	.41	.38	.36	.40	.37	.36	.35
			5	.40	.36	.33	.39	.36	.33	.38	.35	.33	.37	.35	.32	.36	.34	.32	.31
			6	.36	.32	.30	.36	.32	.29	.35	.32	.29	.34	.31	.29	.33	.31	.29	.28
			7	.33	.29	.26	.33	.29	.26	.32	.28	.26	.31	.28	.26	.30	.28	.26	.25
			8	.30	.26	.23	.30	.26	.23	.29	.26	.23	.28	.25	.23	.28	.25	.23	.22
			9	.27	.23	.21	.27	.23	.21	.26	.23	.21	.26	.23	.20	.25	.22	.20	.19
			10	.25	.21	.18	.25	.21	.18	.24	.21	.18	.24	.20	.18	.23	.20	.18	.17
12 — Recessed unit with dropped diffusing glass (1½% ↑, 50½% ↓)	V	1.3	0	.62	.62	.62	.60	.60	.60	.57	.57	.57	.54	.54	.54	.52	.52	.52	.51
			1	.53	.51	.48	.52	.49	.47	.49	.47	.46	.47	.45	.44	.45	.43	.42	.41
			2	.46	.42	.39	.45	.42	.39	.43	.40	.38	.41	.39	.36	.39	.37	.35	.34
			3	.40	.36	.33	.40	.35	.32	.38	.34	.31	.36	.33	.31	.35	.32	.30	.29
			4	.36	.31	.28	.35	.31	.28	.34	.30	.27	.32	.29	.26	.31	.28	.26	.25
			5	.32	.27	.24	.31	.27	.24	.30	.26	.23	.29	.25	.23	.28	.25	.22	.21
			6	.29	.24	.20	.28	.24	.20	.27	.23	.20	.26	.22	.20	.25	.22	.19	.18
			7	.26	.21	.18	.25	.21	.18	.24	.20	.17	.23	.20	.17	.22	.19	.17	.16
			8	.23	.19	.16	.23	.18	.15	.22	.18	.15	.21	.18	.15	.20	.17	.15	.14
			9	.21	.17	.14	.21	.16	.14	.20	.16	.13	.19	.16	.13	.19	.15	.13	.12
			10	.19	.15	.12	.19	.15	.12	.18	.14	.12	.18	.14	.12	.17	.14	.12	.11

Note: Coefficients of Utilization for 20 Per Cent Effective Floor Cavity Reflectance (ρFC = 20).

* Also, reflector downlight with baffles and inside frosted lamp.

Continued

Typical Luminaire	Typical Intensity Distribution and Per Cent Lamp Lumens			ρcc → 80			70			50			30			10			0
	Maint. Cat.	SC	ρw →	50	30	10	50	30	10	50	30	10	50	30	10	50	30	10	0
			RCR ↓	Coefficients of Utilization for 20 Per Cent Effective Floor Cavity Reflectance (ρFC = 20)															
13 Bilateral batwing distribution—clear HID with dropped prismatic lens	V (2½%↑ 45° 71%↓)	N.A.	0	.87	.87	87	.85	.85	.85	.80	.80	.80	.76	.76	.76	.73	.73	.73	.71
			1	.76	.73	.70	.74	.71	.69	.71	.68	.66	.67	.65	.64	.64	.63	.61	.60
			2	.67	.62	.58	.66	.61	.57	.63	.59	.56	.60	.57	.54	.57	.55	.53	.51
			3	.59	.54	.49	.58	.53	.48	.56	.51	.47	.53	.49	.46	.51	.48	.45	.43
			4	.53	.47	.42	.52	.46	.42	.50	.45	.41	.48	.44	.40	.46	.42	.39	.38
			5	.47	.41	.36	.46	.40	.36	.44	.39	.35	.43	.38	.35	.41	.37	.34	.32
			6	.42	.36	.31	.41	.35	.31	.40	.34	.30	.38	.33	.30	.37	.33	.29	.28
			7	.37	.31	.26	.37	.31	.26	.35	.30	.26	.34	.29	.25	.33	.28	.25	.24
			8	.34	.27	.23	.33	.27	.23	.32	.26	.22	.31	.26	.22	.30	.25	.22	.20
			9	.30	.24	.20	.29	.24	.20	.28	.23	.19	.27	.23	.19	.27	.22	.19	.17
			10	.27	.21	.17	.27	.21	.17	.26	.20	.17	.25	.20	.17	.24	.19	.16	.15
14 Clear HID lamp and glass refractor above plastic lens panel	V (0%↑ 66%↓)	1.3	0	.78	.78	.78	.77	.77	.77	.73	.73	.73	.70	.70	.70	.67	.67	.67	.66
			1	.71	.69	.67	.70	.68	.66	.67	.66	.64	.65	.64	.62	.62	.61	.61	.59
			2	.65	.62	.59	.64	.61	.58	.62	.59	.57	.60	.58	.56	.58	.56	.55	.54
			3	.59	.55	.52	.58	.55	.52	.57	.53	.51	.55	.52	.50	.53	.51	.49	.48
			4	.54	.50	.47	.54	.49	.46	.52	.49	.46	.51	.48	.45	.49	.47	.45	.43
			5	.50	.45	.42	.49	.45	.41	.48	.44	.41	.47	.43	.41	.46	.43	.40	.39
			6	.46	.41	.37	.45	.40	.37	.44	.40	.37	.43	.39	.37	.42	.39	.36	.35
			7	.41	.37	.33	.41	.36	.33	.40	.36	.33	.39	.35	.33	.38	.35	.32	.31
			8	.38	.33	.30	.38	.33	.30	.37	.33	.30	.36	.32	.29	.35	.32	.29	.28
			9	.35	.30	.27	.34	.30	.27	.34	.29	.26	.33	.29	.26	.32	.29	.26	.25
			10	.32	.27	.24	.31	.27	.24	.31	.27	.24	.30	.26	.24	.30	.26	.23	.22
15 Enclosed reflector with an incandescent lamp	V (0%↑ 71½%↓)	1.4	0	.85	.85	.85	.83	.83	83	.80	.80	.80	.76	.76	.76	.73	.73	.73	.72
			1	.78	.76	.74	.76	.74	.73	.73	.72	.70	.71	.69	.68	.68	.67	.66	.65
			2	.71	.68	.65	.70	.67	.64	.68	.65	.63	.65	.63	.61	.63	.62	.60	.59
			3	65	.61	.57	.64	.60	.57	.62	.59	.56	.60	.57	.55	.59	.56	.54	.53
			4	.60	.55	.51	.59	.54	.51	.57	.53	.50	.55	.52	.50	.54	.51	.49	.48
			5	.54	.49	.45	.54	.49	.45	.52	.48	.45	.51	.47	.44	.50	.46	.44	.43
			6	.49	.44	.40	.49	.44	.40	.48	.43	.40	.46	.42	.40	.45	.42	.39	.38
			7	.44	.39	.35	.44	.39	.35	.43	.38	.35	.42	.38	.35	.41	.37	.35	.33
			8	.40	.35	.31	.40	.35	.31	.39	.35	.31	.38	.34	.31	.38	.34	.31	.30
			9	.37	.31	.28	.36	.31	.28	.36	.31	.28	.35	.31	.28	.34	.30	.27	.26
			10	.33	.28	.25	.33	.28	.25	.32	.28	.25	.32	.28	.25	.31	.27	.24	.23
16 "High bay" narrow distribution ventilated reflector with clear HID lamp	III (1½%↑ 77%↑)	0.7	0	.93	.93	.93	.90	.90	.90	.86	.86	.86	.82	.82	.82	.78	.78	.78	77
			1	.87	.85	.83	.85	.83	.82	.81	.80	.79	.78	.77	.76	.75	.75	.74	72
			2	.81	.79	.76	.80	.77	.75	.77	.75	.73	.75	.73	.72	.72	.71	.70	69
			3	.77	.73	.71	.76	.72	.70	.73	.71	.69	.71	.69	.67	.70	.68	.66	65
			4	.73	.69	.66	.72	.68	.65	.70	.67	.64	.68	.66	.64	.67	.65	.63	62
			5	.69	.65	.62	.68	.64	.61	.66	.63	.61	.65	.62	.60	.64	.61	.59	.58
			6	.65	.61	.58	.64	.61	.58	.63	.60	.57	.62	.59	.57	.61	.58	.56	.55
			7	.62	.57	.54	.61	.57	.54	.60	.56	.54	.59	.56	.53	.58	.55	.53	.52
			8	.58	.54	.51	.58	.54	.51	.57	.53	.51	.56	.53	.51	.55	.52	.50	.49
			9	.55	.51	.48	.55	.51	.48	.54	.50	.48	.53	.50	.48	.53	.50	.48	.47
			10	.53	.49	.46	.52	.48	.46	.52	.48	.46	.51	.48	.45	.50	.47	.45	.44
17 "High bay" intermediate distribution ventilated reflector with clear HID lamp	III (1%↑ 76%↓)	1.0	0	.91	.91	.91	.89	.89	.89	.85	.85	.85	.81	.81	.81	.78	.78	.78	.76
			1	.84	.82	.80	.82	.80	.78	.79	.77	.76	.76	.74	.73	.73	.72	.71	.69
			2	.77	.73	.70	.76	.72	.70	.73	.70	.68	.70	.68	.66	.68	.66	.65	.63
			3	.71	.66	.63	.69	.65	.62	.67	.64	.61	.65	.62	.60	.63	.61	.59	.57
			4	.65	.60	.56	.64	.59	.56	.62	.58	.55	.60	.57	.54	.59	.56	.54	.52
			5	.59	.54	.50	.59	.54	.50	.57	.53	.50	.56	.52	.49	.54	.51	.48	.47
			6	.54	.49	.45	.54	.49	.45	.52	.48	.45	.51	.47	.44	.50	.47	.44	.42
			7	.50	.44	.40	.49	.44	.40	.48	.43	.40	.47	.43	.39	.46	.42	.39	.38
			8	.45	.40	.36	.45	.40	.36	.44	.39	.36	.43	.39	.35	.42	.38	.35	.34
			9	.41	.36	.32	.41	.36	.32	.40	.35	.32	.39	.35	.32	.38	.35	.32	.30
			10	.38	.33	.29	.37	.32	.29	.37	.32	.29	.36	.32	.29	.35	.31	.28	.27
18 "High bay" wide distribution ventilated reflector with clear HID lamp	III (½%↑ 77½%↓)	1.5	0	.93	.93	.93	.91	.91	.91	.87	.87	.87	.83	.83	.83	.79	.79	.79	.78
			1	.85	.82	.80	.83	.81	.79	.79	.78	.76	.76	.75	.74	.74	.72	.71	.70
			2	.77	.73	.70	.76	.72	.69	.73	.70	.67	.70	.68	.66	.68	.66	.64	.63
			3	.70	.65	.61	.68	.64	.60	.66	.62	.59	.64	.61	.58	.62	.59	.57	.56
			4	.63	.58	.53	.62	.57	.53	.60	.56	.52	.58	.55	.52	.57	.54	.51	.49
			5	.57	.51	.47	.56	.51	.47	.55	.50	.46	.53	.49	.46	.52	.48	.45	.44
			6	.51	.45	.41	.51	.45	.41	.49	.44	.40	.48	.43	.40	.47	.43	.40	.38
			7	.46	.40	.35	.45	.39	.35	.44	.39	.35	.43	.38	.35	.42	.38	.34	.33
			8	.41	.35	.31	.41	.35	.31	.40	.34	.31	.39	.34	.30	.38	.33	.30	.29
			9	.37	.31	.27	.37	.31	.27	.36	.30	.27	.35	.30	.27	.34	.30	.26	.25
			10	.33	.28	.24	.33	.27	.23	.32	.27	.23	.31	.27	.23	.31	.26	.23	.22

Continued

Typical Luminaire	Typical Intensity Distribution and Per Cent Lamp Lumens			ρcc →	80			70			50			30			10			0
		Maint. Cat.	SC	ρw →	50	30	10	50	30	10	50	30	10	50	30	10	50	30	10	0
				RCR ↓	Coefficients of Utilization for 20 Per Cent Effective Floor Cavity Reflectance (ρ_FC = 20)															
19 "High bay" intermediate distribution ventilated reflector with phosphor coated HID lamp (6½% ↑, 75½% ↓)		III	1.0	0	.96	.96	.96	.93	.93	.93	.88	.88	.88	.83	.83	.83	.78	.78	.78	.76
				1	.89	.87	.84	.86	.84	.83	.82	.80	.79	.78	.76	.75	.74	.73	.72	.70
				2	.82	.79	.76	.80	.77	.74	.76	.74	.72	.73	.71	.69	.70	.68	.67	.65
				3	.76	.72	.68	.74	.70	.67	.71	.68	.65	.68	.66	.63	.66	.63	.62	.60
				4	.70	.66	.62	.69	.65	.61	.66	.63	.60	.64	.61	.58	.62	.59	.57	.55
				5	.65	.60	.56	.64	.59	.56	.62	.58	.54	.60	.56	.53	.58	.55	.52	.51
				6	.60	.55	.51	.59	.55	.51	.57	.53	.50	.56	.52	.49	.54	.51	.48	.47
				7	.56	.50	.47	.55	.50	.46	.53	.49	.46	.52	.48	.45	.50	.47	.44	.43
				8	.52	.47	.43	.51	.46	.43	.50	.45	.42	.48	.44	.41	.47	.43	.41	.40
				9	.48	.43	.39	.47	.42	.39	.46	.42	.39	.45	.41	.38	.44	.40	.38	.36
				10	.45	.40	.36	.44	.39	.36	.43	.39	.36	.42	.38	.35	.41	.37	.35	.34
20 "High bay" wide distribution ventilated reflector with phosphor coated HID lamp (12% ↑, 69% ↓)		III	1.5	0	.93	.93	.93	.90	.90	.90	.83	.83	.83	.77	.77	.77	.72	.72	.72	.69
				1	.85	.83	.81	.82	.80	.78	.77	.75	.74	.72	.71	.69	.67	.66	.65	.63
				2	.78	.74	.71	.76	.72	.69	.71	.68	.66	.67	.65	.63	.63	.61	.60	.58
				3	.71	.67	.63	.69	.65	.62	.65	.62	.59	.62	.59	.57	.58	.56	.54	.53
				4	.65	.60	.56	.64	.59	.55	.60	.56	.53	.57	.54	.51	.54	.52	.50	.48
				5	.60	.54	.50	.58	.53	.49	.55	.51	.48	.53	.49	.46	.50	.47	.45	.43
				6	.54	.49	.45	.53	.48	.44	.51	.46	.43	.48	.45	.42	.46	.43	.40	.39
				7	.49	.44	.40	.48	.43	.39	.46	.41	.38	.44	.40	.37	.42	.39	.36	.34
				8	.45	.39	.35	.44	.38	.35	.42	.37	.34	.40	.36	.33	.38	.35	.32	.31
				9	.41	.35	.31	.40	.34	.31	.38	.34	.30	.37	.33	.29	.35	.31	.28	.27
				10	.37	.31	.27	.36	.31	.27	.34	.30	.26	.33	.29	.26	.32	.28	.25	.24
21 "Low bay" rectangular pattern, lensed bottom reflector unit with clear HID lamp (0% ↑, 68½% ↓)		V	1.8	0	.82	.82	.82	.80	.80	.80	.76	.76	.76	.73	.73	.73	.70	.70	.70	.68
				1	.73	.71	.69	.72	.69	.67	.69	.67	.65	.66	.65	.63	.64	.63	.61	.60
				2	.66	.62	.58	.64	.61	.58	.62	.59	.56	.60	.57	.55	.58	.56	.54	.53
				3	.58	.54	.50	.57	.53	.49	.55	.52	.48	.54	.50	.48	.52	.49	.47	.45
				4	.52	.47	.43	.51	.46	.43	.50	.45	.42	.48	.45	.42	.47	.44	.41	.40
				5	.47	.41	.37	.46	.41	.37	.45	.40	.36	.43	.39	.36	.42	.38	.36	.34
				6	.42	.36	.32	.41	.36	.32	.40	.35	.31	.39	.34	.31	.38	.34	.31	.29
				7	.37	.31	.27	.36	.31	.27	.35	.30	.27	.34	.30	.26	.33	.29	.26	.25
				8	.33	.27	.23	.32	.27	.23	.31	.26	.23	.31	.26	.23	.30	.26	.23	.21
				9	.29	.24	.20	.29	.23	.20	.28	.23	.20	.27	.23	.19	.27	.22	.19	.18
				10	.26	.20	.17	.26	.20	.17	.25	.20	.17	.24	.20	.17	.24	.20	.17	.15
22 "Low bay" lensed bottom reflector unit with clear HID lamp (3% ↑, 68% ↓)		V	1.9	0	.83	.83	.83	.81	.81	.81	.77	.77	.77	.73	.73	.73	.70	.70	.70	.68
				1	.73	.70	.67	.71	.68	.66	.67	.65	.63	.64	.62	.61	.61	.60	.58	.57
				2	.64	.59	.55	.62	.58	.54	.59	.56	.52	.57	.54	.51	.54	.52	.49	.48
				3	.56	.50	.45	.54	.49	.45	.52	.47	.44	.50	.46	.43	.47	.44	.42	.40
				4	.49	.43	.38	.48	.42	.38	.46	.41	.37	.44	.40	.36	.42	.39	.36	.34
				5	.43	.37	.32	.42	.36	.32	.41	.35	.31	.39	.34	.31	.37	.33	.30	.29
				6	.38	.32	.27	.37	.31	.27	.36	.30	.26	.34	.30	.26	.33	.29	.25	.24
				7	.34	.27	.23	.33	.27	.22	.31	.26	.22	.30	.25	.22	.29	.25	.21	.20
				8	.30	.24	.19	.29	.23	.19	.28	.23	.19	.27	.22	.19	.26	.22	.18	.17
				9	.27	.21	.16	.26	.20	.16	.25	.20	.16	.24	.19	.16	.23	.19	.16	.14
				10	.24	.18	.14	.24	.18	.14	.23	.17	.14	.22	.17	.14	.21	.17	.13	.12
23 Wide spread, recessed, small open bottom reflector with low wattage diffuse HID lamp (0% ↑, 56% ↓)		IV	1.7	0	.67	.67	.67	.65	.65	.65	.62	.62	.62	.60	.60	.60	.57	.57	.57	.56
				1	.60	.58	.57	.59	.57	.56	.57	.55	.54	.54	.53	.52	.52	.52	.51	.50
				2	.54	.51	.48	.53	.50	.48	.51	.49	.47	.49	.47	.46	.48	.46	.45	.44
				3	.48	.44	.41	.47	.44	.41	.46	.43	.40	.44	.42	.40	.43	.41	.39	.38
				4	.43	.39	.36	.42	.38	.35	.41	.38	.35	.40	.37	.34	.39	.36	.34	.33
				5	.38	.34	.30	.38	.34	.30	.37	.33	.30	.36	.32	.30	.35	.32	.29	.28
				6	.34	.30	.26	.34	.29	.26	.33	.29	.26	.32	.28	.26	.31	.28	.25	.24
				7	.30	.26	.22	.30	.26	.22	.29	.25	.22	.29	.25	.22	.28	.24	.22	.21
				8	.27	.23	.19	.27	.22	.19	.26	.22	.19	.25	.22	.19	.25	.21	.19	.18
				9	.24	.20	.17	.24	.20	.17	.23	.19	.17	.23	.19	.16	.22	.19	.16	.15
				10	.22	.17	.14	.22	.17	.14	.21	.17	.14	.21	.17	.14	.20	.17	.14	.13
24 Open top, indirect, reflector type unit with HID lamp (mult. by 0.9 for lens top) (78% ↑, 0% ↓)		VI	N.A.	0	.74	.74	.74	.63	.63	.63	.43	.43	.43	.25	.25	.25	.08	.08	.08	.00
				1	.64	.62	.59	.55	.53	.51	.38	.36	.35	.22	.21	.20	.07	.07	.07	.00
				2	.56	.52	.48	.48	.45	.42	.33	.31	.29	.19	.18	.17	.06	.06	.06	.00
				3	.49	.44	.40	.42	.38	.35	.29	.26	.24	.17	.15	.14	.05	.05	.05	.00
				4	.43	.38	.33	.37	.33	.29	.26	.23	.20	.15	.13	.12	.05	.04	.04	.00
				5	.38	.33	.28	.33	.28	.25	.23	.20	.17	.13	.12	.10	.04	.04	.03	.00
				6	.34	.28	.24	.29	.25	.21	.20	.17	.15	.12	.10	.09	.04	.03	.03	.00
				7	.31	.25	.21	.26	.22	.18	.18	.15	.13	.11	.09	.08	.03	.03	.03	.00
				8	.28	.22	.18	.24	.19	.16	.16	.13	.11	.10	.08	.07	.03	.03	.02	.00
				9	.25	.20	.16	.21	.17	.14	.15	.12	.10	.09	.07	.06	.03	.02	.02	.00
				10	.23	.18	.14	.20	.15	.12	.14	.11	.09	.08	.06	.05	.03	.02	.02	.00

Continued

Typical Luminaire	Typical Intensity Distribution and Per Cent Lamp Lumens			ρcc → 80			70			50			30			10			0
	Maint. Cat.	SC	RCR ↓	ρw → 50	30	10	50	30	10	50	30	10	50	30	10	50	30	10	0
				Coefficients of Utilization for 20 Per Cent Effective Floor Cavity Reflectance (ρFC = 20)															
25 Porcelain-enameled reflector with 35°CW shielding (II, SC 1.3, 22½%↑, 65%↓)	II	1.3	0	.99	.99	.99	.94	.94	.94	.85	.85	.85	.77	.77	.77	.69	.69	.69	.65
			1	.88	.85	.82	.84	.81	.78	.76	.74	.72	.69	.67	.66	.62	.61	.60	.57
			2	.78	.73	.69	.74	.70	.66	.68	.64	.61	.62	.59	.56	.56	.54	.52	.49
			3	.70	.63	.58	.67	.61	.57	.61	.56	.53	.56	.52	.49	.51	.48	.46	.43
			4	.62	.55	.50	.60	.53	.49	.55	.50	.46	.50	.46	.43	.46	.43	.40	.37
			5	.55	.48	.43	.53	.47	.42	.49	.44	.39	.45	.41	.37	.41	.38	.35	.32
			6	.50	.43	.38	.48	.41	.37	.44	.39	.35	.41	.36	.33	.37	.34	.31	.29
			7	.45	.38	.33	.43	.37	.32	.40	.34	.30	.37	.32	.29	.34	.30	.27	.25
			8	.40	.34	.29	.39	.32	.28	.36	.30	.27	.33	.28	.25	.31	.27	.24	.22
			9	.36	.30	.25	.35	.29	.24	.32	.27	.23	.30	.25	.22	.28	.24	.21	.19
			10	.33	.27	.22	.32	.26	.22	.29	.24	.20	.27	.23	.19	.25	.21	.18	.17
26 Diffuse aluminum reflector with 35°CW shielding (II, SC 1.5/1.3, 17%↑, 66%↓)	II	1.5/1.3	0	.95	.95	.95	.91	.91	.91	.83	.83	.83	.76	.76	.76	.69	.69	.69	.66
			1	.85	.82	.80	.82	.79	.77	.75	.73	.72	.69	.68	.66	.64	.63	.62	.59
			2	.76	.72	.68	.74	.70	.66	.68	.65	.62	.63	.61	.58	.58	.56	.55	.52
			3	.69	.63	.59	.66	.61	.57	.62	.58	.54	.57	.54	.51	.53	.51	.48	.46
			4	.62	.56	.51	.60	.54	.50	.56	.51	.47	.52	.48	.45	.48	.45	.43	.41
			5	.55	.49	.44	.53	.48	.43	.50	.45	.41	.47	.43	.39	.44	.40	.38	.36
			6	.50	.43	.39	.48	.42	.38	.45	.40	.36	.42	.38	.35	.40	.36	.33	.31
			7	.45	.38	.34	.43	.37	.33	.41	.36	.32	.38	.34	.30	.36	.32	.29	.27
			8	.40	.34	.29	.39	.33	.29	.37	.31	.28	.34	.30	.26	.32	.28	.25	.24
			9	.36	.30	.25	.35	.29	.25	33	.28	.24	.31	.26	.23	.29	.25	.22	.20
			10	.33	.26	.22	.32	.26	.22	.30	.25	.21	.28	.23	.20	.26	.22	.19	.18
27 Porcelain-enameled reflector with 30°CW × 30°LW shielding (II, SC 1.0, 23½%↑, 57%↓)	II	1.0	0	.91	.91	.91	.86	.86	.86	.77	.77	.77	.68	.68	.68	.61	.61	.61	.57
			1	.81	.78	.76	.77	.74	.72	.69	.67	.66	.62	.61	.59	.56	.55	.54	.51
			2	.72	.68	.64	.69	.65	.61	.62	.59	.57	.56	.54	.52	.51	.49	.47	.45
			3	.65	.59	.55	.62	.57	.53	.56	.52	.49	.51	.48	.45	.46	.44	.42	.39
			4	.58	.52	.48	.56	.50	.46	.51	.46	.43	.46	.43	.40	.42	.39	.37	.35
			5	.52	.46	.41	.50	.44	.40	.46	.41	.37	.42	.38	.35	.38	.35	.33	.30
			6	.47	.41	.36	.45	.39	.35	.41	.37	.33	.38	.34	.31	.35	.31	.29	.27
			7	.43	.36	.32	.41	.35	.31	.38	.33	.29	.34	.30	.27	.32	.28	.26	.24
			8	.38	.32	.28	.37	.31	.27	.34	.29	.26	.31	.27	.24	.29	.25	.23	.21
			9	.35	.29	.24	.33	.28	.24	.31	.26	.22	.28	.24	.21	.26	.22	.20	.18
			10	.32	.26	.22	.30	.25	.21	.28	.23	.20	.26	22	.19	.24	.20	.18	.16
28 Diffuse aluminum reflector with 35°CW × 35°LW shielding (II, SC 1.5/1.1, 17%↑, 56½%↓)	II	1.5/1.1	0	.83	.83	.83	.79	.79	.79	.72	.72	.72	.65	.65	.65	.59	.59	.59	.56
			1	.75	.72	.70	.72	.69	.67	.65	.64	.62	.60	.59	.58	.55	.54	.53	.50
			2	.67	.63	.60	.65	.61	.58	.59	.57	.54	.55	.53	.51	.50	.49	.47	.45
			3	.61	.56	.52	.58	.54	.51	.54	.50	.48	.50	.47	.45	.46	.44	.42	.40
			4	.55	.49	.45	.53	.48	.44	.49	.45	.42	.45	.42	.40	.42	.39	.37	.36
			5	.49	.44	.40	.47	.42	.39	.44	.40	.37	.41	.38	.35	.38	.35	.33	.31
			6	.45	.39	.35	.43	.38	.34	.40	.36	.33	.37	.34	.31	.35	.32	.30	.28
			7	.40	.35	.31	.39	.34	.30	.36	.32	.29	.34	.30	.27	.32	.29	.26	.25
			8	.36	.31	.27	.35	.30	.26	.33	.28	.25	.31	.27	.24	.29	.25	.23	.21
			9	.33	.27	.23	.32	.26	.23	.29	.25	.22	.28	.24	.21	.26	.22	.20	.19
			10	.30	.24	.21	.29	.24	.20	.27	.22	.19	.25	.21	.19	.23	.20	.18	.16
29 Metal or dense diffusing sides with 45°CW × 45°LW shielding (II, SC 1.1, 39%↑, 32%↓)	II	1.1	0	.75	.75	.75	.69	.69	.69	.57	.57	.57	.46	.46	.46	.37	.37	.37	.32
			1	.67	.64	.62	.61	.59	.57	.51	.50	.49	.42	.41	.40	.34	.33	.32	.29
			2	.59	.55	.52	.55	.51	.49	.46	.44	.42	.38	.36	.35	.31	.30	.29	.25
			3	.53	.48	.45	.49	.45	.42	.41	.39	.36	.35	.32	.31	.28	.27	.26	.23
			4	.47	.42	.39	.44	.40	.36	.37	.34	.32	.31	.29	.27	.26	.24	.23	.20
			5	.43	.37	.33	.40	.35	.31	.34	.30	.28	.28	.26	.24	.23	.22	.20	.18
			6	.39	.33	.29	.36	.31	.28	.31	.27	.25	.26	.23	.21	.22	.20	.18	.16
			7	.35	.30	.26	.33	.28	.25	.28	.24	.22	.24	.21	.19	.20	.18	.16	.15
			8	.32	.26	.23	.30	.25	.22	.25	.22	.19	.22	.19	.17	.18	.16	.15	.13
			9	.29	.24	.20	.27	.22	.19	.23	.20	.17	.20	.17	.15	.16	.15	.13	.12
			10	.26	.21	.18	.25	.20	.17	.21	.18	.15	.18	.15	.14	.15	.13	.12	.10
30 Same as unit #29 except with top reflectors (IV, SC 1.0, 6%↑, 46%↓)	IV	1.0	0	.61	.61	.61	.58	.58	.58	.55	.55	.55	.51	.51	.51	.48	.48	.48	.46
			1	.54	.52	.51	.52	.51	.49	.49	.48	.47	.46	.45	.44	.43	.43	.42	.40
			2	.48	.46	.43	.47	.44	.42	.44	.42	.40	.42	.40	.38	.39	.38	.37	.35
			3	.44	.40	.37	.43	.39	.37	.40	.38	.35	.38	.36	.34	.36	.34	.33	.31
			4	.40	.36	.33	.39	.35	.32	.37	.34	.31	.35	.32	.30	.33	.31	.29	.28
			5	.36	.32	.29	.35	.31	.28	.33	.30	.28	.32	.29	.27	.30	.28	.26	.25
			6	.33	.29	.26	.32	.28	.25	.30	.27	.25	.29	.26	.24	.28	.25	.23	.22
			7	.30	.26	.23	.29	.25	.23	.28	.25	.22	.27	.24	.22	.25	.23	.21	.20
			8	.27	.23	.20	.27	.23	.20	.25	.22	.20	.24	.21	.19	.23	.21	.19	.18
			9	.25	.21	.18	.24	.21	.18	.23	.20	.18	.22	.19	.17	.21	.19	.17	.16
			10	.23	.19	.16	.22	.19	.16	.21	.18	.16	.20	.18	.16	.20	.17	.15	.14

Typical Luminaire	Typical Intensity Distribution and Per Cent Lamp Lumens		RCR ↓	ρcc → 80			70			50			30			10			0
	Maint. Cat.	SC		ρw → 50	30	10	50	30	10	50	30	10	50	30	10	50	30	10	0

Coefficients of Utilization for 20 Per Cent Effective Floor Cavity Reflectance (ρFC = 20)

31 — 150 mm × 150 mm (6″ × 6″) cell parabolic wedge louver (multiply by 1.1 for 250 × 250 mm (10 × 10″) cells) — IV — SC 1.5/1.2 — 0%↑ 58%↓

RCR	80-50	80-30	80-10	70-50	70-30	70-10	50-50	50-30	50-10	30-50	30-30	30-10	10-50	10-30	10-10	0
0	.69	.69	.69	.67	.67	.67	.64	.64	.64	.62	.62	.62	.59	.59	.59	.58
1	.63	.61	.59	.62	.60	.58	.59	.58	.57	.57	.56	.55	.55	.54	.53	.52
2	.57	.54	.52	.56	.53	.51	.54	.52	.50	.52	.50	.49	.51	.49	.48	.47
3	.52	.48	.45	.51	.47	.45	.49	.46	.44	.48	.45	.43	.46	.44	.42	.41
4	.47	.42	.39	.46	.42	.39	.44	.41	.38	.43	.40	.38	.42	.40	.38	.36
5	.42	.37	.34	.41	.37	.34	.40	.36	.34	.39	.36	.33	.38	.35	.33	.32
6	.38	.33	.30	.37	.33	.30	.36	.32	.29	.35	.32	.29	.34	.31	.29	.28
7	.34	.29	.26	.33	.29	.26	.32	.29	.26	.32	.28	.26	.31	.28	.25	.24
8	.30	.26	.22	.30	.25	.22	.29	.25	.22	.28	.25	.22	.28	.24	.22	.21
9	.27	.22	.19	.27	.22	.19	.26	.22	.19	.25	.22	.19	.25	.21	.19	.18
10	.24	.20	.17	.24	.20	.17	.23	.19	.17	.23	.19	.17	.22	.19	.17	.16

32 — 2 lamp, surface mounted, bare lamp unit—Photometry with 460 mm (18″) wide panel above luminaire (lamps on 150 mm (6″) centers) — I — SC 1.3 — 9½%↑ 78%↓

RCR	80-50	80-30	80-10	70-50	70-30	70-10	50-50	50-30	50-10	30-50	30-30	30-10	10-50	10-30	10-10	0
0	1.02	1.02	1.02	.99	.99	.99	.92	.92	.92	.86	.86	.86	.81	.81	.81	.78
1	.86	.82	.78	.83	.79	.75	.78	.74	.71	.73	.70	.67	.68	.66	.64	.61
2	.74	.67	.61	.71	.65	.60	.66	.61	.57	.62	.58	.54	.58	.55	.52	.49
3	.64	.56	.50	.62	.55	.49	.58	.52	.47	.54	.49	.45	.51	.47	.43	.41
4	.56	.48	.42	.55	.47	.41	.51	.45	.39	.48	.42	.38	.45	.40	.36	.34
5	.49	.41	.35	.48	.40	.34	.45	.38	.33	.42	.36	.32	.39	.34	.30	.28
6	.44	.36	.30	.43	.35	.29	.40	.33	.28	.38	.32	.27	.35	.30	.26	.24
7	.39	.31	.25	.38	.30	.25	.36	.29	.24	.34	.28	.23	.32	.27	.23	.21
8	.35	.27	.22	.34	.27	.22	.32	.26	.21	.30	.24	.20	.29	.23	.19	.18
9	.32	.24	.19	.31	.23	.18	.29	.22	.18	.27	.21	.17	.26	.20	.17	.15
10	.29	.21	.17	.28	.21	.16	.26	.20	.16	.25	.19	.15	.23	.18	.15	.13

33 — Luminous bottom suspended unit with extra-high output lamp — VI — SC N.A. — 66%↑ 12%↓

RCR	80-50	80-30	80-10	70-50	70-30	70-10	50-50	50-30	50-10	30-50	30-30	30-10	10-50	10-30	10-10	0
0	.77	.77	.77	.68	.68	.68	.50	.50	.50	.34	.34	.34	.19	.19	.19	.12
1	.67	.64	.62	.59	.57	.54	.44	.42	.41	.30	.29	.28	.17	.16	.16	.10
2	.59	.54	.50	.52	.48	.45	.38	.36	.34	.26	.25	.23	.15	.14	.13	.09
3	.51	.46	.42	.45	.41	.37	.34	.31	.28	.23	.21	.20	.13	.12	.12	.07
4	.45	.40	.35	.40	.35	.31	.30	.27	.24	.20	.18	.17	.12	.11	.10	.06
5	.40	.34	.30	.35	.30	.27	.26	.23	.20	.18	.16	.14	.10	.09	.08	.05
6	.36	.30	.26	.32	.27	.23	.24	.20	.18	.16	.14	.12	.09	.08	.07	.05
7	.32	.26	.22	.28	.23	.20	.21	.18	.15	.15	.12	.11	.08	.07	.06	.04
8	.29	.23	.19	.25	.21	.17	.19	.16	.13	.13	.11	.09	.08	.06	.06	.03
9	.26	.20	.17	.23	.18	.15	.17	.14	.12	.12	.10	.08	.07	.06	.05	.03
10	.24	.18	.15	.21	.16	.13	.16	.12	.10	.11	.09	.07	.06	.05	.04	.03

34 — Prismatic bottom and sides, open top, 4 lamp suspended unit — VI — SC 1.4/1.2 — 33%↑ 50%↓

RCR	80-50	80-30	80-10	70-50	70-30	70-10	50-50	50-30	50-10	30-50	30-30	30-10	10-50	10-30	10-10	0
0	.91	.91	.91	.85	.85	.85	.74	.74	.74	.64	.64	.64	.54	.54	.54	.50
1	.80	.77	.74	.75	.73	.70	.66	.64	.62	.57	.56	.54	.49	.48	.47	.43
2	.71	.66	.62	.67	.63	.59	.59	.56	.53	.51	.49	.47	.44	.43	.41	.38
3	.63	.58	.53	.60	.55	.50	.53	.49	.45	.46	.43	.41	.40	.38	.36	.33
4	.57	.50	.45	.53	.48	.43	.47	.43	.39	.41	.38	.35	.36	.34	.32	.29
5	.50	.44	.39	.48	.42	.37	.42	.38	.34	.37	.34	.31	.33	.30	.28	.25
6	.45	.39	.34	.43	.37	.33	.38	.33	.30	.34	.30	.27	.30	.27	.24	.22
7	.41	.34	.30	.39	.33	.28	.34	.30	.26	.30	.27	.24	.27	.24	.21	.19
8	.37	.30	.26	.35	.29	.25	.31	.26	.23	.27	.24	.21	.24	.21	.19	.17
9	.33	.27	.22	.31	.26	.22	.28	.23	.20	.25	.21	.18	.22	.19	.16	.15
10	.30	.24	.20	.28	.23	.19	.25	.21	.18	.23	.19	.16	.20	.17	.14	.13

35 — 2 lamp prismatic wraparound — V — SC 1.5/1.2 — 11½%↑ 58½%↓

RCR	80-50	80-30	80-10	70-50	70-30	70-10	50-50	50-30	50-10	30-50	30-30	30-10	10-50	10-30	10-10	0
0	.81	.81	.81	.78	.78	.78	.72	.72	.72	.66	.66	.66	.61	.61	.61	.59
1	.71	.69	.66	.69	.66	.64	.64	.62	.60	.59	.58	.56	.55	.54	.53	.50
2	.64	.59	.56	.61	.58	.54	.57	.54	.51	.53	.51	.49	.49	.48	.46	.44
3	.57	.52	.48	.55	.50	.47	.51	.48	.45	.48	.45	.42	.45	.42	.40	.38
4	.51	.46	.41	.49	.44	.41	.46	.42	.39	.43	.40	.37	.41	.38	.35	.34
5	.46	.40	.36	.44	.39	.35	.41	.37	.34	.39	.35	.32	.37	.33	.31	.29
6	.41	.35	.31	.40	.35	.31	.38	.33	.30	.35	.31	.28	.33	.30	.27	.26
7	.37	.31	.27	.36	.31	.27	.34	.29	.26	.32	.28	.25	.30	.27	.24	.23
8	.33	.28	.24	.32	.27	.23	.30	.26	.22	.29	.25	.22	.27	.24	.21	.19
9	.30	.24	.20	.29	.24	.20	.27	.23	.19	.26	.22	.19	.24	.21	.18	.17
10	.27	.22	.18	.26	.21	.18	.25	.20	.17	.23	.19	.16	.22	.18	.16	.15

36 — 2 lamp prismatic wraparound — V — SC 1.2 — 24%↑ 50%↓

RCR	80-50	80-30	80-10	70-50	70-30	70-10	50-50	50-30	50-10	30-50	30-30	30-10	10-50	10-30	10-10	0
0	.82	.82	.82	.77	.77	.77	.69	.69	.69	.61	.61	.61	.53	.53	.53	.50
1	.71	.68	.65	.67	.65	.62	.60	.58	.56	.53	.51	.50	.47	.45	.44	.41
2	.63	.58	.54	.59	.55	.52	.53	.50	.47	.47	.45	.42	.42	.40	.38	.35
3	.56	.50	.46	.53	.48	.44	.47	.44	.40	.42	.39	.37	.38	.35	.33	.31
4	.50	.44	.40	.48	.42	.38	.43	.39	.35	.38	.35	.32	.34	.32	.29	.27
5	.45	.39	.34	.43	.37	.33	.38	.34	.31	.35	.31	.28	.31	.28	.26	.24
6	.41	.35	.30	.39	.33	.29	.35	.30	.27	.32	.28	.25	.28	.25	.23	.21
7	.37	.31	.27	.35	.30	.26	.32	.27	.24	.29	.25	.22	.26	.23	.20	.19
8	.33	.27	.23	.32	.26	.23	.29	.24	.21	.26	.22	.20	.23	.20	.18	.16
9	.30	.24	.20	.29	.23	.20	.26	.22	.19	.24	.20	.17	.21	.18	.16	.14
10	.27	.22	.18	.26	.21	.18	.24	.19	.16	.22	.18	.15	.19	.16	.14	.13

Typical Luminaire	Typical Intensity Distribution and Per Cent Lamp Lumens			ρcc →	80			70			50			30			10			0
	Maint. Cat.	SC		ρw →	50	30	10	50	30	10	50	30	10	50	30	10	50	30	10	0
			RCR ↓		Coefficients of Utilization for 20 Per Cent Effective Floor Cavity Reflectance (ρFC = 20)															

37 — 2 lamp diffuse wraparound — Maint. Cat. V, SC 1.3, 8%↑, 37½%↓

RCR	80/50	80/30	80/10	70/50	70/30	70/10	50/50	50/30	50/10	30/50	30/30	30/10	10/50	10/30	10/10	0
0	.52	.52	.52	.50	.50	.50	.46	.46	.46	.43	.43	.43	.39	.39	.39	.38
1	.45	.43	.41	.43	.41	.39	.40	.38	.37	.36	.35	.34	.34	.33	.32	.30
2	.39	.35	.33	.37	.34	.32	.34	.32	.30	.32	.30	.28	.29	.28	.26	.25
3	.34	.30	.27	.33	.29	.26	.30	.27	.25	.28	.26	.24	.26	.24	.22	.21
4	.30	.26	.23	.29	.25	.22	.27	.24	.21	.25	.22	.20	.23	.21	.19	.18
5	.26	.22	.19	.25	.21	.19	.23	.20	.18	.22	.19	.17	.20	.18	.16	.15
6	.23	.19	.16	.23	.19	.16	.21	.18	.15	.19	.17	.14	.18	.16	.14	.13
7	.21	.17	.14	.20	.16	.14	.19	.16	.13	.18	.15	.13	.16	.14	.12	.11
8	.19	.15	.12	.18	.14	.12	.17	.14	.11	.16	.13	.11	.15	.12	.10	.09
9	.17	.13	.10	.16	.13	.10	.15	.12	.10	.14	.11	.09	.13	.11	.09	.08
10	.15	.12	.09	.15	.11	.09	.14	.11	.09	.13	.10	.08	.12	.10	.08	.07

38 — 4 lamp, 610 mm (2') wide troffer with 45° plastic louver — Maint. Cat. IV, SC 1.0, 0%↑, 50%↓

RCR	80/50	80/30	80/10	70/50	70/30	70/10	50/50	50/30	50/10	30/50	30/30	30/10	10/50	10/30	10/10	0
0	.60	.60	.60	.58	.58	.58	.56	.56	.56	.53	.53	.53	.51	.51	.51	.50
1	.54	.52	.50	.52	.51	.49	.50	.49	.48	.48	.47	.46	.47	.46	.45	.44
2	.48	.45	.43	.47	.44	.42	.45	.43	.41	.44	.42	.40	.42	.41	.39	.39
3	.43	.40	.37	.42	.39	.37	.41	.38	.36	.40	.37	.36	.39	.37	.35	.34
4	.39	.35	.32	.38	.35	.32	.37	.34	.32	.36	.33	.31	.35	.33	.31	.30
5	.35	.31	.28	.35	.31	.28	.34	.30	.28	.33	.30	.28	.32	.29	.27	.26
6	.32	.28	.25	.32	.28	.25	.31	.27	.25	.30	.27	.25	.29	.26	.24	.23
7	.29	.25	.22	.29	.25	.22	.28	.25	.22	.27	.24	.22	.27	.24	.22	.21
8	.26	.22	.20	.26	.22	.20	.25	.22	.20	.25	.22	.19	.24	.21	.19	.18
9	.24	.20	.17	.24	.20	.17	.23	.20	.17	.23	.19	.17	.22	.19	.17	.16
10	.22	.18	.16	.22	.18	.16	.21	.18	.16	.21	.18	.15	.20	.17	.15	.15

39 — 4 lamp, 610 mm (2') wide troffer with 45° white metal louver — Maint. Cat. IV, SC 0.9, 0%↑, 46%↓

RCR	80/50	80/30	80/10	70/50	70/30	70/10	50/50	50/30	50/10	30/50	30/30	30/10	10/50	10/30	10/10	0
0	.55	.55	.55	.54	.54	.54	.51	.51	.51	.49	.49	.49	.47	.47	.47	.46
1	.50	.48	.47	.49	.47	.46	.47	.46	.45	.45	.44	.43	.43	.43	.42	.41
2	.45	.43	.41	.44	.42	.40	.43	.41	.39	.41	.40	.38	.40	.39	.37	.37
3	.41	.38	.36	.40	.38	.35	.39	.37	.35	.38	.36	.34	.37	.35	.34	.33
4	.37	.34	.32	.37	.34	.31	.36	.33	.31	.35	.32	.31	.34	.32	.30	.29
5	.34	.30	.28	.33	.30	.28	.32	.30	.27	.32	.29	.27	.31	.29	.27	.26
6	.31	.28	.25	.31	.27	.25	.30	.27	.25	.29	.27	.25	.29	.26	.24	.24
7	.29	.25	.23	.28	.25	.23	.28	.25	.22	.27	.24	.22	.26	.24	.22	.21
8	.26	.23	.20	.26	.23	.20	.25	.22	.20	.25	.22	.20	.24	.22	.20	.19
9	.24	.20	.18	.24	.20	.18	.23	.20	.18	.23	.20	.18	.22	.20	.18	.17
10	.22	.19	.16	.22	.19	.16	.21	.18	.16	.21	.18	.16	.21	.18	.16	.15

40 — Fluorescent unit dropped diffuser, 4 lamp 610 mm (2') wide — Maint. Cat. V, SC 1.2, 1%↑, 60½%↓

RCR	80/50	80/30	80/10	70/50	70/30	70/10	50/50	50/30	50/10	30/50	30/30	30/10	10/50	10/30	10/10	0
0	.73	.73	.73	.71	.71	.71	.68	.68	.68	.65	.65	.65	.62	.62	.62	.60
1	.64	.61	.59	.62	.60	.58	.60	.58	.56	.57	.56	.54	.55	.54	.52	.51
2	.56	.52	.49	.55	.51	.48	.52	.49	.47	.50	.48	.46	.48	.46	.44	.43
3	.50	.45	.41	.49	.44	.41	.47	.43	.40	.45	.42	.39	.43	.41	.38	.37
4	.44	.39	.35	.43	.38	.35	.42	.37	.34	.40	.36	.33	.39	.36	.33	.32
5	.39	.34	.30	.38	.33	.29	.37	.32	.29	.36	.32	.29	.34	.31	.28	.27
6	.35	.30	.26	.34	.29	.25	.33	.29	.25	.32	.28	.25	.31	.27	.25	.23
7	.31	.26	.22	.31	.26	.22	.30	.25	.22	.29	.25	.22	.28	.24	.22	.20
8	.28	.23	.19	.28	.23	.19	.27	.22	.19	.26	.22	.19	.25	.22	.19	.18
9	.25	.20	.17	.25	.20	.17	.24	.20	.17	.23	.19	.16	.23	.19	.16	.15
10	.23	.18	.15	.23	.18	.15	.22	.18	.15	.21	.17	.15	.21	.17	.14	.13

41 — Fluorescent unit with flat bottom diffuser, 4 lamp 610 mm (2') wide — Maint. Cat. V, SC 1.2, 0%↑, 57½%↓

RCR	80/50	80/30	80/10	70/50	70/30	70/10	50/50	50/30	50/10	30/50	30/30	30/10	10/50	10/30	10/10	0
0	.69	.69	.69	.67	.67	.67	.64	.64	.64	.61	.61	.61	.59	.59	.59	.58
1	.61	.58	.56	.59	.57	.56	.57	.55	.54	.55	.53	.52	.53	.52	.51	.49
2	.53	.50	.47	.52	.49	.46	.50	.48	.45	.49	.46	.44	.47	.45	.43	.42
3	.47	.43	.40	.47	.42	.39	.45	.41	.38	.43	.40	.38	.42	.39	.37	.36
4	.42	.37	.34	.41	.37	.33	.40	.36	.33	.39	.35	.33	.37	.35	.32	.31
5	.37	.32	.29	.37	.32	.28	.35	.31	.28	.34	.31	.28	.33	.30	.27	.26
6	.33	.28	.25	.33	.28	.25	.32	.28	.24	.31	.27	.24	.30	.27	.24	.23
7	.30	.25	.22	.30	.25	.21	.29	.24	.21	.28	.24	.21	.27	.24	.21	.20
8	.27	.22	.19	.27	.22	.19	.26	.22	.18	.25	.21	.18	.24	.21	.18	.17
9	.24	.19	.16	.24	.19	.16	.23	.19	.16	.23	.19	.16	.22	.18	.16	.15
10	.22	.17	.14	.22	.17	.14	.21	.17	.14	.21	.17	.14	.20	.17	.14	.13

42 — Fluorescent unit with flat prismatic lens, 4 lamp 610 mm (2') wide — Maint. Cat. V, SC 1.4/1.2, 0%↑, 63%↓, 60°

RCR	80/50	80/30	80/10	70/50	70/30	70/10	50/50	50/30	50/10	30/50	30/30	30/10	10/50	10/30	10/10	0
0	.75	.75	.75	.73	.73	.73	.70	.70	.70	.67	.67	.67	.64	.64	.64	.63
1	.67	.65	.63	.66	.64	.62	.63	.62	.60	.61	.60	.58	.59	.58	.57	.55
2	.60	.57	.54	.59	.56	.53	.57	.54	.52	.55	.53	.51	.53	.51	.50	.49
3	.54	.50	.47	.53	.49	.46	.52	.48	.45	.50	.47	.45	.48	.46	.44	.43
4	.49	.44	.40	.48	.44	.40	.47	.43	.40	.45	.42	.39	.44	.41	.39	.37
5	.44	.39	.35	.43	.38	.35	.42	.38	.34	.41	.37	.34	.40	.36	.34	.33
6	.40	.34	.31	.39	.34	.31	.38	.34	.30	.37	.33	.30	.36	.32	.30	.29
7	.36	.30	.27	.35	.30	.27	.34	.30	.27	.33	.29	.26	.32	.29	.26	.25
8	.32	.27	.23	.32	.27	.23	.31	.26	.23	.30	.26	.23	.29	.26	.23	.22
9	.29	.24	.20	.28	.23	.20	.28	.23	.20	.27	.23	.20	.26	.23	.20	.19
10	.26	.21	.18	.26	.21	.18	.25	.21	.18	.24	.20	.18	.24	.20	.18	.16

Typical Luminaire	Typical Intensity Distribution and Per Cent Lamp Lumens		ρ_{CC} →	80			70			50			30			10			0
			ρ_W →	50	30	10	50	30	10	50	30	10	50	30	10	50	30	10	0
	Maint. Cat.	SC	RCR ↓	Coefficients of Utilization for 20 Per Cent Effective Floor Cavity Reflectance (ρ_{FC} = 20)															
43 	V	1.4/1.3	0	.78	.78	.78	.76	.76	.76	.73	.73	.73	.70	.70	.70	.67	.67	.67	.66
	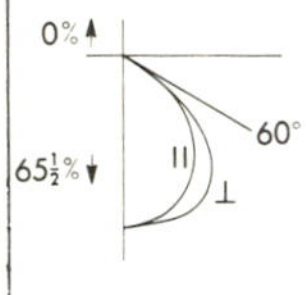 0%↑ 65½%↓ 60°		1	.71	.69	.67	.70	.68	.66	.67	.65	.64	.64	.63	.62	.62	.61	.60	.59
4 lamp, 610 mm (2′) wide unit with sharp cutoff (high angle—low luminance) flat prismatic lens			2	.64	.61	.58	.63	.60	.58	.61	.59	.56	.59	.57	.55	.57	.55	.54	.53
			3	.58	.54	.51	.58	.54	.51	.56	.52	.50	.54	.51	.49	.52	.50	.48	.47
			4	.53	.48	.45	.52	.48	.44	.51	.47	.44	.49	.46	.43	.48	.45	.43	.42
			5	.48	.43	.39	.47	.42	.39	.46	.42	.39	.45	.41	.38	.43	.40	.38	.37
			6	.43	.38	.35	.43	.38	.34	.42	.37	.34	.40	.37	.34	.40	.36	.34	.32
			7	.39	.34	.30	.38	.34	.30	.38	.33	.30	.37	.33	.30	.36	.32	.30	.28
			8	.35	.30	.26	.35	.30	.26	.34	.29	.26	.33	.29	.26	.32	.29	.26	.25
			9	.31	.26	.23	.31	.26	.23	.30	.26	.23	.30	.26	.23	.29	.25	.23	.21
			10	.28	.24	.20	.28	.23	.20	.28	.23	.20	.27	.23	.20	.26	.23	.20	.19
44 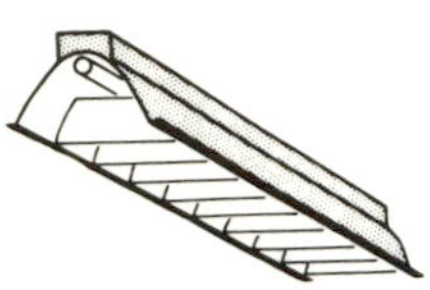	IV	N.A.	0	.71	.71	.71	.70	.70	.70	.66	.66	.66	.64	.64	.64	.61	.61	.61	.60
	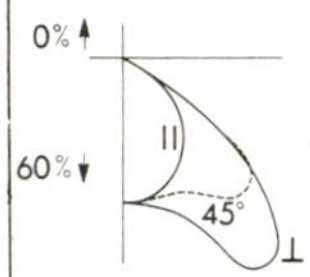 0%↑ 60%↓ 45°		1	.65	.63	.61	.63	.62	.60	.61	.59	.58	.59	.57	.56	.57	.56	.55	.54
Bilateral batwing distribution—louvered fluorescent unit			2	.59	.55	.53	.58	.55	.52	.55	.53	.51	.54	.52	.50	.52	.50	.49	.48
			3	.53	.49	.46	.52	.48	.45	.50	.47	.45	.49	.46	.44	.47	.45	.43	.42
			4	.47	.43	.40	.47	.43	.40	.45	.42	.39	.44	.41	.39	.43	.40	.38	.37
			5	.42	.38	.34	.42	.37	.34	.41	.37	.34	.40	.36	.34	.39	.36	.33	.32
			6	.38	.33	.30	.38	.33	.30	.37	.33	.30	.36	.32	.29	.35	.32	.29	.28
			7	.34	.29	.26	.33	.29	.26	.33	.28	.25	.32	.28	.25	.31	.28	.25	.24
			8	.30	.25	.22	.30	.25	.22	.29	.25	.22	.28	.24	.22	.27	.24	.21	.20
			9	.27	.22	.18	.26	.22	.18	.26	.21	.18	.25	.21	.18	.24	.21	.18	.17
			10	.24	.19	.16	.24	.19	.16	.23	.19	.16	.22	.19	.16	.22	.18	.16	.15
45 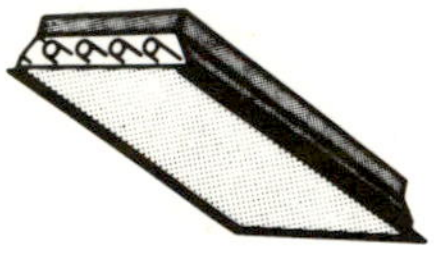	V	N.A.	0	.57	.57	.57	.56	.56	.56	.53	.53	.53	.51	.51	.51	.49	.49	.49	.48
	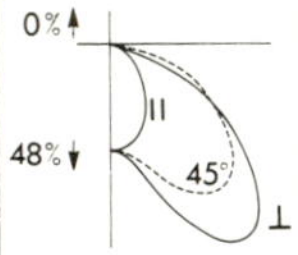 0%↑ 48%↓ 45°		1	.50	.48	.47	.49	.47	.46	.47	.46	.44	.45	.44	.43	.44	.43	.42	.41
Bilateral batwing distribution—4 lamp, 610 mm (2′) wide fluorescent unit with flat prismatic lens and overlay			2	.44	.41	.38	.43	.40	.38	.41	.39	.37	.40	.38	.36	.38	.37	.35	.34
			3	.39	.35	.32	.38	.34	.31	.37	.33	.31	.35	.33	.30	.34	.32	.30	.29
			4	.34	.30	.27	.33	.29	.26	.32	.29	.26	.31	.28	.26	.30	.27	.25	.24
			5	.30	.25	.22	.29	.25	.22	.28	.24	.22	.27	.24	.21	.26	.23	.21	.20
			6	.26	.22	.19	.26	.22	.18	.25	.21	.18	.24	.21	.18	.23	.20	.18	.17
			7	.23	.19	.16	.23	.19	.16	.22	.18	.16	.21	.18	.15	.21	.18	.15	.14
			8	.21	.16	.13	.20	.16	.13	.19	.16	.13	.19	.15	.13	.18	.15	.13	.12
			9	.18	.14	.11	.18	.14	.11	.17	.14	.11	.17	.13	.11	.16	.13	.11	.10
			10	.16	.12	.09	.16	.12	.09	.16	.12	.09	.15	.12	.09	.15	.12	.09	.08
46 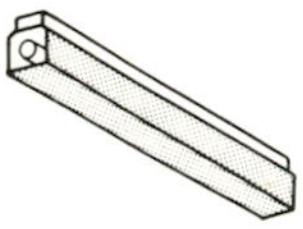	V	N.A.	0	.87	.87	.87	.84	.84	.84	.77	.77	.77	.72	.72	.72	.66	.66	.66	.64
	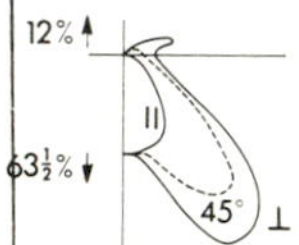 12%↑ 63½%↓ 45°		1	.76	.73	.70	.73	.70	.67	.67	.65	.63	.63	.61	.59	.58	.57	.55	.53
Bilateral batwing distribution—one lamp, surface mounted fluorescent with prismatic wraparound lens			2	.66	.61	.57	.64	.59	.56	.59	.56	.52	.55	.52	.49	.51	.49	.47	.44
			3	.59	.53	.48	.56	.51	.47	.53	.48	.44	.49	.45	.42	.46	.43	.40	.38
			4	.52	.45	.40	.50	.44	.40	.47	.42	.38	.44	.39	.36	.41	.37	.34	.32
			5	.46	.39	.34	.44	.38	.33	.41	.36	.32	.38	.34	.31	.36	.32	.29	.27
			6	.41	.34	.29	.39	.33	.29	.37	.31	.27	.34	.30	.26	.32	.28	.25	.23
			7	.36	.30	.25	.35	.29	.24	.33	.27	.23	.31	.26	.23	.29	.25	.22	.20
			8	.32	.26	.21	.31	.25	.21	.29	.24	.20	.27	.23	.19	.26	.21	.18	.17
			9	.29	.22	.18	.28	.22	.18	.26	.21	.17	.24	.20	.16	.23	.19	.15	.14
			10	.26	.20	.16	.25	.19	.15	.23	.18	.15	.22	.17	.14	.20	.16	.13	.12
47 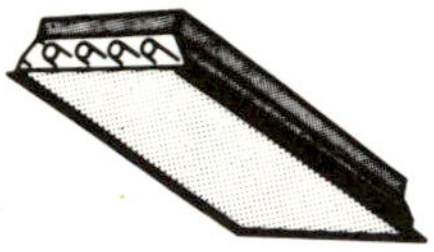	V	1.7	0	.71	.71	.71	.69	.69	.69	.66	.66	.66	.63	.63	.63	.61	.61	.61	.60
	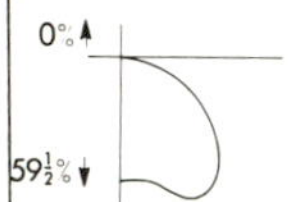 0%↑ 59½%↓		1	.62	.60	.58	.61	.59	.57	.59	.57	.55	.56	.55	.53	.54	.53	.52	.51
Radial batwing distribution—4 lamp, 610 mm (2′) wide fluorescent unit with flat prismatic lens			2	.55	.51	.47	.53	.50	.47	.51	.48	.46	.49	.47	.45	.48	.45	.44	.42
			3	.48	.43	.39	.47	.43	.39	.45	.41	.38	.44	.40	.38	.42	.39	.37	.36
			4	.42	.37	.33	.41	.37	.33	.40	.36	.32	.39	.35	.32	.37	.34	.31	.30
			5	.37	.32	.27	.36	.31	.27	.35	.30	.27	.34	.30	.27	.33	.29	.26	.25
			6	.33	.27	.23	.32	.27	.23	.31	.26	.23	.30	.26	.23	.29	.25	.23	.21
			7	.29	.24	.20	.29	.24	.20	.28	.23	.20	.27	.23	.20	.26	.22	.19	.18
			8	.26	.21	.17	.25	.20	.17	.25	.20	.17	.24	.20	.17	.23	.19	.16	.15
			9	.23	.18	.14	.23	.18	.14	.22	.17	.14	.21	.17	.14	.21	.17	.14	.13
			10	.21	.16	.12	.20	.16	.12	.20	.15	.12	.19	.15	.12	.19	.15	.12	.11
48 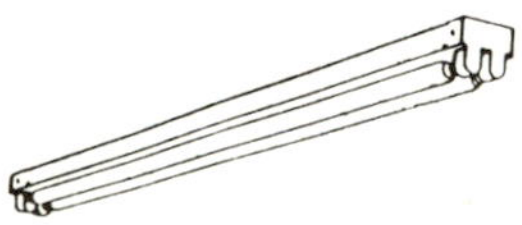	I	1.6/1.2	0	1.01	1.01	1.01	.96	.96	.96	.87	.87	.87	.79	.79	.79	.72	.72	.72	.68
	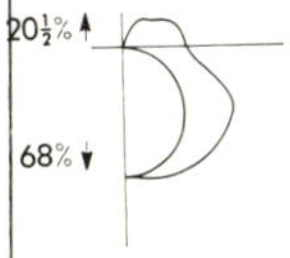 20½%↑ 68%↓		1	.85	.81	.77	.81	.77	.73	.73	.70	.67	.66	.64	.62	.60	.58	.56	.53
2 lamp fluorescent strip unit			2	.73	.66	.61	.69	.63	.58	.63	.58	.54	.57	.53	.50	.51	.48	.45	.42
			3	.63	.56	.50	.60	.53	.48	.55	.49	.44	.50	.45	.41	.45	.41	.38	.35
			4	.56	.47	.41	.53	.46	.40	.48	.42	.37	.44	.39	.34	.40	.35	.32	.29
			5	.49	.40	.34	.46	.39	.33	.42	.36	.31	.38	.33	.29	.35	.30	.26	.24
			6	.43	.35	.29	.41	.34	.28	.38	.31	.26	.34	.29	.24	.31	.26	.23	.20
			7	.39	.31	.25	.37	.29	.24	.34	.27	.23	.31	.25	.21	.28	.23	.19	.17
			8	.34	.27	.21	.33	.26	.21	.30	.24	.19	.27	.22	.18	.25	.20	.17	.15
			9	.31	.23	.18	.30	.23	.18	.27	.21	.17	.25	.19	.15	.22	.18	.14	.12
			10	.28	.21	.16	.27	.20	.16	.25	.19	.15	.22	.17	.14	.20	.16	.13	.11

Continued

Typical Luminaire	Typical Intensity Distribution and Per Cent Lamp Lumens		ρcc →	80			70			50			30			10			0
	Maint. Cat.	SC	ρw →	50	30	10	50	30	10	50	30	10	50	30	10	50	30	10	0
			RCR ↓	Coefficients of Utilization for 20 Per Cent Effective Floor Cavity Reflectance (ρ_FC = 20)															
49	I	1.4/1.2	0	1.13	1.13	1.13	1.09	1.09	1.09	1.01	1.01	1.01	.94	.94	.94	.88	.88	.88	.85
	12½%▲ 85%▼		1	.96	.92	.88	.93	.89	.85	.87	.83	.80	.81	.78	.75	.75	.73	.71	.68
			2	.83	.76	.70	.80	.74	.68	.75	.69	.65	.70	.65	.61	.65	.61	.58	.55
			3	.73	.65	.58	.70	.63	.57	.66	.59	.54	.61	.56	.52	.57	.53	.49	.46
			4	.64	.55	.49	.62	.54	.48	.58	.51	.46	.54	.48	.44	.51	.46	.42	.39
2 lamp fluorescent strip unit with 235° reflector fluorescent lamps			5	.56	.47	.41	.55	.46	.40	.51	.44	.38	.48	.42	.37	.45	.39	.35	.33
			6	.50	.41	.35	.49	.40	.34	.46	.38	.33	.43	.36	.32	.40	.35	.30	.28
			7	.45	.36	.30	.44	.35	.30	.41	.34	.28	.38	.32	.27	.36	.31	.26	.24
			8	.40	.32	.26	.39	.31	.25	.37	.30	.25	.35	.28	.24	.33	.27	.23	.21
			9	.36	.28	.22	.35	.27	.22	.33	.26	.21	.31	.25	.20	.29	.24	.20	.18
			10	.33	.25	.20	.32	.24	.19	.30	.23	.19	.28	.22	.18	.27	.21	.17	.15

Typical Luminaires	ρcc →	80			70			50			30			10			0
	ρw →	50	30	10	50	30	10	50	30	10	50	30	10	50	30	10	0
	RCR ↓	Coefficients of utilization for 20 Per Cent Effective Floor Cavity Reflectance, ρ_FC															
50 Single row fluorescent lamp cove without reflector, mult. by 0.93 for 2 rows and by 0.85 for 3 rows.	1	.42	.40	.39	.36	.35	.33	.25	.24	.23	Coves are not recommended for lighting areas having low reflectances.						
	2	.37	.34	.32	.32	.29	.27	.22	.20	.19							
	3	.32	.29	.26	.28	.25	.23	.19	.17	.16							
	4	.29	.25	.22	.25	.22	.19	.17	.15	.13							
	5	.25	.21	.18	.22	.19	.16	.15	.13	.11							
	6	.23	.19	.16	.20	.16	.14	.14	.12	.10							
	7	.20	.17	.14	.17	.14	.12	.12	.10	.09							
	8	.18	.15	.12	.16	.13	.10	.11	.09	.08							
	9	.17	.13	.10	.15	.11	.09	.10	.08	.07							
	10	.15	.12	.09	.13	.10	.08	.09	.07	.06							
51 ρcc from below ~65% Diffusing plastic or glass 1) Ceiling efficiency ~60%; diffuser transmittance ~50%; diffuser reflectance ~40%. Cavity with minimum obstructions and painted with 80% reflectance paint—use ρ_c = 70. 2) For lower reflectance paint or obstructions—use ρ_c = 50.	1				.60	.58	.56	.58	.56	.54							
	2				.53	.49	.45	.51	.47	.43							
	3				.47	.42	.37	.45	.41	.36							
	4				.41	.36	.32	.39	.35	.31							
	5				.37	.31	.27	.35	.30	.26							
	6				.33	.27	.23	.31	.26	.23							
	7				.29	.24	.20	.28	.23	.20							
	8				.26	.21	.18	.25	.20	.17							
	9				.23	.19	.15	.23	.18	.15							
	10				.21	.17	.13	.21	.16	.13							
52 ρcc from below ~60% Prismatic plastic or glass. 1) Ceiling efficiency ~67%; prismatic transmittance ~72%; prismatic reflectance ~18%. Cavity with minimum obstructions and painted with 80% reflectance paint—use ρ_c = 70. 2) For lower reflectance paint or obstructions—use ρ_c = 50.	1				.71	.68	.66	.67	.66	.65	.65	.64	.62				
	2				.63	.60	.57	.61	.58	.55	.59	.56	.54				
	3				.57	.53	.49	.55	.52	.48	.54	.50	.47				
	4				.52	.47	.43	.50	.45	.42	.48	.44	.42				
	5				.46	.41	.37	.44	.40	.37	.43	.40	.36				
	6				.42	.37	.33	.41	.36	.32	.41	.36	.32				
	7				.38	.32	.29	.37	.31	.28	.36	.31	.28				
	8				.34	.28	.25	.33	.28	.25	.32	.28	.25				
	9				.30	.25	.22	.30	.25	.21	.29	.25	.21				
	10				.27	.23	.19	.27	.22	.19	.26	.22	.19				
53 ρcc from below ~45% Louvered ceiling. Ceiling efficiency ~50%; 45° shielding opaque louvers of 80% reflectance. Cavity with minimum obstructions and painted with 80% reflectance paint—use ρ_c = 50.	1							.51	.49	.48				.47	.46	.45	
	2							.46	.44	.42				.43	.42	.40	
	3							.42	.39	.37				.39	.38	.36	
	4							.38	.35	.33				.36	.34	.32	
	5							.35	.32	.29				.33	.31	.29	
	6							.32	.29	.26				.30	.28	.26	
	7							.29	.26	.23				.28	.25	.23	
	8							.27	.23	.21				.26	.23	.21	
	9							.24	.21	.19				.24	.21	.19	
	10							.22	.19	.17				.22	.19	.17	

Note: Spacing criterion (SC) procedures to determine maximum spacings at which horizontal illuminance will be reasonably uniform between luminaires are given on pages 9-34 to 9-36, *IES Lighting Handbook* (1981 Reference Volume). Maintenance categories (from Maint. Cat. I to VI) are used to determine LDD values according to graphs on page 9-5 of the handbook.

Multiplying Factors for Other than 20 Per Cent Effective Floor Cavity Reflectance

% Effective Ceiling Cavity Reflectance, ρ_{cc}	80				70				50			30			10		
% Wall Reflectance, ρ_w	70	50	30	10	70	50	30	10	50	30	10	50	30	10	50	30	10

For 30 Per Cent Effective Floor Cavity Reflectance (20 Per Cent = 1.00)

Room Cavity Ratio	70	50	30	10	70	50	30	10	50	30	10	50	30	10	50	30	10
1	1.092	1.082	1.075	1.068	1.077	1.070	1.064	1.059	1.049	1.044	1.040	1.028	1.026	1.023	1.012	1.010	1.008
2	1.079	1.066	1.055	1.047	1.068	1.057	1.048	1.039	1.041	1.033	1.027	1.026	1.021	1.017	1.013	1.010	1.006
3	1.070	1.054	1.042	1.033	1.061	1.048	1.037	1.028	1.034	1.027	1.020	1.024	1.017	1.012	1.014	1.009	1.005
4	1.062	1.045	1.033	1.024	1.055	1.040	1.029	1.021	1.030	1.022	1.015	1.022	1.015	1.010	1.014	1.009	1.004
5	1.056	1.038	1.026	1.018	1.050	1.034	1.024	1.015	1.027	1.018	1.012	1.020	1.013	1.008	1.014	1.009	1.004
6	1.052	1.033	1.021	1.014	1.047	1.030	1.020	1.012	1.024	1.015	1.009	1.019	1.012	1.006	1.014	1.008	1.003
7	1.047	1.029	1.018	1.011	1.043	1.026	1.017	1.009	1.022	1.013	1.007	1.018	1.010	1.005	1.014	1.008	1.003
8	1.044	1.026	1.015	1.009	1.040	1.024	1.015	1.007	1.020	1.012	1.006	1.017	1.009	1.004	1.013	1.007	1.003
9	1.040	1.024	1.014	1.007	1.037	1.022	1.014	1.006	1.019	1.011	1.005	1.016	1.009	1.004	1.013	1.007	1.002
10	1.037	1.022	1.012	1.006	1.034	1.020	1.012	1.005	1.017	1.010	1.004	1.015	1.009	1.003	1.013	1.007	1.002

For 10 Per Cent Effective Floor Cavity Reflectance (20 Per Cent = 1.00)

Room Cavity Ratio	70	50	30	10	70	50	30	10	50	30	10	50	30	10	50	30	10
1	.923	.929	.935	.940	.933	.939	.943	.948	.956	.960	.963	.973	.976	.979	.989	.991	.993
2	.931	.942	.950	.958	.940	.949	.957	.963	.962	.968	.974	.976	.980	.985	.988	.991	.995
3	.939	.951	.961	.969	.945	.957	.966	.973	.967	.975	.981	.978	.983	.988	.988	.992	.996
4	.944	.958	.969	.978	.950	.963	.973	.980	.972	.980	.986	.980	.986	.991	.987	.992	.996
5	.949	.964	.976	.983	.954	.968	.978	.985	.975	.983	.989	.981	.988	.993	.987	.992	.997
6	.953	.969	.980	.986	.958	.972	.982	.989	.977	.985	.992	.982	.989	.995	.987	.993	.997
7	.957	.973	.983	.991	.961	.975	.985	.991	.979	.987	.994	.983	.990	.996	.987	.993	.998
8	.960	.976	.986	.993	.963	.977	.987	.993	.981	.988	.995	.984	.991	.997	.987	.994	.998
9	.963	.978	.987	.994	.965	.979	.989	.994	.983	.990	.996	.985	.992	.998	.988	.994	.999
10	.965	.980	.989	.995	.967	.981	.990	.995	.984	.991	.997	.986	.993	.998	.988	.994	.999

For 0 Per Cent Effective Floor Cavity Reflectance (20 Per Cent = 1.00)

Room Cavity Ratio	70	50	30	10	70	50	30	10	50	30	10	50	30	10	50	30	10
1	.859	.870	.879	.886	.873	.884	.893	.901	.916	.923	.929	.948	.954	.960	.979	.983	.987
2	.871	.887	.903	.919	.886	.902	.916	.928	.926	.938	.949	.954	.963	.971	.978	.983	.991
3	.882	.904	.915	.942	.898	.918	.934	.947	.936	.950	.964	.958	.969	.979	.976	.984	.993
4	.893	.919	.941	.958	.908	.930	.948	.961	.945	.961	.974	.961	.974	.984	.975	.985	.994
5	.903	.931	.953	.969	.914	.939	.958	.970	.951	.967	.980	.964	.977	.988	.975	.985	.995
6	.911	.940	.961	.976	.920	.945	.965	.977	.955	.972	.985	.966	.979	.991	.975	.986	.996
7	.917	.947	.967	.981	.924	.950	.970	.982	.959	.975	.988	.968	.981	.993	.975	.987	.997
8	.922	.953	.971	.985	.929	.955	.975	.986	.963	.978	.991	.970	.983	.995	.976	.988	.998
9	.928	.958	.975	.988	.933	.959	.980	.989	.966	.980	.993	.971	.985	.996	.976	.988	.998
10	.933	.962	.979	.991	.937	.963	.983	.992	.969	.982	.995	.973	.987	.997	.977	.989	.999

Appendix D:
Electrical Symbols for Lighting Layouts

The table below presents electrical symbols which can be used on plan drawings to show the locations of lighting fixtures, outlets, and switches. To distinguish wiring circuit layouts from standard architectural drawing symbols (e.g., dimension lines), use thick curved lines on the drawings to connect switches to outlets and fixtures. Lighting fixtures to be used on a project should be identified in a table, called a *fixture schedule*. For example, fixtures, lamps, and mounting heights listed in the schedule can be referenced to symbols on drawings by sequential letter-symbol notations.

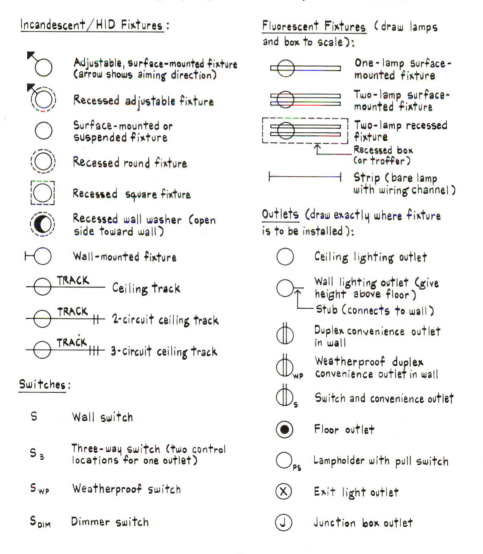

Incandescent/HID Fixtures:

Adjustable, surface-mounted fixture (arrow shows aiming direction)

Recessed adjustable fixture

Surface-mounted or suspended fixture

Recessed round fixture

Recessed square fixture

Recessed wall washer (open side toward wall)

Wall-mounted fixture

Ceiling track

2-circuit ceiling track

3-circuit ceiling track

Switches:

S   Wall switch

S₃   Three-way switch (two control locations for one outlet)

S_WP   Weatherproof switch

S_DIM   Dimmer switch

Fluorescent Fixtures (draw lamps and box to scale):

One-lamp surface-mounted fixture

Two-lamp surface-mounted fixture

Two-lamp recessed fixture

Recessed box (or troffer)

Strip (bare lamp with wiring channel)

Outlets (draw exactly where fixture is to be installed):

Ceiling lighting outlet

Wall lighting outlet (give height above floor)

Stub (connects to wall)

Duplex convenience outlet in wall

Weatherproof duplex convenience outlet in wall

Switch and convenience outlet

Floor outlet

Lampholder with pull switch

Exit light outlet

Junction box outlet

Note: The letter "E" (for electrical) can be placed in circle outlet symbols if the open circle could be confused with columns or plumbing symbols on drawings.

Appendix E:
Lighting Organizations

Listed below are organizations which can provide technical and educational materials about lighting design.

American Home Lighting Institute (AHLI)
435 N. Michigan Avenue
Chicago, IL 60611

General Electric Lighting Institute (GELI)
Nela Park
Cleveland, OH 44112

Illuminating Engineering Society of North America (IES)
345 E. 47th Street
New York, NY 10017

International Association of Lighting Designers (IALD)
40 E. 49th Street
New York, NY 10017

United States National Committee of the
 Commission Internationale de l'Éclairage (CIE)
National Bureau of Standards
U.S. Department of Commerce
Washington, DC 20234

Indexes

NAME INDEX

McGowan, T. K., 240
McGuinness, W. J., 242
Mackey, R. L., 240, 242
MacLeod, R. B., 223
Mayo, E., 84
Millet, M. S., 181, 190
Mills, S. M., 27, 30, 110, 241
Moore Grover Harper, 221
Mormon Tabernacle, 115
Mueller, C. G., 240
Munsell Color Company, 13
Murdoch, J. B., 184

National Electrical Manufacturers
    Association (NEMA), 52
National Fire Protection Association
    (NFPA), 121
National Oceanic and Atmospheric
    Administration (NOAA), 76
National Research Council of Canada
    (NRCC), 112
New England Journal of Medicine, 121
Nuckolls, J. L., 240, 241

Ohm, G. S., 239, 248

Panero, J., 108
Parsons, H. M., 84
Philips Technical Review, 80
Phillips, D., 241
Pohl, J., 242
Porretta, P., 220
Progressive Architecture, 240
Purkinje, J., 16

Rodman, H. E., 223
Rohles, F. H., 61
Rosco, 210
Rosenfeld, A. H., 187
Ross, D. K., 37
Rubin, A. I., 240
Rudolph, M., 240

Saks Fifth Avenue, 210
Science, 84
Sears, Roebuck and Co., 210
Segil, A. W., 186, 241
Selkowitz, S. E., 187
Shaw-Walker Company, 240
Shellko, P. L., 109

Shemitz, S. R., 104
Simpson Electric Company, 85
Smith, Hinchman & Grylls, 125
Snell, W., 66, 236
Snellen, H., 10
Southern Methodist University, 170
Spencer, D. E., 107
Spencer, V. E., 107
Steffy, G. R., 118
Sylvania, 213

Taylor, J. R., 223
Tektronix, 85
Thompson, D., 220

U.S. General Services Administration
    (GSA), 121
U.S. National Bureau of Standards
    (NBS), 36, 84, 113, 121, 175,
    240, 264
University of California (Berkeley),
    219
University of Virginia, 115
University of Washington (Seattle),
    219

Virginia Polytechnic Institute and
    State University, 219

Western Electric Company, 84
Westinghouse Electric Corporation,
    110, 240, 242
Whitesides, F. E., 83
Williams, H. G., 109, 126

Yilmaz, H., 15
Yonemura, G. T., 36, 84

Zekowski, G., 103
Zelnik, M., 108

SUBJECT INDEX*

Abney's law, 135, 142
Accent light, 101
Accommodation, 4, 9
Adaptation, 16

Adapted brightness, 25
Additive primary colors, 231
Altitude angle, solar, 172
Ambient light, 109
Ambient luminescence, 110
Amenity curve, 80
Angle:
    altitude, solar, 172
    beam cutoff, 65, 226
    bearing, solar, 172
    mirror, 32, 100
    nadir, 138
    shielding, 64
    solid, 237
    viewing, 32, 34, 238
    visual, 10
Aperture fluorescent lamp, 225
Apparent brightness, 22, 24
Aqueous humor, 3
Area sources, 246
Artificial skies, 219
ASA designation, 217
Atria, 192

Ballasts, 52-53
Batwing beam spread, 66, 132
Beam cutoff angle, 65, 226
Beam daylighting, 187
Beam spread:
    angle of, 103
    batwing, 66, 132
    length of, 102
    pattern of, 66
    width of, 102
Bearing angle, solar, 172
Bilateral clerestories, 183
Bilateral openings, 176, 180
Binocular vision, 6
Binocular visual field, 8
Biological needs for visual informa-
    tion, 40
Bipin base, 47
Bisection illusion, 20
Black-and-white print film, 217
Black hole effect, 117
Blackbody color temperatures, 227
Blind spot, 4
Blinds, 189
Body shadow shield, 125
Brightness:
    adapted, 25
    apparent, 22, 24
    control of, 38-39

*For easy reference, checklists, example problems, and tables are listed on page 270.

CHECKLISTS

EXAMPLE PROBLEMS

TABLES